Are You Watching,
Liverpool?

Jim White

Are You Watching, Liverpool?

HEINEMANN : LONDON

First published in Great Britain 1995
by William Heinemann Ltd
an imprint of Reed Consumer Books Ltd
Michelin House, 81 Fulham Road, London SW3 6RB
and Auckland, Melbourne, Singapore and Toronto

Copyright © Jim White 1994
The author has asserted his moral rights

A CIP catalogue record for this title
is available from the British Library
ISBN 0 434 00115 5

Phototypeset by Intype, London
Printed and bound in Great Britain
by Clays Ltd, St Ives PLC

To my Dad

who didn't make it to see the Double

Contents

Acknowledgements

There are a lot of people interviewed in this book, who all gave of their time freely, and without whom there wouldn't have been a book: so thanks.

But before I got to talk to anyone, there were a bunch who gave advice, background, encouragement and help. Particularly: Andy Mitten, Patrick Barclay, Joe Lovejoy, Rob Hughes, Richard Williams, Johnny Flacks, Steve Bentley, Barney Chilton, Jon Shine, John Cunningham, Martin O'Neill, Richard Trengrove and the ever-lovely Peter Boyle. Also Leo Robson, who supplied the beard at Elland Road.

And there were others who were around throughout the year, sharing the ups and ups of an amazing season. David Robson turned a blind eye to all that time off; Chris and Karen in Manchester supplied enough hospitality to have made Rocco Forte green with envy; Michael Crick was astounding with a stat; Tom Weldon was an ace of an editor; and Cat Ledger was a double winner of an agent who kept the concept on the road after the derailment in Turkey.

But maximum thanks are due to Arabella, who lived it more than anyone. Not a football enthusiast, she said something halfway through the season I never expected to hear coming from her mouth. 'If Blackburn loses and United wins,' she said as I left for a game towards the end of the season, 'then United have got the title.' Let's hope there's an Aga in it.

Introduction

Below me, the Oldham Athletic fans, many wearing blue mop-top wigs for their big day out, jigged in an unfocused stew of celebration. Then, with that telepathic speed with which ten thousand people can in an instant find one voice, they started singing. 'Always look on the bright side of life,' they chanted. 'Duh-do, duh-do, duh-do duh-do duh-do.' It was our cheery anthem they were singing, thrown back at us with relish, with irony. Ha ha, they meant by the hijacking, this season of yours, which had apparently promised so much red rapture, which had at one time offered the first trophy-sweep in English football history, was falling apart; ha ha, you arrogant bastards; ha ha, what fun to see you falling off a roof, flat on your smug faces.

The bright side of life, all right. Within a fortnight, Manchester United's apparently unstoppable march through 1994 had come to this: losers in the Coca-Cola Cup final, wavering in the league and now, with seconds of the FA Cup semi-final remaining, about to be humiliated by the second most incompetent team in the Premier League.

Oddly, I was not surprised. This is what you expect the football team you love to do to you: hint at glory and then falter. United, who had swaggered through the first two-thirds of the season like pigeons on the pull, had suddenly developed mange. Three of our best players, Roy Keane, Andrei Kanchelskis and Eric Cantona, the newly crowned King of Old Trafford, sat in the stands, suspended from action for a series of minor (or in the case of his 'royal highness', major) misdemeanours. In their absence their colleagues had lost faith, they were labouring. Peter Schmeichel, the goalkeeper whose hands for six months had been like quick-setting cement – firm, safe, adhesive – had started behaving like John Major's government, dropping bollocks at every corner; Dion Dublin, in for Cantona and by reputation good in the air, had not received a pass to forehead all afternoon; Ryan Giggs played as if his knee-length Stanley Matthews memorial shorts were acting as windbreaks; Lee Sharpe had misplaced the art of dancing past fullbacks and looked about as rhythmic as your dad at a disco. Oldham, ordinary at their best, remained untroubled as the most woeful FA Cup semi-final on record creaked to its conclusion. Wembley, in its long history of crap games, had seldom seen one crappier.

The semi had been staged in north London, instead of, as tradition dictated, a geographically convenient neutral ground, for no more tangible reason than greed – higher prices, higher profits. Some more principled United fans staged a boycott, unwilling, unable to part with yet more dosh to follow their team, their loyalty stretched beyond its fiscal limit. All season, tickets for United games had been as difficult to get hold of as Duncan Goodhew's head in a bubble bath, but for the semi I had landed four. I had taken my son and two mates, one of whom had last seen United in their magnificent, spiritually enriching demolition of Wimbledon in the fifth round, seven weeks previously. Never, he said as the game ground its goalless way into extra time, had he seen such a decline in a football team in so short a time. But it was to get worse. With less than six minutes of the game remaining, Schmeichel made another major mistake. He punched weakly at a cross, the ball landed at the feet of Neil Pointon, the Oldham defender, whose haircut suggested he had stepped on to the Wembley pitch from the Tardis, transported direct from 1985. Pointon smacked the ball into the back of the United net. This was what had sent, after a second's blinking disbelief, the Oldham supporters below me into their carnival of taunt. Always look on the bright side of life.

That's it, I thought. I'd started out to write a book about United in Europe. Knocked out of that, I stayed on for the treble. Now it looked as if I could pack up the double. I sat with my head in my hands, looking up only when the United fan next to me touched my shoulder. He was off home. Couldn't bear to see the boys like this, he said. For the first time in a football-watching life in which I had never done the four-thirty 'excuse me', I felt like joining him. It would have been a mistake. As he was making his way to Wembley Park tube, with less than a minute of extra time to go, and with the Oldham defence mentally measuring themselves up for their Cup-final suits, the young United substitute Nicky Butt headed the ball towards their area. Brian 'Choccy' McClair flicked it hopefully forward, over the heads of a mixed line of red and blue. And then Mark 'Sparky' Hughes, for ten years an unimpeachable hero of the United faithful, watching it as it fell over his left shoulder, volleyed the thing goalwards. It was the noise that struck me: an angry thwump of leather on leather you could hear forty yards away. The ball, moving with an Exocet's vicious intent, left his right foot and billowed into the netting at the back of the goal before the Oldham keeper could move.

I'm not sure what Hughes did next, or what the Oldham players did, but I know what the man in front of me and I did. We stood, in a piece of instant male bonding seldom seen since the heyday of the San Francisco bath-houses, roaring in each other's faces, an incoherent bawl of triumph and relief. Below us the Oldham festivities had stopped more abruptly than a teenager's party when their parents come home. As we embraced, my new lover and me, my son looked at us with that look five-year-olds reserve for adults who behave like children.

'What you doing, Dad?'

'Celebrating.'

'Why?'

'It was a great goal,' I told him. 'It was a bloody, bloody, bloody great goal.'

I was wrong. It was more than a great goal. It was a goal to be

immortalised to the tune of 'Winter Wonderland' in the oral history
that is the United song repertoire:

> All the Oldham were cheering
> Ordering their beer in
> Then Choccy chipped it
> And Hughesie smashed it
> Made the Oldham goal look totally shit.

It was a goal that put the whole grand ambition back on the tracks;
a goal that saved Manchester United's season; the most extravagant
season in their extravagant history.

What follows here is the story of that season: a tale of stratospheric
highs and subterranean lows, of victory on the field and the loss of
a founding father off it. It is a story of artistry and brutality,
of Giggsy, Incie, Sparky and Eric the King. Of Fergie the Boss and
Sealey the Folk Hero. It is also the story of Boylie the cheerleader,
Barney the T-shirt man and Scotty, who spent twenty-six days in a
Turkish prison in the red cause. It is the story of merchandising and
commercialisation, of power and politics, of queues and touts, the
story of a formidable footballing business. And it is a story told
unapologetically through red-tinted spectacles. This doesn't mean,
I hope, that it is uncritical, or that if you are a fan of another club,
or even not a fan at all, you won't find something of interest in
here. It is just that red-tinted is the only view I've ever known.

'When I was selling copies outside Selhurst Park for the Wimbledon
game,' Andy Mitten of the best-selling fanzine *United We Stand*
told me towards the end of the season, 'I was selling them to people
I'd never seen before and they'd obviously never seen United
before. I heard someone say: "Ooh, I'm actually going to see Ryan
Giggs in the flesh." They were tourists, people who'd suddenly
jumped on the bandwagon because United are doing well. I hated
them. Glory-hunters.'

The thing I didn't want to tell Andy was, I was a glory-hunter.
In 1968 I jumped on the red bandwagon because it was rolling

along very nicely. In the playground of my primary school in a Manchester suburb you were either blue or red, and bugger that City had just won the title to become champions, I went for the greater glory. I went for the champions of Europe. From the moment Matt Busby kissed the European Cup, I was one of those in the playground in a little scarlet football shirt with a white vicar's collar (well, pink actually, it ran in the wash) taunting those who wore sky-blue. At every playtime through the following winter, when we played football we gave each other the names of our heroes as we picked the teams. If you got selected first you were Denis the King and could tug your cuffs over your fists. Second, you were Best and had a licence not to pass. Third, you were Charlton and were obliged to shoot from the halfway line. I was usually Tony Dunne, the left back.

For my seventh birthday my sister bought me a copy of Bobby Charlton's autobiography, *This Game of Soccer*. Perhaps she couldn't find Tony Dunne's. It read in the front: 'To Jim, a true fan. Happy Birthday, Bobby Charlton.' I spent much of my time with that book; I loved its pictures of Mexican goalkeepers making extravagant dives and exposing their midriffs as they failed to keep out huge shots from Bobby Charlton. My friend Malcolm and I used to reconstruct great moments from the book in the back garden, lifting our shirts as we tumbled.

But it never occurred to me that I could see Charlton, Denis the King, Bestie and their mates (I was convinced they were all the best of pals, otherwise why would they pick each other?) in the flesh. The closest I got to seeing the big three in action was once when my mum, dad, sister and me drove out on a Sunday afternoon to have a look at the house that Georgie Best had built for himself in Bramhall. There were crowds of people there, just standing, looking, saying the place looked like a toilet.

'Poor man,' I remember my mum saying.

And my dad, he missed the plot entirely and took me along every fortnight to see Altrincham in action in the Cheshire League.

I got to see Sidebottom, Houston and Forsyth play, though. Perversely, I finally started going to matches when United were in the

Second Division, and the fans had embarked on a nine-month terror campaign through the provincial towns of England. At Manchester Grammar School, tales circulated about how crazed these reds were, about them smashing up special trains on their way to Nottingham or Bristol with axes liberated from the emergency cupboard in the guard's van. The axes would be taken to your heads, too, the stories went, if you didn't fit in. So when I finally arrived at Old Trafford, aged fourteen, with my mate Jon and his brother, for the top of the table game against Sunderland, I was equipped. A black acrylic scarf with red-and-white stripes was tied in a thick knot around my neck and strapped around each wrist were a couple of mock-silk numbers with pictures of Willie Morgan on them. Willie was my hero. It wasn't so much his bandy-legged wing play glimpsed on 'Match of the Day' or Granada's 'Kick-off Match' that I admired – it was his three-tier, wedding-cake coiffure, a carefully constructed confection which became my sartorial blueprint. This style was no easy option: it required a full range of hairdressing appliances to maintain its architecture. One of my moments of last season was when I saw Morgan in the Old Trafford press box; he's now a match commentator for Piccadilly Radio, and in bomber jacket, tight jeans and plimsolls looked like an unusually well-preserved seventies' rock star. Particularly since, twenty years on, he appears still to employ the same barber.

As we approached the stadium on that January day in 1975 I adopted the walk that was needed in order to survive without ridicule at the time, a bent-knee shuffle in which the principle aim was to keep the toes obscured beneath the tips of your flares. I thought I looked the part – rock-hard. When we got to the steps of the railway bridge which led across to the Stretford End, a boy was challenging junior passers-by to a fight: 'You reckon you're 'ard, coomon then, I'll see you afftoh.' He was no more than seven, but when he ignored me I nearly wet my pants with relief.

Inside I couldn't believe it. At Altrincham they only had one chant: 'Alty, Alty.' To hear the variety at Old Trafford, the myriad ways 15,000 people in the Stretford End could snarl at the tumbling mass of Wearsiders at the other end of the stadium – 'You'regonna-

getchyourfuckinedskickedin,' 'You'regoinomebyfuckinambulance' –
was a vicarious thrill scarcely hinted at by 'Match of the Day'. We
stood in the Stretford Paddock, the non-contributory section of the
Strettie, and I couldn't keep my eyes off the terraces to my left.
When the Kop stopped standing last season, much was made of the
Scouser's alleged wit, the instant humour of their chants. With
the Strettie there wasn't any pretence of that. The lightest touch
there was was when an opposing player went down injured and
they sang, 'Bring on the dustbin.' I loved it.

From then on I went to almost every home game and the convenient away games (Stoke, Everton, City). I collected programmes,
pasted tokens on to my token sheet and queued for big-match
tickets. I had the best day of my teenage life when Jon and I went
to Hillsborough to see United beat Derby County in the semi-final
of the Cup in 1976. Ten years before disaster, we were in the
Leppings Lane end, spilling down the terraces, taken whichever
way the force took us, crushed by the emotional energy of being
back in the big time. That evening I got an early taste of the double.
I lost my virginity in front of 'Match of the Day' as the highlights
of the afternoon's game were being shown. In 1980, I bumped into
the girl in question in a pub. She told me she had just been intimate
with Joe Jordan. It made me unfeasibly proud at the time, beating
a hero by four years. But then Joe was always a little slow getting
into the box.

The luck couldn't last: we lost the Cup to Southampton in what
was my second visit to Wembley of the year. In March my mate
Roger, unstinting in his evangelical efforts to colour me blue, took
me to the final of the League Cup, as it was quaintly known then,
to see Manchester City beat Newcastle. I am, therefore, a rarity: a
person still alive who has witnessed Manchester City landing
a trophy. His efforts didn't work: even in impressionable ado-
lescence, I preferred to see United lose than City win.

For the next fifteen years I watched United unstintingly as they
won far more frequently than they lost. We seemed to be always at
Wembley, and I was always there too: blagging, begging, pulling
strings for tickets as you have to do if you're a United fan. In 1979

I had got to the Friday of Cup-final week without a sniff. That morning at the end of a lecture, a student stood at the front of the hall and asked if anyone liked football: I was the only person to say yes (it was a Middle English lecture). I thought he was organising a kickaround, but he said did I want a Cup-final ticket? His dad was a director at Middlesbrough, he said, had sent him one and he didn't really like football (he was going through a difficult phase). He wanted the thing to have a decent home. The home I could give it was in the Buckingham Palace class. I didn't even have to pay.

Later I found a sure-fire method of obtaining tickets: go in the press box. But though I went to Wembley as often as I wanted (1976, 1977, 1979, 1983 – three times including a replay – 1985, 1990 – twice – 1991, 1992, not to mention the Charity Shields), I never saw United win the title. Three managers, Docherty, Sexton and Atkinson, fell failing to do it, while down the East Lancs Road they won the thing at will. At Old Trafford the ten years since we were last champions quickly became fifteen became twenty became twenty-five. And Liverpool marched on relentlessly.

In 1992, I thought the wait was over. So, Paul Ince told me this year, did the players. They reckoned they were the best team in it. Which is probably why they didn't win it. Besides, they reckoned without Leeds, a club led by a Frenchman with, we thought at the time, no more to distinguish him than a large nose. That night at Upton Park when we finally blew it was the worst night of my watching career: the diametric opposite of my Hillsborough double whammy. No matter what all these new football writers suggest, there is nothing romantic or intellectually stimulating about losing. It was horrible. The last game of the season was at Anfield and did they enjoy seeing us fail. After the game, Ryan Giggs told me, their fans, the ones renowned for their humour, asked him for his autograph as he boarded the team coach. He obliged and they ripped it up and threw the paper back in his face. In May that year, I thought, that's it, we'll never do it now.

Which is why I loved 1993. That year United, electric at Loftus Road, razor sharp at Norwich, pulsating at Palace, produced the best football I had ever seen. I'd never experienced Law, Best and

Charlton, but this seemed as good as it could be. On the wings Kanchelskis, Giggs and Sharpe tore with pace. At the back Bruce, Pallister, Parker, Irwin and Schmeichel were less generous than a Tory social security minister. In the middle Ince, McClair, Robson and Hughes harried and snapped. And up front the Frenchman, spirited away from Elland Road, scored with regularity and aplomb.

This time it was not United who cracked in the run-in, it was our rivals, Aston Villa. Without stepping on the pitch, we won the title when Villa lost at home to Oldham; Alex Ferguson was playing golf that afternoon, and learnt the news from a motorist passing the course. Twenty-six years of waiting, expecting, anticipating, as well as suffering the mockery of Merseyside, combined in the celebrations which erupted when Robson and Bruce picked up the new FA Premier League trophy after the penultimate match of the season against Blackburn Rovers.

On his fifth birthday, I took my son to Selhurst Park to see the last game of that year, to see the champions, to see his heritage. I held him up to watch as Robson scored and I taught him how to sing 'the Marseillaise'. The highlight of his day was spotting a streaker who paraded at half-time: 'Look,' he said, 'one of the players hasn't got any clothes on.'

As we walked back to the car he said, 'Dad, when was the last time United won the league?'

'Twenty-six years ago,' I said. 'If it takes them as long to do it again, you'll be my age.'

War Is Declared

When you're Man United,
everyone wants to do you.
                    Les Sealey

The noise could be heard about half a mile away. A high-frequency keening, as if a number of dogs were in pain. As I walked up the hill of a quiet suburban street, past the mock-Tudor black-and-white Edwardian houses, it grew louder. Past the cars clogging driveways, past tourist coaches parked haphazardly on the pavement's edge, it grew louder yet. Through a pair of big, green, wooden double gates, into a car park beyond which a playing field stood thick and green in the summer haze, it was now loud. Very loud. And there, in one corner of the car park, amid a forecourt-load of expensive German cars, was the source of the noise. A red Golf GTi was engulfed by about two hundred prepubescent girls. They were upset these girls: wailing, panting, thrusting their half-formed breasts on to the car's windows. Around the car park, another thousand teenagers squealed and showed their dental metal work as a tanned young man opened the car door and made his way slowly across the tarmac, pushing patiently through the crowd, signing an autograph or two if he could work his hands free from the flail of adolescent limbs. It took him nearly twenty minutes to traverse about twenty yards and disappear into the two-storey brick building at one end of the car park. After he had gone, a girl in a black shirt with 'Sharp Viewcam' written across the chest, leant against a new Audi and sobbed.

'Ryan, Ryan, Ryan,' she was saying to her friend whose face was buried in her shoulder. 'He looked at me. Ryan Giggs, he looked at me.'

Manchester United were back in training.

For nearly twenty-five years I had been following Manchester United, and for twenty-five years just before the season started was the best bit. When expensively acquired tans neatly offset freshly laundered white shorts; when Bob and Jimmy on 'Football Focus' said: '. . . and you can't write off Manchester United, perhaps this will be their year'; this was the time that optimism had yet to be shattered by experience. Twenty-five years of managers arriving with plans and departing with pay-offs, a quarter-century of players not up to the job, had not dulled the tingle of that time, that just-before-they-started-just-before-they-blew-it moment.

But this year was different. This year the boys in red were the real thing: arrogant, overendowed with skill, competitive, resourceful, fully capable of repaying extravagant expectation. As I stood there in the car park, surrounded by an anticipation that ran through the veins with the charge of Bolivia's finest, I felt that this year the beginning really was only the start of things.

Where I was standing is called The Cliff. While Old Trafford, United's muscular headquarters, with its sweeping steel stands and hectares of plush hospitality suites, oozes money, style, success, the club's training ground is another world. Three miles of unprepossessing Salford away, The Cliff has no fancy peripherals. In the changing rooms into which Ryan Giggs had just disappeared, the floor is covered with pimply lino. Upstairs there are cupboard-sized rooms full of physiotherapy equipment; an old-fashioned canteen is up there, where jaunty dinner ladies serve high-energy food through a hatch and the sauces on the tables are in plastic containers that make farty noises when squeezed. The whole complex is smaller than the lavatory block at Milan. But it is here that the real work of Manchester United is done: the planning, the graft, the sweat and the reckoning out how to cope with a near-post corner.

About ten-thirty on a muggy summer morning the work began for the new season. Never mind that the FA Premier League trophy, won three months previously, was sitting in the museum at Old Trafford where fans were lining up to be photographed holding it (an opportunity not to be missed, and only £6.95 a time). Now work was required to defend it. Work was needed too, to campaign for the FA Cup and the Coca-Cola Cup. Most of all, it would take work here at The Cliff to mount a challenge for the European Champions Cup, the competition which the club won in 1968 and for which they had now qualified for the first time in a quarter of a century; to challenge for this cup, we supporters assumed, without the benefit of any empirical evidence, was our right and privilege.

That's the thing about professional football: accumulation is all in the future.

By now there was a bigger crowd at The Cliff to watch these United boys in pre-season training than many Third Division teams would draw on match day. About two thousand people were there; they had arrived, some of them, by specially chartered coach. Press photographers toyed with phallic lenses, small boys clung to libraries of autograph books and middle-aged men in nylon rainwear peered through the windows of the cars parked in the forecourt.

'I thought Sparky had a Porsche,' one man said to his friend.

'Oh aye,' said the friend, adopting the superior tone of one in the know. 'But he uses his club car for coming to training.'

Most of the crowd, though, were teenaged girls, hair tied in topknots, chewing like cows at the cud, taking in the free show in the middle of a school holiday. They were there to see Giggs and Sharpe, the pair who, in their manager's words, are 'photogenic boys' and whose presence in the team ensured that everywhere United were to go this season, the air would be thick with adolescent pheromones.

Gradually the spectators made their way to the grass bank surrounding The Cliff's training pitch, making sure not to stray over the low fence with its signs saying 'Strictly no admittance past this point'. As they went, they squashed past the parked cars and pinged the wing mirrors. No wonder Sparky left his Porsche at home.

Around half past ten, the champions of England began, haphazardly, in ones, twos, threes, to jog out of the changing room on to the pitch. There was Schmeichel, the Danish keeper built like an oarsman; there was Bruce the captain with the nose, broken countlessly in the red cause, all over his face; there were Parker and Irwin, full backs and thus interest-free zones; Pallister, long and ragged of limbs, tagged behind, not brimming with enthusiasm. There were Robson, the warhorse, and Hughes, the centre forward with the on-pitch disposition of something let loose on the streets of Pamplona; there was Ince who, the previous season, had begun to fill Robson's boots and become United's engine. There were several reserves, whose pictures appear on the team photo at the beginning of the season, but then would not resurface in the public consciousness for the rest of the year. And there was Cantona, the genius, the man whose arrival the previous November had started the roll towards the title. While the others jogged and jiggled their arms to warm up, he performed elaborate, balletic stretches of leg and back, sitting on the grass, legs spread, stroking his thighs. The French sophisticate amid the British yeomen. Whatever they were doing, they did it with the self-consciousness of someone trying to perform an everyday task knowing that two thousand people are studying their every nose clearance.

Up on the bank, the older supporters applauded the champions' arrival, the girls jumped up and down and pointed at Ryan and Lee, several young lads started to chant 'champeeonays, champeeonays, olay, olay, olay,' the new cry at Old Trafford, the Italian shout of triumph, learnt off the Channel 4 football and filtered through a Salford accent.

Out on the pitch before the players Brian Kidd, the well-preserved former member of United's European Cup-winning team and now assistant manager, was constructing geometric patterns with traffic cones and trawling net loads of footballs behind him. As the players ran past, warming themselves up, he shouted at them to accelerate, to up the pace. Some of them, Paul Ince, for instance, shouted back that they were not that keen.

Running marginally ahead of everyone, trying a bit harder, was the new signing, Roy Keane, transferred from Nottingham Forest during the summer for a record £3.75 million. Everyone had wanted him, Arsenal had tried, Blackburn had offered to employ two body-builders to help carry his wages to the bank. He had decided on United, because, he said, he wanted to win things. Money wasn't everything, he said. Which is the sort of thing you can say when you're on £8,000 a week. No matter how generous the remuner-ation, now he was here, Keane looked nervous. Not surprising, really: there is a long and ignominious tradition of players moving from the City Ground to Old Trafford for large fees, failing and then returning Trentwards, hoots of Stretford End derision speeding their departure. Storey-Moore, Birtles, Davenport, Webb: Roy wasn't keen to join the list.

Then, walking across the pitch, dressed in shorts and T-shirt, came the manager Alex Ferguson, known to the players as the Boss: they seem to find it uncomfortable to call him anything else. He was beaming cheerfully, nodding and saying 'How yer doin?' to everyone he passed, the master surveying his domain. He laughed at the players, pointed at the crowd, some of whom shouted to him by name ('Alex, Alex, all right?'). He shadow-boxed with Ince, ruffled Sharpe's hair. He gathered them together, said something to them, and then the real work began.

This is Graham Taylor's idea of how a footballer should train: at a session at Bisham Abbey when he was manager of England, Taylor, at the suggestion of the sports psychologist he used to listen to, told Lee Sharpe to go out into the centre circle of the training pitch. There Sharpie was instructed to play keepy-uppy, juggling the ball in the air off head, foot, chest and shoulder for as long as he could. While he did it, Taylor told him, he should count out loud. Backwards in multiples of five.

This is how Manchester United train: they put a goalkeeper in the goal and then the players whose job it is to cross the ball cross it and the players whose job it is to score, try to score. The goal-keeper tries to stop them.

Which partly explains why Alex Ferguson now drives a Mercedes bigger than the house he grew up in and why Graham Taylor manages Wolves.

It is Brian Kidd, an insatiable student of international training methods (he studies how Wigan rugby league team prepare) who worked out that this was the best way of doing things.

'Kiddo went to Italy,' Paul Ince told me. 'Went to watch Milan and Parma train, came back and said, "Listen, all they do is shoot, shoot and more shooting." Volleys, half-volleys, chesting it, knocking it aside, shoot, shoot, shoot. So that's what we do. And you know what? It gets results.'

So Kidd had directed Robson, Pallister, Bruce, Ince and Brian McClair to stand in the centre circle, firing balls out to the wings where Parker, Sharpe, Andrei Kanchelskis, Giggs, Irwin and several of the faceless ones hurtled along and crossed them into the box where Hughes, Cantona, Keane and Dion Dublin tried to put them into the net past Schmeichel. 'Go, go, go,' Kidd said as he dropped balls at their feet. When they had had enough of that, Kidd varied the routine, with passes through the middle, one-twos on the edge of the box, practising the little build-up manoeuvres which would surface later in games.

On this muggy summer day before the season began, the players might have arrived gagging about how they couldn't be bothered and that Incey was a lazy bastard, but during this routine they concentrated. Really concentrated. As the balls pinged around, thumped on to foreheads and hurtled off boots, they seemed particularly anxious to inflict maximum damage on their goalkeeping colleague, Peter Schmeichel, to smash the ball as hard as possible past him. Alone in the goal at The Cliff, watching as Mark Hughes, Roy Keane and Dion Dublin bore down on him, Schmeichel must have known how that bloke who stood in front of the tank in Tiananmen Square had felt as ten tons of armour approached at speed. But the more the balls flew, the more he seemed to love it, throwing himself around, laughing in a crisp, staccato burst when Hughes missed. Within ten minutes, the joking, mickey-taking atmosphere had been replaced by one of hard competition. The crosses started to come over quicker, the shots came in quicker, the curses were quicker to fly.

'Shit,' Mark Hughes spat when a rasping volley wobbled the aluminium crossbar above Schmeichel's head.

'Shite,' said Schmeichel when his prodigious leap was not enough to keep out a shot from Dublin.

'Shit,' said Eric Cantona, miskicking and thus confirming this as the Esperanto curse of the cockup.

As the session progressed, as everyone in the squad tried their hand at scoring past him, Schmeichel became possessed: screaming, bawling, leaping, thwapping his thighs when he did a good save, applauding himself, sweat washing down the back of his training shirt.

'Shite,' said Irwin, as the goalkeeper pulled a top-corner-bound header out of the air as others might remove fruit from a tree.

'So sorry Den,' said Schmeichel, showing a fine Nordic grasp of the ancient English art of sarcasm. 'Sorry for being in the right place at the right time. Sorry for doing my job.'

'Lucky,' said Ince.

'Fuck you,' said Schmeichel, not amused.

Alex Ferguson had asked the players when they had gathered that morning whether they were hungry. He wanted to know if they were satiated by their success the previous year, satisfied by breaking the twenty-six-year curse and lifting the title. Or if they had enjoyed that achievement so much they wanted more.

'I told them,' he told me, 'that the bus was going on. This club has to progress. And the bus wouldn't wait for them. I told them to get on board.'

On the evidence of that early training session they didn't want to miss the stop. They looked ravenous, greedy, compulsive. If this is what they are like in rehearsal, I thought standing there watching them, then on the night, the opposition could do with some celestial assistance.

Later I was to ask Les Sealey, the reserve goalkeeper, whether it was always like that. 'Listen,' he said, 'when you're Man United, everyone wants to do you. When you're Man United and you're the champions, everyone wants to do you times ten. If you want to make sure they don't, you have to be harder, tougher, stronger. You have to be ready. It's going to be war. You're going out into the trenches.'

Out there for nine months, no amount of squealing girlie fans will protect you.

When the war started, it started well: victories against Arsenal in the Charity Shield (on penalties), against Norwich, Sheffield United, Southampton and West Ham in the league. There was a draw with Newcastle, when Andy Cole equalised, and a screamer of a win at the previous year's rivals Aston Villa. Lee Sharpe scored twice there, and each time undertook a hip-swivelling celebratory dance by the corner flag. Among the girlies, there wasn't a dry seat in the house.

By September, with only a month of the season gone and sixteen points accrued from six games, the bookies had decided that the war was already past its critical phase. The odds on a retention of the title shortened to the Ronnie Corbett. In the press, drooling at the fleet-footed, super-skilled football that General Ferguson and his troops were unleashing, the speculation was about how many trophies they would land. The double? The treble? The quadruple? The European Cup, it seemed, was merely a matter of getting on the plane.

'United are the best team in England,' Trevor Francis of Sheffield Wednesday was reported as saying. 'They will be a very big threat to Barcelona or Milan.'

Or, as Paul Ince put it to me: 'If we're not better than Barcelona, then I'm not a black man.'

I caught up with them at Chelsea, the weekend before their first trip to the Continent. It was like old times at Stamford Bridge, a big, excited crowd shoving at the narrow entrance gate. A policeman on horseback rapidly losing his dignity and control as the surge bore past him. A polyglot of accents – American, Scots, Irish,

Scandinavian – people travelling from all over to see United, the champions, continue their barn-storm at the top. And Ken Bates, the Chelsea chairman, charging us £25 to watch from what elsewhere would constitute the cheap seats, the top tier of the white elephant stand, the great rusting Chelsea structure which almost bankrupted his club when it was built in the seventies; £25 to watch from a position not much more adjacent to the pitch than the airship hovering overhead; £25 to sit in front of a plane-load of Danes, waving little cardboard red and white flags at their national hero. He was down there somewhere, ant-like, the one in the goalkeeper's green jersey decorated by a motif which looked as though a toddler had emptied its lunch down the front. You couldn't miss him.

From wherever you watched, though, this was a game which suggested it might not be all over by Christmas, after all. This was one to remind you that optimism is the least resilient of football emotions. In the middle of the first half, Cantona attempted a lob from the halfway line. It cleared the Chelsea keeper and bounced goalward. On 11 September, I thought, Cantona has scored the goal of the season. But the ball hit the bar, shot upfield, broke to them, Schmeichel fumbled a shot and Peacock popped it away. The Danes behind me looked like you would if you had come all this way to see your man balls it up.

It was the only goal of the game. At the end, the generously jowelled Chelsea fan in front of me stood up and turned round. 'Haaaaaa,' he yelled at me, his neck wobbling over the collar of his replica shirt. 'Haaaaaa. Waaaaa. Fuck off.'

I was to encounter his sort again.

After the game, my mate Nigel and I stood outside a pub on the Hollywood Road closed to protect it from football rabble like us and decided we couldn't see the point of Roy Keane. He had played wide on the right, and had been tentative, ineffectual, Webb-like. The eager-to-please new boy had looked tactically lost. The reason why he had played out of his usual run-up-and-down-the-middle position was because the team which had lost to Chelsea was the team Alex Ferguson was to be forced to play in Europe: no Hughes, no Kanchelskis. This was the problem that made Paul Ince's aggressive statement of intent look fallible. Though the backbone of this United team had already won a European trophy, the Cup Winners Cup in 1991, that was before UEFA had snuck in their rule that teams could only field three foreign players. From 1992, the year the EC introduced free movement of labour, UEFA went insular. In England any Irish, Welsh and Scots players were to count as foreign. 'Scandalous,' Alex Ferguson called the rule.

After a year of lobbying the FA had managed to have the restriction softened somewhat. Irish, Welsh and Scots internationals who had played their youth team football for English clubs were reclassified 'assimilated foreigners'. So you could now pick up to three assimilated foreigners, but only in addition to two genuine foreigners; or if you wanted three foreigners, you could only add two assimilated. Get that? It was a procedure about as straightforward and logical as the Italian electoral system. What it amounted to was that United had five outright foreigners – Schmeichel, Keane, Cantona, Kanchelskis and McClair – and three assimilated foreigners – Hughes, Giggs and Irwin – from which they could select five. And what it meant was that in European competition Alex Ferguson could not field his strongest team. He was to be constantly, as it were, at the mercy of his permutations.

'I never thought I'd see the day,' he said at Manchester airport as the team gathered the following Tuesday for a flight to Budapest to play Kispest Honved in the first round of the European Cup, 'when I said I needed more Englishmen in a squad of mine.'

2

The European Cup

*Your first trip abroad and it's with Manchester
United in the European Cup.*
        Bobby Charlton, talking to youth players,
                            14 September 1993

Milan have their own club plane. American basketball teams, travelling for exhibition games in Europe, come by Concorde. For the
flight to Budapest, ferrying the champions of England to the club's
first appearance in the European Cup since before several of their
players were potty-trained, Manchester United went Manx. A tiny
turbo-prop, a plane which generally ferried passengers the short
hop from Ringway across to the Isle of Man, had been hired from
Manx Airlines.

'Manx Airlines?' someone had said before we boarded. 'Does
that mean it hasn't got a tail?'

They weren't that far wrong.

On foreign trips, football organisations charter themselves a plane
and then offset some of the cost by selling spare places to the
media. For England matches, the players and officials are screened
off in a different section from the press pack, unwilling to share air
space with people who routinely call them turnips and planks. On
the Manx plane, there wasn't room for segregation. So here were the
players, dressed in their black Umbro travel suits (£74.99 from
the Old Trafford superstore), white or red Umbro piqué polo shirts
(£21.99 from high street outlets) and a variety of fancy training
shoes (from reps' car boot), shoe-horned into seats alongside the
ambassadors of the British press, in their shabby macs (£14.99, Mr
Byrite), scuffed brogues (£22.50, Hush Puppy) and hangover scowls

(£45.75, on expenses). Here was the chairman and his fellow directors, in their United blazers and crisp white shirts, sitting three to
a row, knees tickling chins. Here were Bobby Charlton, United
director, and Denis Law, media pundit, swapping yarns about the
old days in a plane that would have taken them back a bit.

Hitching a ride as a member of the fourth estate, to write a book
about United's progress through Europe, I took my place on the
plane and looked round to see something approaching thirty million
pounds' worth of footballer squeezed in within feet of me. And
everywhere, this expensive accumulation of talent complained about
the leg-room: Gary Pallister, the gangly six-foot-four England centre
back, and not the best of air travellers, looked particularly
uncomfortable, preparing for physical endeavours ahead with his
legs trussed up beneath him like a Sunday roast.

There was a variety of ways to take one's mind off the discomfort.
At the back of the plane, Steve Bruce, clubbable and friendly, sat
with the tabloid boys, swapping jokes and flicking through a copy
of *90 Minutes* magazine. To my right, Paul Ince browsed through
The Face and said 'Fuck off will ya' to Lee Martin when he tried
to snatch his Walkman. Three rows behind me Eric Cantona read
a paperback (*Confidences* by Marcel Pagnol) and said '*Oui, bien*'
when the jolly man from the *Daily Express* said '*Ça va, Eric?*' In
front of him was Ryan Giggs. Sitting away from the senior players,
Giggsy preferred the company of the boys newly signed up from
the youth team – Nicky Butt and Ben Thornley – who were on the
trip for the experience. He passed the time rolling up little paper
missiles, which he flicked at the inviting acreage of Dion Dublin's
bald head three rows in front and ducking down behind his seat
when his victim turned to see what was going on. Dublin himself
was preoccupied with the back page of the *Daily Mail*: 'Dublin's
Giant Leap' was the headline. The story said he was going to play
in Hungary. Never believe what you read in the papers was to be
the valuable piece of European experience he picked up from this
trip.

And in the row in front of me, Bryan Robson showed all his
international experience. The father figure of Old Trafford, he was

the only passenger on the plane with a row of seats to himself. Everything about him was cool, calm, unflustered, even the neat manner in which he ate his in-flight meal, carefully folded the napkin afterwards and reassembled the packaging to make it easier for the steward to take away. He knew how to idle away the time, too. After discussing arrangements for a Bryan Robson Scanner Appeal function with Danny McGregor, United's commercial manager, he pored over a crossword in *The Puzzler*. ''Scuse me mate,' he said to me after about half-an-hour's poring, leaning back across the seats. 'Can you help us with this clue?'

But with his soft County Durham accent and the hair-drier drone of the aircraft's engines, I didn't hear him properly. I thought he said the clue was: 'Head of school beginning with a B; four letters.'

'Beak?' I offered.

'Beak?' he said, frowning, running his pen over the blank squares. 'No, beginning with a P.'

'Oh, P,' I said. 'Head of school, beginning with a P, four letters.'

My mind went into a turmoil of lexicography, churning away in a desperate attempt to impress him as he had never ceased to impress me. 'Er, er, er.'

'I thought you journalists was meant to be good with words,' he smiled.

'Er, er, er. Head of school, beginning with a P. Er, er,' I spluttered. 'Prefect?'

He looked at me, looked at his crossword, and looked back at me much as he might at a referee after a decision with which he took issue.

'Eh? Prefect? You what?'

Next to me Patrick Barclay, of *The Observer*, sensing a problem, offered assistance. Robson passed him the magazine.

' "Head or skull, four letters, beginning with a P," ' read Barclay. 'Pate.'

'Ar, pate. That's the one. Thanks, Paddy,' said Robbo.

So there it was, my first conversation with a hero and I came across like Bertie Wooster's idiot younger brother.

Most of the time, unable, unlike the press and directors, to savour an in-flight drink or five, most of the players slept. And as the plane banked into Budapest, only Brian McClair and Michael Phelan looked out of the windows to check the scenery below them.

As we got off the plane, Ferguson was in charge, mother-henning both the press and the players.

'Nicky Butt, you help Norman here with the kit,' he instructed, nodding in the direction of Norman Davies, the man who ensures everyone has something decent to wear on the pitch.

'And you Giggsy,' said Ince.

'Oh aye,' said Steve Bruce. 'Fifteen million quid's worth of kit man.'

In the airport baggage-reclaim area, standing by a luggage carousel, Ferguson gave a short press conference.

'Lee Sharpe's feeling his thigh strain a touch,' he said. 'I'm hoping he'll be fit, we need all our Englishmen. He's a young lad, possibly if he was a little more experienced he would have told me he wasn't fit earlier and we would have planned accordingly. But obviously he's desperate to play.'

What would be the formation, Alex? the man from the *Sun* wanted to know (everyone called him Alex).

'Same as Saturday, at Chelsea.'

When you lost?

'Ar.' He smiled.

And what did he know about the opposition? someone asked.

'Well, Puskas used to play for them, but they're not quite what they were then. Hungarian football's going through a bit of a dip at the moment. So it'll be a big game for them. We've had them watched five times. They're a young team, and in Europe it's all about experience.'

A passing American, spotting all the microphones and notebooks, said to me, 'Hey, are you guys here for the world series soccer?' so I missed what Ferguson said about his chances.

'Good,' the man from the Press Association repeated for me,

indulging in the old journalistic tradition of sharing quotes. 'He said United's chances were good.'

Glad he told me.

The luggage took an age to arrive, the white heat of free enter-prise efficiency had not yet fully filtered through to Budapest air-port. As they waited around the lounge the players were collared for pre-match interviews by the pressmen. The tabloid reporters, anxious that none of their colleagues got a quote they didn't, eyed each other making contact carefully, muscling in if it was looking promising. At the same time, they tried to find a little exclusive of their own. The man from the *Daily Star* had his own way of doing things. He chatted to Roy Keane in an Irish patois so strong that no eavesdropper could understand a word. In a corner, Cantona and Robson posed for one of those pre-match photographs where players stand with their arms round each other and look embar-rassed. The photographer had supplied them with a prop each: an inflatable Red Devil's trident, with which they fenced halfheartedly.

No one, however, approached Giggsy. The press weren't allowed to speak to him. Alex Ferguson had made that clear, and the press lads accepted the restriction absolutely: they knew Fergie, knew the temper, knew he would be quite happy to send them home on the next plane if they snuck so much as a quiet word. So while his colleagues chatted about thighs and calfs and groins and said 'very much so' and 'as I say' and 'hopefully', Giggs sat with Butt and Thornley, yawning and studying the laces on his Reeboks. Bobby Charlton came over to the threesome and, ignoring Giggs, addressed the juniors.

'First trip abroad is it lads?'

Butt and Thornley nodded.

'And it's with Man United in the European Cup, my, my.'

They smiled indulgently at the avuncular Charlton, then, when he had walked away, looked at each other and raised their eyebrows.

And when the luggage eventually appeared, Giggs, as Ince had jokingly suggested, did help Butt, Thornley and Norman the kit man push the big metal skips of playing gear through customs. In the concourse, the one Hungarian fan there to meet us, assuming the teenage heart-throb of British football to be a no-interest lackey-type, walked straight past him and asked Michael Phelan for his autograph.

Once on terra firma, that was the end of the mixing. The players and directors had one coach, the press another, and we were billeted in different hotels. On the route in, past the evidence of advancing capitalism (Top Shop, Pizza Hut, McDonald's, inevitably), past the evidence of decaying communism (several broken-down Trabants), the press coach drew level with a local tram. Standing by the door was a blousey woman with hair-colour fresh from the bottle. The ageing lads of the pack, freed of family responsibilities for a day or two, all whooped as they copped a load of her. When the door of the tram opened, an up-draught caught the woman's skirt and exposed her in the manner of Marilyn Monroe in *The Seven-Year Itch*.

'Bloody hell,' said Joe Lovejoy, now of the *Sunday Times* but then my colleague at *The Independent*, and a man always ready with an appropriate footballing metaphor. 'She just showed me her Pesci Muncas.'

That evening the pack divided up. The tabloid lads (and Joe) went off one way, the intellectual wing the other. I tagged along with the intellectuals: Patrick Barclay, David Lacey of *The Guardian*, Rob Hughes of *The Times* and Colin Malam of the *Daily Telegraph*. Eric Cantona regards journalists as the lowest items on the food chain, and after his experiences who can blame him. But these men should not be confused with those who write sneering columns from a desk in London, or conjure up headlines about 'Norse Manure': they are the Boswells to Cantona's Johnson, the men who give daily expression to his genius and whose prose fuels the passion of fans.

As we sat in a pricey restaurant in the old quarter, amid the Japanese trade delegations and expensively shod American political tourists, they all agreed that reporting on United in Europe was a pleasure compared to following England. In part, this was because United played good football and when you are professionally

obliged to sit on a Saturday afternoon through a game involving
Sheffield United, good football is to be cherished. But also it was
because the relations between England and the press had reached
such poisonous depths that it was almost impossible to report sen-
sibly any more.

'I call it BT and AT,' said David Lacey trying to make himself
heard above a gypsy violinist clad in a Dunhill belt, scratching away
at his fiddle. 'Before Turnip and After Turnip. There's no doubt
that all that slagging off took its toll. He came in full of ideas of
how to co-operate with the media and the turnip stuff finished that
off. You couldn't talk to him, and if you tried he became paranoid
that you were trying to do him down.'

Ferguson, on the other hand, everyone agreed, while making no
attempt to pretend he was the media's friend, had mellowed since
United won the championship, and was now easier to approach.
Besides, he had not suffered the regular character assassination
attempts in the way Taylor had. Yet.

We also discussed United's chances. It was the three-foreigner
rule that was hamstringing Ferguson, they reckoned. On this
occasion his choice was made easier because Hughes was suspended
from European competition for a misdemeanour in the previous
year's UEFA Cup; Kanchelskis, in a decision which would prove
particularly odd as the season unfolded, wasn't even considered.
Which meant neither of them travelled: they stayed at home in
Manchester, to watch the match on the telly with a beer in hand.
But there would come a time, Rob Hughes suggested, when the
manager would have to make a choice; and fiddling with his formation was not his greatest strength – witness his nervy selection-
tinkering in the run-in in 1992. Moreover, once a foreigner or two
was unable to be considered, United's much-vaunted squad looked
less impressive than its admirers attested: the venerable Robson
was now central to the team, with Phelan, Martin, Dublin and
Sealey only a knock away from joining him. A couple of injuries
beyond them, and the cover was untried youth.

'He should have bought English,' said Patrick Barclay. 'It's not
like Milan, he couldn't run a shadow squad for the league and the

European Cup. What you'll find is United can't really compete on equal terms with the big boys in Europe. It's the same with Old Trafford. In England it's the great club stadium. Compared to the San Siro or the Bernabau it's the Loftus Road of Europe.'

'A nice little ground,' I said.

'Exactly.'

'Mind you, I think you'll have more than one round to write about,' Rob Hughes added. 'If they don't beat this lot and don't qualify for the mini-league then English football really is in trouble.'

After dinner, with the rain damping the cobbles, four of us caught a taxi back to the hotel. The driver, clocking our sort in the mirror, pulled a brochure from under his dashboard. 'Nightclub, gentlemen,' he said, handing it back to us. It was a well-thumbed item advertising a mucky bar, offering 'twenty-five beautiful girls'.

'Lesbie show, very good,' the driver continued. 'Fuck fuck show. I take you there, yes?'

And one of our number, who will remain nameless lest word percolates out of how badly he besmirched the reputation of football writers abroad, said: 'No, no. Straight to the hotel, if you don't mind. We want to get an early night tonight.'

When Everton once played in China, Pat Nevin took a merciless ribbing in the Goodison dressing room because he took time out to go and look at the Great Wall. What was he interested in that for? several players wanted to know, he was never a bricklayer. In Budapest, the Hungarian National Gallery boasts five Goyas and seven El Grecos: United's players preferred the twelve channels on their hotel room televisions.

On the plane back I asked Gary Pallister if he or any of his colleagues ever took the opportunity to go sightseeing in foreign cities.

'Nah, not really,' he said. 'There isn't really the chance to, like. You have to rest, get yourself prepared and that. Also you always leave immediately after the game. A few of us might go on one of Mickey Phelan's walks, but that's about it.'

Indeed on the morning of the game, Phelan could be seen leading

Robson, Pallister and Irwin along the promenade which skirts the banks of the Danube, strolling in the late summer sunshine. They were filmed every step by a crew from Granada Television, recording events for the new Manchester United video magazine. So they didn't walk far.

They missed out: Budapest was glorious. Its fringes may be smudged by great grey swathes of municipal tower blocks that make Hulme look like Hale Barnes, but the centre is a gem. Unlike in Moscow, the locals appeared optimistic, well turned out, making an effort towards elegance. Of course you still saw people wandering the streets in ill-fitting, badly designed garments made of man-made fabric. But they were United fans. Everywhere they were, about five thousand of them. Hungary's capital had not seen so many black shirts on its streets for fifty years.

By the bus station, about eight hours from kickoff, I climbed aboard an ersatz vintage bus which was advertising sightseeing trips. My fellow travellers were a local guide, a couple from Orlando ('host city of the soccer world cup, whatever that is,' said the man) and a middle-aged United fan who introduced himself as Tony. Tony was an ex-sailor – smoked Capstan full strength, and had fingers the colour and consistency of the soles of a rocker's shoes. He wore a red United shirt, which stretched unforgivingly over his midriff. He came originally from Stretford, he told me, but now ran a small business in Weston-super-Mare and retained a season ticket to Old Trafford, which was an expensive business. He had paid £900 for this trip and no, the wife hadn't come, though he was on the look-out for a blouse for her, something nice.

'You know that geezer what runs the programme stall in Warwick Road?' he said. 'Well I found out he come down here in a van. I could've hitched a ride and saved meself a few quid for the next round.'

Tony had followed United on every overseas game since English clubs were readmitted into Europe five years after the Heysel massacre, and tried to learn something of the history of the places he visited. He had certainly learnt something about Budapest. As the bus chugged through the glorious baroque streets, past the parks and opera houses, past equestrian statues apparently on every corner, he kept up a spirited commentary in opposition to the dreary autopilot of the official guide.

''Course, this was all part of the Ottoman Empire,' he said pointing at a mosque. 'Hence the Turkish influence in them mina-fuckin-rets over there.

'This is called the Square of Heroes,' he said, when we stood in a big square lined with pompous statues of men in moustaches on horseback. 'Bit rich havin' a Square of Heroes when you're on the wrong side in two world wars.

'Give the Hungarians their due,' he said as we passed a war memorial (a man on a horse). 'They refused to hand over their Jews until nineteen forty-two. Didn't do them much good, but at least they made the effort.'

As the bus spluttered on, and the American couple had started to rely on Tony for all their information (''course there's a big refugee problem here: it's yer ethnic Hungarians getting out of Romania, i'n't it'), Tony told us Budapest was the best city he had seen. In Madrid he had got piles sitting on the bare concrete benches at Atletico's ground ('there were cushions for hire outside, but I didn't discover that till after, did I?'). Rotterdam he remembered little of ('had a few') and Moscow had frankly bored a learning hound like him.

'There was nothing to do in Moscow except the hookers,' he said. 'If I was younger and still in the navy I might have had a go. But now I've learnt not to dip yer wick where an Arab's been. One lad went with this bird for three hundred dollars. He said it was the experience of a lifetime. Well, in my wide experience of females and their anatomy, she must've had an extra part to be worth three hundred bucks.

'No, me, I prefer sightseeing,' he said. 'Make sure every day's full. I went on a trip yesterday and I got it well wrong. Four hours up the bloody motorway to see some bloody collective farm.'

The bus's last stop was on top of a huge hill which overlooks Budapest. We stood, Tony and I, looking down on the Danube waltzing its way through the city laid out like a model train set below us.

'Great view,' I said.

'Aye,' said Tony. 'Too bloody good for foreigners.'

After the bus tour, I headed up to the old quarter, and wandered round a magnificent baroque church. Purity and simplicity were obviously anathema to Hungarian architects, every inch of the interior was covered in devotional paintings and strange hiero- glyphics, as if the chief designer from Umbro had got hold of the place.

There were United fans in here too, looking interested, checking their guidebooks as around them, in the nave, a gamelan outfit was setting up its gongs and cymbals, bonging and crashing as it went.

'Bloody hell,' said one of the reds when someone dropped a big, bass gong. 'Sounds like that old cow from Maine Road, Ellen, with 'er bleedin bell.'

Most of the reds, though, were gathered in the city centre, drinking. A group had laid out their flags around a fountain in the pedestrianised shopping area. There was a cheery variety: 'MUFC, Brickhouse Reds: from Newton Heath to Munich, from Rotterdam to Eternity' read one. The legend on another stated simply, '17 Years' – an important reference that, in United-speak: it was that long since Manchester City had won a trophy. It went up to eighteen years on 1 March 1994. Someone else, with an optimistic piece of loyalty, had brought along a Manchester Olympic 2000 flag, liber- ated from some public building back home. As they sang their songs (the best was to the tune of 'You've Lost That Loving Feeling': 'We've got that Micky Phelan/Woe-oh that Mickey Phelan/We've got that Mickey Phelan/And he's sub, sub, sub/Woe-woe-woe'), tourists took snaps and shook their hands and wished them well.

I bought a T-shirt from a lad, also called Tony, who was sitting in a bar with a pile of about twenty of them. They had been made specially for the tie, he explained, to be worn to the next round, a veteran's battle honour. They had the date of the match and the crests of the two clubs. For additional authenticity, Honved's name was spelt incorrectly. 'You can't buy them in the shops, these,' T-shirt Tony said. 'Only a fiver, we brought about four hundred with us. We'll sell the lot, definitely. Pay for the trip and a few of these.'

He downed a lager and asked me who I had travelled with.

Came on the press trip, I said.

'Oh no,' he said, rolling his eyes. 'You're not doing one of them there-was-no-trouble-but-you-could-sense-the-undercurrent-of-hatred articles are yer? Listen we're pussy cats compared to them daft old days. We had some geezer from the *Star* do that on us when we played Pesci Muncas. He stayed with us in the hotel; we'd gone over, a crowd of us, like, for a few days before the game. Thought we'd never see the article, didn't he? But someone brought one over with them on the day of the match. He'd made it all up, bollocks and that. Right bollocks. Give him a hard time? Christ we fuckin' crucified the feller. I felt sorry for him in the end.'

No, I said, I wasn't doing anything like that.

At six o'clock, two hours before kickoff, the press party made its way to the field of battle. The Kispest district is not Budapest's most scenic. Through grimy streets the press bus went, on every corner there was a bar, and every bar was filled with United fans, singing and beering. Just before we got to the ground, we saw the blue sweep of a police light, and heard the whelp of a siren.

'Eh up,' said a couple of the tabloid boys, jumping up towards the front of the bus.

'Trouble.'

But no, it was just a policeman testing his electrics. By a gate into the stadium itself, a tubby United fan and a tubby Honved follower were exchanging shirts and shaking each other warmly by the hand. Nothing to report there, then.

Honved's ground, overshadowed by a big, steamy industrial complex with lots of chimneys pumping out a stink, was comfortingly familiar to anyone who had been to Altrincham's Moss Lane. Except Moss Lane has seats. And at least one gents. The line of poplars which had been planted along one side of the ground, apparently in an attempt to hide the factory, were, it transpired, there for a different purpose: the only poplars in Europe to survive on a diet of urine. There was a small stand squatting down one side of the pitch, the rest of the accommodation was open terracing. On a balmy September evening no one much minded. But if this had been January in an acid rain storm, the reds, occupying a pen at the opposite end of the ground to the locals (who advertised themselves as the Ultra Red Boys Kispest) would have been in less cheerful voice. As it was, encouraged by the hospitable prices of the local brew, they were already in good song when we arrived and didn't stop singing throughout. One lad entertained himself before the kickoff by climbing a giant advertising hoarding behind the terracing and obscuring an incitement to buy Shell with the '17 Years' flag I had seen decorating the town square earlier in the day.

'What's that for?' one of the pressmen said. 'I thought it was twenty-five years since they were last in the European Cup.'

The press boxes were exactly that, tiny prefabs, probably made of asbestos, with glass fronts and no air. After the night some of those boys had enjoyed, a box with no air is no place to watch a game. Instead I wandered up into the stand, and sat on a concrete bench which Tony the sightseer would have been relieved to miss out on. Around me the Hungarians ate packets and packets of sunflower seeds; 'for the nerves' one told me, and it looked as efficient a way to quell the football-match terrors as smoking or chewing gum; the only unfortunate side effect is that you end up cheeping. To one side, in the directors' box (they had chairs), Bobby Charlton and Ferenc Puskas, old sparring partners, greeted each other with the kind of mutual respect the great reserve for each other. Next to me sat a bloke working for the English-language newspaper in Budapest, the *Hungarian Times*. He told me that Joel Cantona, Eric's brother, had recently been playing for Ferencvaros and that Eric had been spotted during the summer paying a fraternal visit, taking in the local culture. 'Apparently he was out on the town until two, three, four in the morning every night,' he said. 'Really enjoying himself.'

That's the thing about being a United player, you can never

escape it; even a thousand miles away, there are plenty of eyes on the scan for indiscretion.

To a mass cheer from the five thousand visitors and a lone firework from the locals, United trotted out on to a pitch which appeared to possess more grass than the rest of Hungary. They wore green and yellow with, in a touch which warmed the hearts of traditionalists, the numbers 1–11 on their backs and no sign of names on shoulders. Robson, back at number 7 and in charge, issued lengthy instructions to Cantona and Giggs. Then, at 8.04 p.m., on 15 September 1994, United kicked off in the European Cup.

The ball was played by Cantona to Giggs, who slipped over. Then Sharpe slipped, then Keane slipped. When Pallister slipped, letting in their number 8 for a shot at Schmeichel, it was apparent that whoever advised them on stud selection had clearly slipped.

Gradually, growing more sure-footed, United began to dominate the game. After less than twenty minutes, Giggs and Sharpe carved up their defence down the left and Keane, becoming agoraphobic because he was getting so much space on the right, stole into the area to score. So that was the point of him that Nigel and I had missed.

Ten minutes later, after Sharpe, showing little sign of any injury strain, had again destroyed them on the left, Keane popped in another. It was rousing stuff, until Parker slipped in our box and they scored. The Ultra Red Boys celebrated, as did the electronic scoreboard: 'Goooool', it flashed, and I thought European slip-ups like that could come back to haunt us.

But I had thought without Giggs. He was rampant, flicking, feinting, doing disco shimmies and swivels of the hip.

An American voice behind me kept on saying: 'Yes, oh, yes, that is beautiful, beautiful,' every time the boy performed part of his repertoire. After another piece of dreamy play, the voice tapped me on the shoulder.

'Hi, I'm from the American embassy,' it said. 'Who is that guy? That number eleven?'

'His name's Ryan Giggs,' I said.

'Ryan Giggs,' he said. 'Beautiful name, beautiful athlete.'

The voice nearly creamed itself when, just before half-time, the beauty whipped in a beauty of a cross; their centre back slipped and Cantona poked it home.

In the second half United could have had a bucketful. Cantona missed, Robson missed, Phelan, on as a less attractive replacement for Giggs, met a corner with a thump of his ever-expanding forehead, which the keeper tipped over. And that goal-scoring Phelan was gone, gone, gone. Instead the only strike that counted came from them, another lapse, another 'Goooool'; 3–2 when it could have been 6–0.

At the final whistle, I picked my way through the drifts of discarded sunflower kernels, down under the stand to the dressing rooms.

Brian McClair, the non-combatant foreigner, brought over in case one of the others had broken down in training, had been sent out of the dressing room with Ben Thornley, the non-combatant youth, and they stood in the corridor like a pair of naughty schoolboys removed from class. Through the thin commie-built walls, you could hear Ferguson's voice, raised in anger, yelling at those who had taken part.

'Bit wet out there,' I said to McClair.

'Aye, a bit,' he said.

'Their number five was useful,' I said.

'Aye, all right,' he said.

'Reckon you could have won it by four or five tonight,' I said.

'Aye, mebbes,' he said. It was difficult for him to speak to me, I realised, with his ear cocked, trying to catch the bollocking going on within.

'I agree with yer, mate,' said Thornley, anxious perhaps for his first press interview. 'Their number five? Different class.'

McClair looked at him, looked at me and frowned.

When the door eventually opened and Ferguson appeared, he had rearranged his features into a look of calm, diplomatic ease as he made his way up to the directors' bar for a press conference. First up were the Hungarian media. A young student interpreter stood next to Ferguson translating. He spent most of the conference looking confused at the pronunciation. 'Well, it was a three–two win and we're disappointed,' Ferguson said. 'Before the game we would have been happy with three-two of course, but just now we're kicking ourselves for not winning it by six. We could have sent some signals round Europe tonight if we'd done that, I tell you. Instead we let silly goals in: the lads are insistent their second one was a mile offside, but I'm not so sure. I've always said this about Europe, lose concentration for five minutes and the roof falls in on you. Tonight we were lucky in that respect, we will be going back to Old Trafford with a win, and so long as we don't go mad there, we're through. And that's the important thing. Tonight we have shown we can play, but we have some concentration problems. Mebbe we've learnt the lesson. I hope so.'

A local asked him what he thought of their team.

'Good, skilful. But young, you need to learn.'

The pitch was very slippery, I said.

'Ar,' he said. 'Apparently they've had a bit of a drought over the summer, so with all the rain last night, it just sat on the surface. But we should be used to rain. And they'll have to get used to it. When they come to Manchester, the one thing we can guarantee them is rain.'

Standing behind him, Bobby Charlton, wearing a Manchester 2000 badge on his lapel (motto: 'the precipitation in Manchester during the Olympic period is the equivalent of a wipe with a damp cloth'), didn't find that one funny.

Then Ferguson spotted Denis Law, hovering in the press pack, his commentary duties done. He wrapped his arm around the great man's shoulders, then announced to the Hungarians that he was the man they ought to speak to.

'Here we are,' he said. 'Two great Scots footballers, sixty-five international caps between us. He got sixty-five and I got fuck all.'

As Ferguson conducted some interviews with the television crews, I spotted Roy Keane coming out of the dressing room into the corridor. I congratulated him.

'Always nice to score,' he said, eyes alight with elation.

Was he nervous I wondered, on his European debut?

'Nah, it wasn't really a big game,' he said. 'Well, it was like, but I wasn't.'

As I asked him about playing wide on the right, a couple of other press lads joined in on the interrogation: there were quotes on offer here, quotes they didn't want to miss.

'Well, it's not really me best position,' he said, being worked into a corner by the gathering pack. 'It gives me too much time to think, and I'm not so good at that. I prefer running all the time down the middle. You get too much time on the ball out on the wing and I'm not good on the ball. Mind you, I'm such a squaddie, I'll play anywhere he asks me. I'd go in goal to get a game. If the Boss tells me the right wing, I'll play there.'

It had worked well tonight, one of the boys said. Unlike at Chelsea.

'Ar, against Chelsea I was fucking crap. To be honest widcha, I was so shite I thought I was lucky to be in the starting line-up today.'

I asked him how he was settling in at United.

'It's a dream just to play for Manchester United. The day I signed I was settled. People will be asking me in two years if I'm settled. They'll probably ask me in ten. But, honest, I feel well settled now.'

I was just about to ask him what the point of Roy Keane was when Ferguson, spotting out of the corner of his protective eye that one of his younger players was being interviewed, shouted: 'Oi, youse cunts, leave the guy alone. What do you want out of him, a book or something?'

The smile suggested he was about 40 per cent in jest.

On the plane home, everyone relaxed. The players, unable to share Manx Air's hospitality on the way out, were already an hour into the drinks trolley by the time the press – copy dispatched, pictures wired – arrived at the airport. As we stepped on to the plane we were greeted with a relaxed rendition of 'Where the fucking hell were you?'

While the plane trundled its way back to Manchester, everyone was up and in the aisles, talking: Ince collared Rob Shepherd of

Today, wanting to know why his coverage of England matches was so negative. Shepherd, not one to shirk a challenge, even from Paul Ince, explained it was because England are crap.

'Yeah, but it doesn't help the boys, does it?' Ince said.

'Is that my job?' asked Shepherd.

'Yeah,' said Ince.

Ferguson worked the aisles, easy with his players: now was the time for spirit to be built. He chatted for twenty minutes with Cantona, sitting, as usual, away from the rest; he upbraided Thornley and Butt for drinking ('Are youse two old enough? What am I gonna tell your parents?'); he listened patiently to David Meek, the *Manchester Evening News*'s venerable United correspondent, as he presented the press corps' complaints about the plane; he shmoozed Pallister and Ince: 'Excuse me,' he said to Rob Shepherd as he leant over him to talk to Ince, 'I have to butter up my prima donna superstars from the England squad.'

'England team, actually,' said Pallister.

And he had a drink himself.

Over the next fortnight, United scooped up two more league wins, the points against Arsenal won by a free kick from Cantona of fearful power. Twenty-two points and rising.

They also played the first leg of the Coca-Cola Cup at Stoke. Ferguson fielded Martin, Phelan and Dublin to give them some running. Rather proving the intellectual wing of the press's point about the depth of United's squad, they lost at the Victoria Ground 2–1: Dublin got the goal.

Then came the return fixture against Honved, a tie which did not set the Mancunian pulse racing: the stands had more gaps than a seven-year-old's smile; it was the lowest crowd of Old Trafford's season. This time Keane was the unlucky foreigner. He sat in the stand, an Umbro track coat covering a checked jacket and tie combination loud enough to have been heard in Rotherham. Ferguson had not relished the choice, which, with Schmeichel, Cantona, Giggs and Irwin certainties, had rested between Hughes and Keane.

'You know Sparky is not the most understanding of people,' he explained. 'But I'd rather have a punch-up with him than Keane. Have you seen the size of Roy's forearms?'

It wasn't much of a game the missing thousands missed. United won at a canter. Giggs was again beautiful; twice he essayed that little trick of his where, in possession, with his back to his marker, he flicks the ball over his own shoulder and the defender's and is round and on it before his opponent has time to turn.

He wasn't the only one displaying tricks. At one point Cantona did an extravagant overhead kick on the touchline, a piece of aplomb which earned him a kick up the backside from a defender. As Cantona got up, he kicked the offender on the shin, then glowered at the linesman standing but a yard away, daring him to do something about his bit of retaliation. The linesman took one look at those flared nostrils and decided to keep his flag sheathed.

But it was won in a less fanciful manner. Bruce, his head swathed with bandages which protected a forehead slice open from a collision with an Arsenal boot ten days earlier, scored twice – with headers. It was a feat which sent one reporter into raptures when Bruce arrived to answer questions in the press room afterwards.

'Steve you have a tremendous scoring record, don't you? That's two tonight and you scored in every round in the Cup Winners Cup. I reckon that's pretty good for a centre back.'

'Er, thanks,' he replied, still eating a piece of pork pie. And then he left.

But one thing struck me more than any other during the game. Around the pitch those new revolving advertising boards had been installed; the ones that flip electrically so that you can display three different ads in the space normally taken up by one – for 'Ooh Aah *Daily Star*', maybe, or 'Harcros Building Supplies' – thus trebling the income from the one space. During the periods of *longueur* in the first half, Old Trafford was so quiet that the only sound you could hear was a gentle electric swish, clump, as the perimeter advertising boards rotated. As a metaphor for the new way of things at United, I was to discover, it would take some beating.

3

Money, Money, Money

*Exploitation? Who's exploited? If it gives them
enough money to buy a Roy Keane or two,
and pay Cantona's wages why should I worry
if it means selling jumpers to kids in
Portsmouth.*
    Red Eye, contributor to *Red Issue* fanzine

Once before a game, because the press can use the same gents as
the directors at Old Trafford, I found myself standing in the middle
trap when two plushly coated men came in and stood either side of
me. They were talking over my head, continuing a conversation
begun elsewhere, possibly in one of the myriad executive dining
facilities which have sprouted underneath the new stands.

'The year before last we did three million,' said one of the leakers.
'Last year, even with the title we only did five. This year we're
looking at ten.'

As I shook and left, I clocked that the speaker was Martin
Edwards, chairman and chief executive of Manchester United Football Club PLC.

If you like money Old Trafford is a great place to be. On match
days the whiff of it is everywhere, striking nostrils with even more
force than that traditional Saturday aromatic cocktail of hot dogs,
police-horse manure and beery farts. Once a fortnight this quarter
of a Manchester industrial estate hosts more than just a football
match. It transmogrifies into a bazaar, as teeming, colourful and
chaotic as anything in the Middle East. Every centimetre of pavement within half a mile of the ground is occupied by commerce.
Fast-food wagons churn out cholesterol by the coronary load; stalls
sell souvenir scarves, hats, badges and posters; several men trade in

rare match programmes; boys with bin-liners jammed with T-shirts yell 'get your Cantona only a fiver'; youths by the dozen off-load piles of magazines, newspaper supplements, lottery tickets; a woman under a golf umbrella paints adolescent complexions red, white, yellow or green; and men with shifty faces move against the tidal flow calling out their mantra: 'Anyone need tickets? Buy or sell.'

But the most extraordinary sight is reserved for once you have fought your way into the shadow of the ground itself. There, snaking round crush barriers that are permanently cemented into the fore-court, is the queue for the Manchester United superstore. It is made up of people already burdened by United apparel – shirts, sweaters, jackets, earrings – lining up for up to an hour behind at least two thousand others in all the filth the Manchester sky can throw down on their heads, for the privilege of buying yet more stuff: 3-D posters of Lee Sharpe (£5.99), Peter Schmeichel souvenir drinking mugs (£9.99), Giggsy duvet covers (£25.99). Also ladies' goat-skin leather purses with embossed club crest (£12.99), toddlers' romper suits with embroidered away colours (£14.99) and official United fleece tops by Umbro (appropriately named, price £34.99). A range of fifteen hundred items of United memorabilia is available to empty the pockets of the day-trippers.

'Sometimes on a match day,' said Edward Freedman, United's energetic merchandising manager whose office overlooks this swarm of profitability, 'the chairman comes here, and we both just stand and look out over the queue. Then we smile at each other.'

As in their results on the pitch, so in their financial dealings, United did rather well in 1994. In an economic sector which has tradition-ally involved about as much chance of a good return on investment as opening your wallet over a drain, at Old Trafford they have introduced a new word to the football vocabulary: profit. During 1993–94, profits topped £10 million.

'Manchester United,' said a stock market analyst I rang to ask to recommend a football club to buy into. 'They are the only ones remotely likely to give you a return on your investment.'

United have always been that little bit sharper with money than the rest of football. When Martin Edwards's father Louis ran the place, he had a shrewd eye for making a commercial return on other people's fanaticism, not least in the manner in which he used to supply the club's catering outlets with pies from his own meat company, items which, so legend has it, were not fully acquainted with the phrase 'sell by date'. He realised, too, that the well-heeled middle classes of south Manchester and Cheshire had plenty to offer his club: plenty of readies. In 1965 United were the first club in the country to build executive boxes; some of the companies which took a lease back then still retain them, making the boxes the most expensive pieces of hire-purchased real estate in the north. When Louis Edwards died in 1980 – hounded to his death, the family maintained, by a Granada Television documentary sniffing corruption – his son took over the bailiwick.

Martin Edwards, a decent public school and club rugby player, was not in the cut of the usual football club owner, not the local-boy-made-good who used to stand on the terraces and who ploughs money into his club as an expensive piece of local philanthropy; he was no Jack Walker of Blackburn, or Jack Hayward of Wolves, or Lionel Pickering of Derby; in fact he had no obvious qualification for the job. It was as if Darren Ferguson became manager on the nod after his dad retired. Many of the supporters, who had always fondly assumed that Sir Matt Busby, the people's champion, would succeed Louis Edwards, were wary of him from the start. His interests, they suspected, were more Edwards than United.

'There is no question,' said Johnny Flacks, of the Football Supporters Association, a United season ticket-holder and a harsh critic of the Old Trafford regime, 'that some of the activity he sanctioned in his early days undermined the performance on the field.'

In 1986, Flacks points out, when United appeared to be romping to the championship, Edwards negotiated to sell Mark Hughes, who couldn't stop scoring goals, to Barcelona midway through the season. But as soon as the transfer was organised, Hughes stopped scoring and United fell off the top. Edwards did not become any more popular with the fans when it was later revealed he received 1 per cent of whatever profits the club made on transfer dealings.

Fans' suspicions about his commitment to their cause were further fuelled when twice in the eighties, dancing to the tune of the times, he tried to flog the family silver. First, in 1984, he agreed to sell his majority stake to Robert Maxwell for £10 million; a flotation which didn't float, so to speak. Then, in 1989, a consortium led by a businessman with interests on the Isle of Man offered to buy him out for a cheerful £20 million.

It was not the most dignified episode in Manchester United's history. After a summer of speculation, before the first game of the new season, a small man with a moustache, easy to pass in the street, paraded in front of the Stretford End juggling a football. He was introduced as Michael Knighton, the new owner of Manchester United and, to be fair, he wasn't bad with a ball. The fans loved it (anyone was better than Edwards). But the deal fell through, Edwards was less impressed by his touch in the penalty area. Nevertheless he was given a seat on the board, which he has subsequently relinquished. I saw the would-be chairman at the 1991 Rumbelows Cup final, incidentally, standing by the door of Wembley's banqueting suite. I recognised him at once, but my mate Nigel didn't. Assuming him to be a steward, he asked for directions.

For one fan, the BBC journalist Michael Crick, this ghastly dash for cash epitomised the Edwards reign. In 1990 Crick wrote a critique of the club's financial direction: *Manchester United – The Betrayal of a Legend*.

'One can only pray that Martin Edwards hands over control to an owner prepared to return to some of the Busby philosophy,' was Crick's anguished conclusion. 'The magic of Manchester United will only be cast again if control of the club is restored to people prepared to represent those who inspired Sir Matt – the fans.'

Martin Edwards didn't take Crick's advice. He remains in his lavish suite of Old Trafford offices, just along the corridor from the windowless box-room Sir Matt used to grace. And how glad he must be he didn't manage to find a buyer back then. At a conservative estimate, five years on, the club is worth more than four times what Knighton offered him. In the 1993 published accounts, Edwards's bank balance improved to the tune of £174,500 in salary and by more than £600,000 in dividend payments on his 3.38 million shares; his shareholding value of £20 million rated him a place in the 1994 *Sunday Times* list of richest people. I tried to interview him during the course of last season, but he declined, writing me a charming letter saying he was too busy to see me. Fair enough: it's a time-consuming business filling out all those paying-in books.

Three important things have happened since Edwards tried to sell, which have sent United's finances to the top of the City premiership. First, United and the other big clubs broke away from the Football League and negotiated an astral-sized television deal of their own; an arrangement in which, unlike the past, the gargantuan fees were not shared with the poorer, lower-division clubs. It was a deal, many say, engineered by Edwards. You can see his point. United had twenty-six of their matches screened live by television last season. Only a utopian would have expected them to share the spoils of such overexposure with Hartlepool, Northampton and Wycombe; Bruce Forsyth, after all, feels under no obligation to hand over part of his earnings to the bloke who reads the local news on Granada. In the 1992–93 season they picked up £2,611,115 from the BBC and Sky and they didn't have to give a penny of it to Rochdale.

Secondly, in 1991, the club floated on the Stock Exchange. The idea was that the ordinary fan could take a stake and at the same time help to raise funds to rebuild the Stretford End. Plenty did: I know of at least two season ticket-holders who finance their United habits entirely from dividend payments on their shares. At the same time, though, institutions also took the opportunity to buy in: the BBC staff pension fund owns over 3 per cent of the shares, which, oddly, gives the 'Match of the Day' team a stake in the well-being of the club. Pressure from such big investors meant a host of professional expertise was brought in to assist Edwards, to ensure that the shareholders had a regular dividend fix. So in came men who knew what they were doing, like Edward Freedman, head-hunted from Tottenham, and from outside football altogether came

Robin Launders, the financial director with wide City experience. (Great name for an accountant, Launders.)

Thirdly, and most significantly, a team emerged under Alex Ferguson which started playing the most beautiful football seen for twenty-five years. The latent support throughout the country, which United had enjoyed since half its team were destroyed in the Munich aircrash of 1958, emerged from its torpor and blossomed into a free-spending celebratory bloom. And it focused Edwards's mind that the real money to be made out of United would come not from selling up, but from success on the pitch.

'We took one look at what was happening and started to exploit the opportunity,' said Danny McGregor, a long-time Edwards associate and now commercial manager at Old Trafford. 'In the nicest possible way, of course. The thing is, in this business of ours, you never know what's around the corner, so you would be sensible to make the most of today.'

Make the most of it they did. In a way Liverpool singularly failed to do in their period of pre-eminence. When I first went to Old Trafford, what you would spend was the 80p entrance money, 10p for a programme and, if you could stand the queues, 15p for a pie. That would be it, until next time. Now, the United follower is looked upon as a seven-day-a-week selling opportunity: his or her whole life can be financially orientated around the club. When I visited McGregor in his office, he sent me away with a holdall full of brochures for United schemes which have nothing to do with football. You can now drink Champs Cola, shop with a United Visa card, take a holiday with a United executive break, have your wedding reception in a club suite, hold your children's party in the museum canteen, and organise your pension through United financial services: fortunate, then, that Robert Maxwell didn't take over in 1984.

'What you have to realise,' said the ebullient McGregor, 'is that in the old days this place was only open for business on twenty-six days of the year. Now we are trying to make it a year-round facility.'

He's right: You can even come to Old Trafford and spend your money when the team isn't on display. Every day bar match days, a guided tour of the stadium is conducted. It is a brilliant piece of money-spinning: last season more than 100,000 people went on the tour; at £4.95 for an adult, £2.95 for children, it generated on its own more income than a Third Division club might make in half a season. And the cunning part is, if the tour I joined one afternoon was representative, these were people who were not regularly engaged in filling the United coffers.

More than fifty of us gathered in the trophy room underneath the main stand. In the corner a video played slow-motion replays of a recent goal. Three French students were watching the screen.

'*C'est Giggs, ça?*' said one, pointing at the goal-scorer.

'*Non,*' said his friend. '*C'est Sharpe, je crois.*'

It was Ince.

Behind them a woman in a wheelchair was disappointed she had forgotten her camera and was to miss the opportunity of having pictures taken of herself in front of the trophies in their cabinets. No problem, said the steward, we've got a camera on hand specially for such situations, we can take polaroids. So she was snapped alongside the FA Premier League trophy, a replica of the Cup Winners Cup, and the monstrosity that is the Barclays Manager of the Season award (on loan from Alex Ferguson, said the notice in front of it, and who could blame him not wanting it cluttering up the house). When she'd finished, a few more quid popped into the till: they charged her for the prints.

The tour guide, after he had shooed us upstairs to the under-stand concourse, asked how many of us had been to a match at Old Trafford. Unless they were all like me and couldn't be bothered to make their experience known, this was a tour full of United virgins. And how they loved being seduced by the place, by the little dis-carded pads of chewing gum around the manager's dugout, by the press room (available, so the guide told us, for hire for conferences and sales conventions), by the players' lounge ('which one,' said an excited seven-year-old bouncing on a chair, 'do you reckon Giggsy's sat in, Mum?'). In the home dressing room a man with a camcorder videoed the bars of Imperial Leather in dishes round the bath, and in the security monitoring room a woman asked how many policemen would be on duty for a match.

'When Liverpool or Leeds or City come, about two hundred and fifty,' said the guide. 'When Wimbledon come, three. But naughtiness has been eradicated inside this ground. The last time there was major trouble here was back in nineteen seventy-nine.'

Now if he'd asked if anyone had been at that match, against Forest, when the Scoreboard End erupted, I could have put up my hand.

The thing, though, that made everyone's tour, was when Mark Hughes trotted out on to the pitch for a photo shoot to promote a new Wales kit. When he had finished, as the fifty of us stood by the touchline, respecting the instruction in five languages not to walk on the playing surface, he came over. Showing remarkable patience, he proceeded to sign every autograph, pose for every snapshot, pull a face for every camcording that was asked of him.

And that, fundamentally, is what has United's bottom line looking so healthy: the players. Not only is this team a winning one, but it is stuffed with photogenic teenage idols and newsworthy foreign geniuses. It is a running, kicking, scoring, year-round advertisment for Martin Edwards's brand.

'Oh, there's no question that this team has made everyone's job easier,' said Danny McGregor. 'Hey, if the team's winning, no one complains if the rolls are stale in the hospitality restaurants.'

If only Louis Edwards had thought of that.

It is in merchandising that the players' influence is most telling. Three years ago, merchandising's contribution to the spreadsheet of Theme Park United was negligible; this year as Martin Edwards predicted over the porcelain, it topped £10 million, more than 30 per cent of turnover. Sitting in his office before a game one Saturday in the season, surrounded by sample products and sales-figure data, Edward Freedman was a happy merchandising manager indeed. He rolled off, for my benefit, a long list of his financial superlatives.

'We have the best-selling replica football shirts in the country.

We have seven titles in the top-selling videos in the country, including the number one. Our *Manchester United Magazine* sells more than a hundred thousand copies a month, making it the biggest-selling football title. We . . .'

So it went on. In the two years since Freedman arrived from Tottenham Hotspur he has set about marketing United with the unabashed enthusiasm of a McDonald's executive.

'There is no question,' he said, 'that the football souvenir business will be the growth business in this country in the nineties. And Manchester United is uniquely equipped to lead the growth. Manchester United is a unique brand. Arsenal, you see, despite all their huge success on the pitch, are big only in north London. United are national, international, global. So, with skilful marketing you can achieve anything.'

As well as a huge mail-order operation ('clock these,' he said, handing over a pile of orders a goalpost high, 'that's just today's'), Freedman, through a franchise deal with Birthdays, a greetings-card retail chain co-owned by Bryan Robson, has opened up United superstores in the high streets of Belfast, Dublin, Plymouth and Manchester. By 1996, long-suffering parents will be able to equip their offspring's requirements for red paraphernalia in Sydney and Tokyo too.

Freedman's biggest seller in all the outlets are the replica shirts, items manufactured by Umbro, an American-owned company, based in Wythenshawe, south Manchester. There are three types of shirt: the scarlet home number, complete with a watermark inlay picture of Old Trafford stadium; the black-and-gold change shirt for when the opposition wears red and the referee wears lime; and, for when the opposition wears red but the referee wears black, the yellow-and-green heritage shirt, as worn when the club was formed as Newton Heath (though presumably in the 1870s the shirts did not have Umbro and MUFC woven into the fabric).

Now you might think that yellow and green would be a usable substitute for red in every conceivable circumstance of colour clash and that black might appear to be superfluous to any playing

requirements. And you would be right. Umbro's marketing manager, Simon Marsh, admits as much:

'The black shirt is principally a fashion-driven item,' he told me
when I visited his factory. 'There is not a footballing need for the
kit in the sense that the yellow-and-green shirt will avoid a clash in
all instances. But we make a considerable investment in the club
and we seek a return on that investment.'

Return on investment (how much he wouldn't tell me) is what
Umbro get. These garments sell by the factory load: the day the new
red kit was launched, the queue outside the superstore stretched the
entire circumference of the ground. Small children are particularly
fond of the outfits and by embracing the junior market, Umbro and
United have attracted endless charges of exploitation. The charges
are: the shirts cost a packet, come complete with built-in obso-
lescence – since the design changes every other year – and generally
make parents' lives a misery.

Me, I don't subscribe to that view. This is a commercial world we
live in and if parents cannot resist temptation on their offspring's
behalf, then that's their problem. Besides, if my son's experience is
typical, kids derive considerable pleasure from playing football in
the garden dressed in the same kit as Ryan Giggs wears; it would
require industrial quantities of vaseline and a crowbar to separate
my boy from his constant green-and-yellow companion. Call me
irresponsible, but £32.95 seems a reasonable price to pay for six
months of smiles.

No, my argument is that my club should entrust their image to
an outfit with the visual sense of Ray Charles. Umbro manufactures
solely from a form of artificial fibre which, when pulled over the
head, generates more electricity than Sizewell B. Apparently, in
order to make the shirts impossible to pirate, this material is then
decorated by an inlaid, 3-D, hieroglyphic scribble motif which looks
as though a gorilla has been attempting *The Times* crossword on
the front. Add to that an onanistic fascination for its own tradename
and you have a garment which even Cantona, Paco Rabane's man,
by turning up the collars and lacing the redundant laces down the
front, cannot invest with any style.

As such the shirts entirely fit the United merchandising brief: no items of any taste, be it bed linen or wallpaper, calendar or egg-cup shall be sold within the environs of Old Trafford. Lack of style, though, does not stop the match-day buying frenzy when, according to Danny McGregor, 'There are more buggers in that shop down there than there were in *Ben Hur*'. The average spend in the souvenir shop by match-goers is now £2 per head per game.

And Edward Freedman is after more. Over the close season he took over an erstwhile car-spares warehouse which abuts the Stretford End. It comprises 57,000 square feet, the size of a fringe-of-town megastore, which he transformed into a souvenir supermarket which makes the one on the front concourse look like Mr Khan's on the corner; a monster shop, where United stuff can be bought by the trolley load; Red 'R' Us.

'When I looked at those queues on a match day and the fact it took an hour to get into the shop and I thought of how many people must be put off from coming in, I realised something had to be done,' said Mr Freedman of his new imperial headquarters. 'Our critics talk about exploitation. I prefer to call it satisfying a demand. Besides, it means Arsenal won't be able to claim they have the biggest souvenir shop in England any more.'

He grinned at that thought: the former Spurs employee with the recalcitrant Arsenal-loathing gene.

There are, it seems, no limit to what United can do, what angle they can exploit, no end to the ways they can make money. It is money which they need to make. In 1993 the wage bill was £6,182,000. There were 114 permanent staff then (43 professional players – the youth team are YTS – 28 ground staff, 13 in the ticket office and 30 in administration), plus some 250 part-timers (from chefs to programme sellers) employed on match days. This meant the average wage in that first champion season was nearly £55,000, an astonishing figure bettered only by a handful of City of London financial institutions and Blackburn Rovers. But by 1995, with some of the contracts Martin Edwards has signed to keep his highly marketable squad together, this figure could go up by 50 per cent. Such a rapacious beast takes feeding.

'It does and we will play our part doing it,' Edward Freedman said. 'But you asked if there were limits. Yes, there are limits. We will not sanction anything which diminishes the good name of our club. That is why we need to sort that lot out.'

He pointed out of his office window, down on to Sir Matt Busby Way, where the match-day open market sites itself, where the free-lances live, where money is made which does not find its way through United's tills. And that hurts.

There are four chip shops within a potato's throw of Freedman's office. On match days, beneath pictures of the great heroes – Best, Law, Hughes and, in the Lou Macari Chip Shop, Lou Macari – half the annual agricultural output of Lincolnshire is fried up to line rumbling beer bellies.

How much food is actually handed over the four shops' counters can only be guessed at. When I asked the manageress at the Lou Macari shop (once owned by the man himself) how many portions of chips she sold, she behaved as if she had signed the official secrets act.

'I can't tell you that, it's confidential,' she said.

Could she at least give an estimate of how many people came in to the shop, I asked.

'I'm not prepared to say,' she said, turning her back on me.

Or, I suggested, who on earth she sells stuff to during the summer?

'Will you leave now, please.'

At Marina's Restaurant and Grill, round the corner on Matt Busby Way, the man bailing out the tuck was more forthcoming, if no more specific.

'Fuck knows, mate,' he said. 'All I know is I go home Sat'dee with a sore fucking wrist from doing this all day.'

Serving chips, presumably.

Further down the road, the woman under the big golf umbrella who paints cheeks, chins and noses for £2 a time (the teenage girls usually just want Giggs on their face), told me she was a drama teacher during the week.

'I'm here every home match, weather permitting, usually do about sixty or seventy,' she said. About £120 on a good day; for five hours' work it sounded like a more lucrative pursuit than encouraging children to stand around like trees.

Elsewhere there are T-shirt salesmen offering items of a more robust visual humour than might be found in the souvenir shop: a parody of the lettering on the Liverpool sponsor's logo, which reads 'Cocksuckers' instead of Carling; a picture of an empty piece of furniture with the legend, 'For sale: one trophy cabinet, unused for 17 years, apply Mr P. Swales, Maine Road, Manchester'; or the more simple and direct 'Scum', the affectionate local term for Leeds United.

It is these last which arouse Freedman's ire: the swag workers, as they are known. Manchester is the centre of swag culture: most of the shirts outside any football ground will have come from the city, as will most of the salesmen. T-shirts sold unlicensed and pirated at pop festivals in Glastonbury come from Manchester; a Manc swag worker was spotted selling shirts outside Giants Stadium during the World Cup. Their biggest market is on their own doorstep, however, and United are not happy about it.

'We cannot allow things like that to be sold within sight of the ground,' Edward Freedman told me. 'Partly because "Scum" T-shirts are not the kind of thing we want associated with our club and partly because they sell shoddy goods which rip off our customers.'

And partly because they are creaming off some of the money you would like?

'Look, no one objects to fish and chip shops and face-painting, they are supplying a service which we don't and good luck to them. These pirate merchandisers are a different matter: they are making money from our good name. We have taken steps to stop that kind of thing, we have brought a lot of the stall holders into the fold, said if you want to supply goods, then we will supply you, license you. We have also trademarked our name and logo. It is now a criminal offence to pass off a piece of merchandise as genuine when it is not.'

Which is why, outside Wembley, scarves which say things like 'Red Army', and 'Manchester on the march' are on sale: unlicensed.

'Those who have chosen to stay outside the fold, we have pursued in the courts. We have undercover teams working as we speak, infiltrating the firms which supply the fake goods. We are not messing around here.'

'Licence from them?' said Steve Bentley, who makes unlicensed T-shirts. 'It's me what should be on a percentage from them, for services improving their image. Because their cool rating's gone right down. You wouldn't be seen dead in the stuff they produce; the only thing a lad might buy from them is a badge.'

Steve, by day a sign-maker, by night calls himself Barney's Football Chic – Barney after his former penchant for a bundle in United's cause. He is bespoke T-shirt-maker to the hard-core reds. Not to be confused with the swag workers, Steve's material is chic, clever and not profit-motivated. Witty visual parodies of American sportswear labels, his range includes shirts decorated 'Champions' (in the Champion-style), 'Studwiser' (like Bud) and the cult item, the 'L'Eric Sportif', with a cartoon of the great Frenchman in place of the Coq Sportif's cockerel.

'I've got another ten designs coming soon,' Steve said. 'My favourite is a picture of Remi Moses with just the word "Respect" underneath. 'Cos he deserves maximum respect.' The idea of these T-shirts came to him, he said:

'Because there isn't anything for the lads out there. I've never sold anything to anyone wearing a football shirt. I don't sell them outside the ground, it just cheapens it all. It's a cliquey thing, if too many people get hold of them, then they're not exclusive. It's like a new nightclub. You think it's great and then the ordinary Joe gets to hear about it, comes along and it's not great any more. I like to keep things elite and exclusive. It's like I used to get my Ts bulk, but I wasn't happy. They got saggy in the neck and I'd rather be dead than have Barney Ts with a saggy neck, so now I get them from Russell Athletic. They cost a bit, but there you are.'

This is the way of fan enterprise at Old Trafford. While the club itself is expert in satisfying the astonishing demand for Giggsy and Dannie Behr his-and-hers bath towels, some fans have found a handsome market selling each other items of more grassroots interest. A lad who wants something cool from Barney's can get it only by mail order; forms available only where reds-in-the-know are likely to find them.

'I used to run a stall in Affleck's Palace,' said Steve, 'selling both United and City T-shirts. It was a shop of two halves, like. But with me doing a full-time job I had to staff it with kids. And the coloured lads used to come in and tax them. They were taking so much clobber it wasn't worth carrying on.'

Now he is happier, selling enough to keep him in match tickets.

'I do about two hundred a month altogether,' he said. 'My most popular United one is the "L'Eric". I could do a lot more, but you'd lose the ethic of it, wouldn't you?'

Towards the end of the season, while Steve was ensuring exclusivity by turning down orders from people he thought uncool, someone less scrupulous of their cool rating was making hay in the Warwick Road open market. Imitations of the 'L'Eric Sportif' T-shirt I acquired from Barney's were selling by the back-heel load. Only at Manchester United: a pirate of a pirate.

What do the players think of all the commerce? Well, since they benefit directly and indirectly (it does no harm to their marketable image) they are generally tolerant with their time.

Danny McGregor attests that: 'The chairman, manager and players are all fantastic here. If I want one of them for a function, they always do their best to make themselves available. That's the thing about Manchester United, despite its size, this is still a family club. Everyone, from the chairman down, is interested in only one thing: what's best for Manchester United.'

One big happy family, then, corralled by Our Martin, as the fans, with a twinge of irony, term the chairman?

Not quite.

Plenty of reds I know think Edwards is doing a good job maximis-
ing the club's earnings and, as the man who has delivered success
off the pitch to match Ferguson's on it, deserves his handsome
reward. Others find it hard to disguise their lingering dislike and
the suspicion born in the eighties. The fanzines, for instance. There
are four of them at United – *Red Issue, Red News, United We Stand*
and *Walking Down the Warwick Road* – all of them publications
dating from the dim days of 1988 and 1989 when they were born
from a desire to expose what hard-core fans thought was going
wrong with the club.

'We were cheesed off with what was happening on the pitch and
off it,' John Daniels of *Red Issue*, the senior fanzine told me. 'I
suppose we wanted to put some fun back in our lives which were
a bit grim.'

Martin Edwards might enjoy the irony, given their consistent
attacks on the financial arrangements of his club, that as interest in
United has reached meltdown, all four fanzines have started to
make money. The hawkers down the Warwick Road and at selected
away grounds ('not Elland Road or Anfield, for obvious reasons,'
said John Daniels) are selling more and more. *Red Issue* and *United
We Stand* now print well over 5000 copies an edition; *Red News*, by
its own admission less regular, is not far behind.

'As we got more money in, we just reinvested it,' Andy Mitten
of *United We Stand* told me. 'Printed better, more regularly. Then
we used the profits to finance our football, paying for travel
and that. But now it's reached the point where I've had to
employ an accountant, run it as a business. I've become an Edwards.'

But while the fanzines recycle their profits, upgrading the
quality of their product all the time while keeping the price low,
there is a suspicion in their pages that this is not the Edwards
agenda.

Here is a typical letter to the fanzine, *Red News*, headlined 'A
Rich Martin's World', and signed 'A poor United fan who just about
affords his league match ticket-book.'

Nice to know that Our Martin is continuing the high standards of the Club that we fully expect from such a noble and wonderful Chief Executive!

This years' development lottery tickets sent to United members contain not one extra-money-for-Martin-making schemes, but two!

Firstly, if any reds do sell some tickets (a rare event I know), they complete a section entering the amount of tickets sold . . . fair enough.

But below that you are then asked to fill in a section which says, 'I enclose a donation of . . . towards stadium improvements.' What a cheek! Not only do they try and sell you lottery tickets, they then expect you to make an extra donation towards OT which They (the Club) should be funding. They earn all this money from gate money, merchandise, sponsorship, TV money, etc., need I go on, etc., and they still want an extra pound of flesh. And secondly . . . on the envelope in which you are supposed to send back your unsold tickets, they inform us that it is a Freepost letter (no stamp required) but if we use one it saves on their costs!!!

Anyone would think we were supporting Halifax Town and not the biggest club in Britain. No need to ask why Our Martin is so popular with the shareholders or why United's shares are doing so very very well.

Events may have proven Michael Crick entirely wrong when he made his prognosis five years ago in *Manchester United – The Betrayal of a Legend*, but he still remains in the camp of sceptics.

'I was completely mistaken because I predicted that Edwards's money obsession would hamstring any efforts on the pitch,' Crick said (he told me this when I bumped into him at an away match at West Ham). 'And what's gone on down there is thanks to Ferguson. Edwards was either very shrewd or very lucky to get him. But I still feel that I was valid in my criticism of the direction the club is taking, particularly becoming a PLC. They are now locked into a cycle where they are obliged to produce dividends at all costs, and since the directors are all shareholders they might not prove the most objective decision-makers if difficult choices have to be made.'

That is not all that worries Crick. There is also the question of the increasing middle-classing of the club. This is not carried out through any affection for social engineering, but because the middle classes have more money to part with. Effectively, over the past four years, a significant proportion of the traditional cloth-cap element among United's supporters has been priced out. For the 1990–91 season a league match ticket-book cost £110.50 for a seat in K stand, where the lads go; for the 1994–95 season the same annual tickets cost £266, an increment way above the rate of inflation. At the same time, the number of places available for the less well-off have declined as the stadium has gone all-seater. The invention of 'club class', an expensive, hospitality-led way of flogging ordinary seats, has swallowed up much of the new Stretford End. Once, after a match, on the train back to London, I met a bloke who had just sat in a club-class seat. His company owned two. They cost £900 the pair for the season, for which the customer was entitled to use the club-class facilities, such as the restaurant sited where we used to queue up for pies in the old days. A meal there was included in the price, I assumed.

'Oh no,' he said. 'You pay extra. But it's good grub.'

And more club means fewer cheap seats.

If it seems a perfectly usual business proposition – demand means that price can be lifted appropriately – what must be remembered is that football is not a perfectly usual business. It is has emotion stitched through it like Umbro's emblem on an away shirt.

'United's is such a short-term, high-risk strategy,' Johnny Flacks said to me. 'If they start to slip on the playing field, this new support will fade away. Can you see anyone buying the *Manchester United Magazine* if it's full of reports of defeats? What businessman wants to entertain clients by taking them to watch losers?'

Indeed who will buy the third-strip pantie liners, the Lee Sharpe hi-energy disco drink, the Eric Cantona autographed studs?

'We middle classes just don't show the same head-down, go-and-watch-the-grass-grow dedication that a football club needs as its bedrock,' continued Johnny. 'We've got better things to do with our time. At United if times get bad, the hard core won't be there to fall back on, as it still is at Liverpool, say. And even if people like me are dedicated, our sons will never become footballers. The people whose sons might play for United in the future are being told we don't want the likes of you, you can't give us enough money.

United shouldn't be holding on to their traditional support because they are some sort of social service, but because it is in their best interests not to alienate their future seed-bed. If I were Martin Edwards in his position, I'd make sure I had Ferguson by the balls for life. Because he's got to be certain someone keeps doing the business for him on the pitch.'

As I left Johnny's comfortable house in a comfortable street in comfortable south Manchester, I thought it takes an act of copper-bottomed, die-hard pessimism to predict United's imminent financial collapse. Here they are winning everything in sight, with a profit forecast that would send City stockbrokers galloping to their screens, and with more people outside the ground demanding tickets than most clubs get inside.

What's more, I thought, how could it go wrong? They were about to qualify for the money-printing exercise that is the mini-league stage of the European Cup.

4

Stuffed

*Galatasaray, Galatasaray, 2–0 up and fucked
it up, Galatasaray.*
          Manchester City fans, 7 November 1993

When it was announced that United were to play Galatasaray of
Istanbul in the second round of the European Cup, a friend sent
me a postcard. 'What a draw!' he wrote on it. He was right: qualification for the mini-league was now the most certain thing this side
of a date with a nurse. After the necessary mopping up, there would
be trips to Milan, Barcelona, Moscow, Monaco – well stocked with
duty-free. And Fergie, while making all the right noises about com-
placency and no such thing as an easy game in Europe, sounded
like a man who had just landed an easy game in Europe. 'The Turks
are lovely people,' he said on hearing the news. 'We're looking
forward to going over there.'

What did we know about Galatasaray? I caught the train up to
Manchester for the first leg with Michael Crick who, in addition
to documentation about Martin Edwards, keeps a sheaf of red
statistics in his briefcase. He revealed some important information:
unless there was a Finnish side called Aanaanan of which he was
unaware, Galatasaray were the only team in Europe with five As
and no other vowel in their name. He also knew they had been
required to win their last game of the season 8–0 away from home
to take their domestic championship. After a performance of grit,
determination, skill and composure and not a hint of bribe, back-
hander or bung, they had managed it.

But most of all, what we both knew was that they were from Turkey, a country whose last big moment in Europe was when the Ottoman Empire bequeathed its name to an item of household furniture; a country, moreover, whose footballers are about as resolute under pressure as England's cricketers. An early goal, we agreed, and they would crumble like the pastry on one of Louis Edwards's old meat pies.

Oddly, Michael forgot to mention that, like United, they were unbeaten at home in Europe. Also that in 1988, nearly a decade more recently than the reds, they had made it to the semi-final of the European Cup. And, more particularly, that the spine of their team was German.

I got to Old Trafford an hour before kickoff, to find that six thousand Turkish supporters had set up camp in the main stand, many of whom had travelled from as far away as Green Lanes, the kebab house quarter of north London. They were all men, wore yellow-and-scarlet headbands, banged drums, blew air horns and smoked cigarettes which, the smell suggested, were rolled from the contents of the laundry basket. Every one of them joined in chants about Cim Bom, their club's nickname. They made a huge and joyful noise; a noise, I jotted in my notebook, that 'was a triumph of hope over expectations'.

Just as the atmosphere had been, so the perimeter advertising boards were commandeered by the visitors: in addition to exhortations for Efes Pilsen and Turkish Airlines, there, in front of the Stretford End, was the poster that had become gigglingly familiar from televised England matches in Izmir and Istanbul. Any nation that had a commercial product called Arcelik could scarcely be taken seriously as a force in world football. Disappointingly, it turned out, this is a chain of television rental stores, their version of Rumbelows, so presumably Galatasaray once entered the Arcelik Cup.

As kickoff approached, and the United fans made their late and blasé way to their seats, it was clear this was no sellout: 'I'm keeping my powder dry for the big teams,' a mate had said. But the visitors' section of the directors' box was well occupied; Galatasaray's nobs greeted each other with pecks on the cheek and big shrugs of the shoulder which you didn't have to be Harry Enfield to translate as 'let's enjoy it while we can.' Oddly, Lou Macari was in there among them, on his way from Stoke to Glasgow. 'Just here to watch the stuffing,' he explained.

It seemed he was right. Within two minutes, Robson, dragging the ball past a centre back who possessed the turning circle of an oil tanker, had stabbed in a goal. The Turkish hordes were silenced, the United fans made gloating noises. For the next ten minutes the Turks gave the ball away with a frequency which suggested they were coached by Graham Taylor. After a moment of panic in their defences not seen since the Dardenelles were attacked, they conceded a needless corner which Pallister headed on and one of their players posted the ball into his own net. Pallister got no more than a handshake from one or two colleagues: this was routine.

'A procession', I wrote. Plus something about 'floodgates'.

At this stage Giggs decided to go solo, as if keen to advertise his wares to anyone watching from Milan, say. He jinked and jogged and lost the ball taking on his fifth defender. Usually this occurred with Cantona, lurking unmarked in the penalty area, turning the air Betty Blue with frustration.

'An exhibition', I wrote. 'Pack your bags for the San Siro.'

Then, from nowhere, they scored. Tugay, a ringer for Lee Chapman except that he could run, stuck in a belter of a drive from thirty yards. And, just before half-time, they scored again. Martin and Schmeichel got into a tangle and as Schmeichel readied himself to scream blame at his colleague, Hakan, a big, fast centre forward, scooped it in to the Stretford End goal. In the directors' box the Turks went Greek.

'If we're not careful,' Alex Ferguson had told me on the return flight from Hungary, 'we'll be watching "Coronation Street" on Wednesday nights.'

United started the second half like a team of soap devotees anxious not to miss an episode. With the sound of broken crockery ringing in their ears, they played with the kind of nervous tension of which they are uniquely capable. The clever triangles around the centre circle broke down as Hughes put two-yard passes into Sharpe's shins at net-bursting pace; Giggs and Keane were showing all the tactical acumen of beheaded poultry; Cantona was having the kind of game that would make Howard Wilkinson glow with satisfaction at off-loading him; in defence, nervy passing between Bruce, Pallister and Martin were sending 'just boot it' jitters through the home crowd.

Inevitably there was another cockup just inside our half involving Martin (who was soon – was he watching the same game? – to be bought by Lou Macari for Celtic). Kubilay galloped forward and, via a post, did the unthinkable: he put them into the lead. He ran towards his fans to celebrate, but was caught and drowned by a pile of colleagues who proceeded to conduct some sort of sexual congress on the touchline. In the directors' box the Turks hugged each other and jumped up and down on their seats chanting their love of Cim Bom. In front of them, Robin Launders turned grey at the sight of millions wiping themselves off his balance sheet. The United lads looked like a team that had just gone behind to a bunch whose giblets they should have basted.

Worse was to follow. As Galatasaray played keep-ball in their own half, a man ran on to the pitch brandishing a burning rag, another man joined him and danced a jig towards the centre circle. Before the police and stewards could reach the pair, Schmeichel, showing a liking for leaving his penalty area in search of trouble that would have disastrous consequences later in the season, chased after them. To vociferous approval from K stand, he grabbed the rag-burner and started treating him in a manner not dissimilar to the way he behaves towards Bruce on a weekly basis. The Turks, however, didn't see the positive side of Schmeichel's citizen's arrest, and all bundled in for a bit of handbags. Never pass up the opportunity to waste some time.

While this was going on the French journalist beside me, there to cover Eric's regal progress, shook his head and asked if it could really be true that United had never lost a European tie at home. It was, I said.

'And now this, the Turkeys,' he said, raising his eyebrows heavenward.

Perhaps it was pride, perhaps it was the sight of Ferguson's face going plum-coloured with fury on the touchline, perhaps it was Schmeichel's bit of community policing, perhaps it was the thought of thirty-six years of unbeaten-at-Old-Trafford history about to go down the newly installed under-pitch drainage system, but something got United going. Suddenly, an hour too late, they started to play.

Sharpe, marooned at left back because Irwin had been omitted as the excess foreigner (it seemed a good idea at the time), pushed forward and began to accelerate past derailed defenders, swiping in incendiary crosses. Hughes found some room, Ince found some snap, the lads at the Scoreboard End found their voices, and Cantona found himself stepping through the Galatasaray defence to equalise off his shin. A tidal wave of relief poured from the stands as Cantona vaulted the hoardings and, PR man to the last, embraced the badge on his shirt.

The last five minutes, during which Keane almost pulled off the great escape when he whiskered a post, passed in a bedlam of Turkish whistling and desperate English roaring. At the final whistle the Galatasaray players, substitutes and officials hunkered down in a gleeful centre circle scrum. In the stand their fans looked ready to sing their way back to Stoke Newington. Giggs's eyes didn't leave the turf as he walked off.

Afterwards, Rainer Hollmann, their coach and like much of his team, a German, swished into the press conference wearing a Kevin Keegan haircut (grey stripes), a Ron Atkinson trenchcoat (very long) and a Terry Venables grin (very wide). He sat down, smiled and said something in German. An interpreter told us that 'If anyone is telling Mr Hollmann before the game that he is drawing with Manchester United three–three, he is being very surprised.'

He is not being the only one.

'He is also being very surprised to see his team come back after being two down in ten minutes. This is not the usual way in Turkish football. Now he is looking forward to the second leg.'

And would, someone wanted to know, the fans have a hot welcome for United in Istanbul? Hollmann gave a sly grin.

'They will be waiting for you,' he said, sweeping out of the room. 'At the airport.'

It was ten minutes before Alex Ferguson arrived. He stumbled on to the press room platform, his mouth had disappeared into a tight knot, his cheeks were flecked with anger veins, a nerve flickered under his right eye. He was a man battling not to loose the invective about fanny merchants and fuck-ups you could see simmering in his throat.

'To be honest with youse I'm in shock,' he said eventually, his voice barely loud enough to reach the front row. 'I think part of the problem at our club is we get in front and it gets a carnival, one or two players start to run away with it. This is a throwaway. How can players risk throwing everything away by lack of team play? After that, I can tell you, there's a long way to go before we're the finished article, a long way. I've seen these signs recently. Mebbe they've learnt their lesson. They'd better. We've a hell of a job on our hands now. A hell of a job.'

He then left, head down, teeth clamped, silent.

Into his place bounced Peter Schmeichel. An oddly chirpy Peter Schmeichel, a Peter Schmeichel who had obviously learnt the first rule of media relations: never let the bastards know you're down. Looking forward to the second leg, Peter? someone asked.

'Think about it,' Schmeichel said, in his mix of south Manchester and south Copenhagen, not a common combination, 'that's why you play football, for the big games like this.'

What about assaulting the fan, though, Peter, someone else said, a tad rash perhaps?

'He was a Turk, came on with a burning United flag. You never know what he is intending, he came from behind us all and I saw him first. It was frustration really that made me do it. We were losing and you don't know if the referee is going to add time for this sort of thing, so I wanted him off the pitch quickly. That's all.'

A Turkish journalist spoke up: 'He was not Turkish fan,' he said. 'He was Kurd, burning Turkish flag. This was political.'

Schmeichel looked perplexed.

'It was a red, white and black United flag he was burning.'

'No,' said the man. 'It was Turkish flag. He was Kurd.'

'Well then,' smiled Schmeichel, 'they'll love me in Istanbul won't they, beating up a Kurd.'

It was generally considered in the press that this was United's fault, not Galatasaray's. United had squandered it, not shown the killer touch, fannied it up. Giggsy was the headless chicken who shouldered the blame. He sat out the wins against Everton and Leicester in the following fortnight, wins conducted with an ease that made you wonder how the same bunch could bugger things up so comprehensively against the Turks. But he was there as the highly remunerated glory-boys of English football gathered at Manchester airport, looking relaxed as they were surrounded by the less well-remunerated ambassadors of the British press. Standing in the middle of a forest of Dictaphones, Alex Ferguson gave a here's-something-for-your-preview-pieces press conference, which centred on Robson's blocked sinuses, Pallister's dicky knee, and, the now familiar question, which foreigner would get the drop this time.

I asked him if he had ever faced a position like this before.

'With Aberdeen we drew at home with Gothenburg and then couldn't find a goal at their place,' he said, sounding rather alarmed at the prospect of history repeating itself. 'They'll be the favourites, but that's the way we want it. To be honest with youse, I don't think they've got the mental toughness of the Spaniards and Italians to go for a nil-nil. The crowd will be behind them, though. It'll be tough. If we win, it'll be our best ever.'

The flight was delayed and, as the hacks changed their money ('fuck me, I'm a millionaire, I got a million Turkish lire'), the team grazed the book shop. Phelan bought *Fever Pitch* ('heard on the grapevine it was all right'), Schmeichel a Robert Ludlum (footballer's standard issue) and Hughes, Melvyn Bragg's hefty biography of Richard Burton. He would need, as things turned out, something to occupy his time.

After all the complaints about the plane to Budapest, this time a big-bodied jet had been laid on, with club-class facilities, a movie screen and encouragingly for some, limitless free drink. This was an option not open to the team, who were billeted away from the pack, up the front of the plane: 'We had to go up there to keep out of the stink of your booze,' explained Brucie.

As the plane veered out of the charcoal Manchester sky, the crew introduced themselves over the tannoy.

'My name is Paul Rosato and I am your chief steward today,' a voice said. 'And my companions here to help you are Amanda, Belinda and Samantha.'

Richard Williams, *The Independent on Sunday*'s cultured sports writer, who knows these things, pointed out that Rosato was the name of the Milan player who had marked Denis Law during the 1969 European Cup semi-final. Law, on duty for ITV and sitting three rows behind us, confirmed it was true.

'Aye, bastard held my shirt at every corner,' he chirped. 'Mind you, I don't remember Amanda, Belinda and Samantha playing for them.'

As scene-setting pieces for the next day's papers were mentally prepared, the conversation was all about which foreigner would be left out. Irwin was definitely to play ('seems sensible', Ferguson had said at Manchester airport, understating wildly) as was Schmeichel. Which left three to be picked from Keane, Cantona, Hughes and Giggs; Kanchelskis was once again left in Altrincham. The consensus was it was a choice between Keane (tactically disposable) and Giggs (tendency to being a fanny merchant).

'One thing's for sure,' reckoned Rob Hughes of *The Times*. 'He daren't leave Cantona out or he'll be on the first plane back to Charles de Gaulle.'

As for Hughesie, well, he'll terrify them.

When the plane touched down at Istanbul we were told to prepare £5 each, to hand over as airport tax.

'Pay yer fiver,' said Brucie, as players, officials and press queued up together at passport control, 'and ask for a doner or shish.'

Once we were through into the main airport concourse, Rainer Hollmann was right. They were waiting for us. The luggage-reclaim area was over-run with the over-excited. Everywhere there were television cameras, yabbering technicians, men with clipboards claiming to be official guides, pushy policemen adding to the anarchy. Flashbulbs popped and arc lights probed. Schmeichel was grabbed and did an interview in faltering German. Robson was ambassadorial, Ferguson polite and Giggsy tried to lose himself among the youth players. A confused cameraman even pointed his lens in my face. 'Hello, Turkish television,' he said. 'What do you think the chances of Manchester City?'

Behind a glass screen about a hundred and fifty local fans, with bad banners and big chants, kept up a cascade of noise which a full Carrow Road would be pushed to match.

'Welcome to the Hell,' one banner read. And, 'Welcome Mr Cantona. After the match you say goodbye Mrs Cantona'. And, 'You call us barbarians, but we remember Heysel, Hillsborough'.

'Jesus,' said Brucie, nodding towards the banner boys. 'There was a hell of a crowd when we got to South Africa in the summer. But they were pleased to see us.'

'We're all together behind the goalkeeper,' said Parker, as Schmeichel led the way outside, pushing through the baying, bubbling reception committee. Cantona slowly shook his head in distaste as the natives folded in around him, poking, prodding; Robson, the last one through, fighting the tide, was a lesson in patience. As the big metal skips of kit were slung aboard, the team coach was surrounded by the overeager chanting and gesticulating predictions of the score (always 5–0 for some reason). Pallister, Sharpe and Ince pressed their noses to the windows, grinning at the hand signals and replying in kind. It was loud, it was chaotic. You wondered what this welcome mob would be like if they had recourse to chemical stimulants, and it was about as spontaneous as a prefight publicity spat between two heavyweights managed by Don King. There, in the midst of the mob, clearly directing operations, was a man in headphones and a Galatasaray scarf; a producer, as it turned out, from local television.

On the press coach – which (as if anyone would be interested in it) was granted a siren-blazing police escort – our guide asked if anyone had any questions. A photographer, who had drained Amanda, Belinda and Samantha of in-flight hospitality and was seconds from a slobbery, mouth-open sleep, said he did indeed have a question.

'Where's the fucking whorehouse?' he guffawed.

Nobody else laughed. They were too busy writing up their story.

The next morning, Joe Lovejoy was apoplectic.

'Just had the bloody office on the phone,' he said. ' "What's all this about a riot at the airport?" they were going. Apparently it's all over the pops. They want me to do a follow-up. I told them there wasn't a bloody riot. You were there, you can back me up.'

All over the pops it was. Pages of it – 'Welcome to the Hell' figured prominently – in the *Daily Mirror*, the *Sun* and *Today*. They had bought the Turkish telly man's hype hook, headline and stinker. And why not, it made for a good story.

Back home in Manchester, the players' families had read that the night before's contrived and boisterous welcome was a nightmare gauntlet of hate. They thought their lads were in mortal danger when in fact they were watching videos in a converted sultan's palace of a hotel down by the Bosphorus. On the plane back, Peter Schmeichel cornered some of the tabloid men.

'How can you write that shit, you know it wasn't true,' he yelled. 'After what happened in Manchester my wife was really worried.'

There was no answer to that.

The Turkish press, already as paranoid as a room full of coke-heads, took this characteristic piece of pre-match hyperbole as an open declaration of war. On the way to Ferguson's afternoon press conference at the team palace, I spotted on a newsstand a piece in English on the front page of the local evening sports paper *Fotospor* (a publication owned, it turned out, by Asil Nadir's son).

'To our dear English friends, sort yourself out,' it began, before chasing itself up a cul-de-sac of self-righteous indignation that would have gained the writer a job at Wapping. 'And to think for years we believed you were true "English gentlemen". God we were wrong. Please don't be too offended, but it was your own mindless articles and statements that made us believe this. Stuff Turkey, stuff this, stuff that. We will see tomorrow who gets stuffed.'

In the former ballroom of United's palatial accommodation where Fergie was due to address the 'English gentlemen', I showed the paper to a couple of the pack (a move which Richard Williams, incidentally, said revealed a lack of European experience: 'you could have had an exclusive there'). Steve Curry, the jolly Les Dawson lookalike from the *Daily Express*, had the reception desk make a dozen photocopies and soon everyone was poring over it, mocking – their own hands, of course, pristine in this matter – its absurd exaggeration. It turned out a man from *Fotospor* was at the conference. Seeing me with a copy of the paper, he asked me what I thought of the article. I said I thought it was funny, but why did he ask.

'We are very interested in what you English think of us Turks,' he said.

When Fergie arrived, brisk, matter-of-fact, he looked anything but a man caught up in a war.

'Some place, huh?' he said, looking around. 'The directors are away on a boat trip up the Bosphorus. I wouldn't mind joining them, so hurry up youse lot.'

What, was the first question, did he think of the reception at the airport?

He smiled and raised his eyebrows.

'But have you ever been through a riot like that?' someone pressed.

'That was a riot was it lads?' he said. 'Youse obviously never seen a Glasgow wedding.'

'What happens at a Glasgow wedding, Alex?' Steve Curry wanted to know.

'Well if you don't have at least a dozen fights, it's considered a waste of everybody's time. But no, the Turks are lovely people, though they can be a bit volatile. This is a big town, there's twelve million people here and things can happen. So the boys will stay here, in the hotel. It's a sensible precaution.'

And did he think they would get the result the following night?

'If we go out it'll be our own fault. It's a great thing to be in Europe and we can't get enough of it. I'll be saying to them, do you want to play against the likes of Milan, Barcelona or Benfica? No, hang on, Benfica aren't in it.'

Everyone laughed, as you do when Fergie laughs.

'Actually, in a perverse way, I'm looking forward to tomorrow night. That's the acid test. If we can't do it, we'll hold up your hands and say we aren't good enough.'

After the conference, as Ferguson went off to juggle with his foreign permutations, a group of us were given a guided tour through the palace. It was some place, indeed. Through the Turkish baths with their cake-icing plasterwork, we went, under chandeliers which, the guide said, contained the largest acreage of glass south of Versailles. We went along the waterfront walk, just behind the players, wandering around bored in their tracksuits. Across the water the most stunning city skyline in the world glistened in the late afternoon sun; the mosques on the hilltops, forceful, dynamic, looking like upturned spider crabs, minarets gently swaying in the heat haze. But it was the sight I saw as I looked back up at the hotel which made it all worthwhile: there, on the balcony of one of the bedrooms, confirming everything I had always wanted to believe, were Cantona and Schmeichel playing chess.

The day of the match dawned, hazy in the smog. The players were out of bounds. Most of them spent the afternoon catching up on the sleep they had missed the night before: the desk staff at the palace had conscientiously put telephoned death threats through to their rooms throughout the night. Just doing their bit for Cim Bom.

I did what they were unable to do and went for a walk through the city.

Istanbul, like Manchester, had just failed to land the millennium

Olympics. Their bid, like ours, had been stuffed by Sydney's. The city seemed to regard this match as a reasonable substitute: tickets, it was said, were changing hands for over a month's wages. Walking through the streets, where all life is conducted in Istanbul, you were blinded by the yellow and red of Galatasaray. Traders sitting on blankets on the pavement, selling single cigarettes from broken packets, selling individual fish hauled straight from the Bosphorus, selling you your own weight on bathroom scales, were united for Cim Bom. In the posh restaurants, well-heeled ladies bought flags and yellow neckbraids from salesmen passing from table to table. In the Grand Bazaar, red-and-yellow balloons were strung in lines from shop to shop, pictures of the players were pasted to every shop window.

There were reds out and about, but they were discreet: there was nothing like the cheery drink-in of Budapest. It was like an away game at West Ham, compared to one at Coventry. Two lads I met in the Grand Bazaar had no sign of any colours.

'Not advisable,' they said, as in the background someone cranked up their air horn and chanting could be heard. 'They can be volatile.'

These boys were particularly excited to have bumped into Martin Edwards, browsing for knick-knacks (to take home for a special friend, perhaps).

'I shook his hand,' said one.

Odd that, four years ago they would have tried to chin him.

As an experiment I decided to take off my jacket and walk through this maze of volatility displaying my United T-shirt.

I was completely mobbed, pulled this way and that by locals. 'Hey Manchester,' said a man at a carpet stall. 'You will lose, come buy my carpet and you will have something to take home.'

'Hey Manchester,' said another yellow-toothed grin. 'Your Cantona is a peach.'

Indeed, I agreed, a peach of a player.

'No, no. You no understand. Cantona, son of a peach.'

What they all wanted to know was why the British papers called the Turks animals.

'We are friends,' they said, in an overfriendly way. 'Turkish are gentlemen. Why print these lies?'

It wasn't until about two o'clock that a waiter in a restaurant where I stopped for barbecued fish gave me a very hard time. News had just filtered out about an incident at a hotel, involving a group of reds who, I think he said – his English wasn't brilliant – had done fucky fucky on pavement outside their hotel and abused the Turkish flag. He held me responsible. 'Why do you act as scum?' he fumed. 'Why do you piss on Turkish flag. See this bottle,' he said, grabbing hold of my Pilsen, 'we will shove it up you tonight. We will fuck you Manchester.'

Which, given the size of his moustache, sounded ominous.

We were bussed to the ground two hours before kickoff. The night before we had visited the place; it was empty, peaceful, serene under the floodlights. I had stood on the centre spot looking up at the empty terraces paraboling away, noting that Arcelik was here too. Rather disappointing I had learned from our driver that this was pronounced Archieleech, as in Cary Grant's real name. In the background you could hear muezzin chanting from the minarets ('. . . sounds just like Bethnal Green,' Joe Lovejoy had said). Denis Law had stood beside me, doing air side-foots from the centre spot. I asked him what he had experienced of the Turkish atmosphere in his time. 'Played here for Scotland,' he said. 'We shat ourselves.'

Now, two hours before the start of a game a whole country had wanted to see, the area around the ground was still deserted. No sign of any life, no street traders, no touts, no queues, just a couple of riot-control water cannon hiding out up a side street.

'Where is everyone?' someone asked as we got off the coach.

'They are all inside,' said the driver. 'Since nine o'clock this morning.'

If they were excited in the Grand Bazaar and in the Blue Mosque ('You Manchester,' said the man at the door, whose job it is to tell visitors to take off their shoes as a mark of respect, 'you will lose five–nil, ha ha!'), inside the ground the atmosphere was as if a Cup-final crowd had been mainlining adrenalin for a fortnight. The upper tier of stands were lined with bass drums, thumping out a constant, rib-threatening rhythm. It looked like Hades up there, shadowy figures enveloped in pink clouds vomited out by flares that were being torched by the minute. Everyone in the ground was chanting through their repertoire of songs in a manner which Cardiff Arms Park in the seventies would have been pressed to match. A thick smog of gunpowder smoke palled the pitch. It was some sight.

There were five thousand riot policemen in the ground, most of them ringing the perimeter running track. Up in the corner of the stand, surrounded by a human shield of cops twenty deep, the forlorn rump of United fans, no more than three hundred and fifty of them, looked monochrome against the sea of red and yellow around them.

'Where are they all?' I asked David Meek. 'I thought there would be more of our lot than that.'

'Got themselves arrested, apparently,' he replied.

Suddenly about a hundred police tore over to one of the entrances to the underground dressing rooms and formed an enormous tortoise of riot shields. Since you would have had to be Steve Backley to chuck anything from the terraces on this part of the pitch, it seemed this was merely done to intimidate visiting teams, worry them about what lay ahead. Amid a cacophony of whistles so loud it would have worried dogs throughout Asia Minor, the United players emerged. As they made their way to salute the brave few who had followed them there, every Turk in the ground (most of the police included) treated them to the traditional Galatasaray welcome song: 'Fuck you, fuck you, fuck you, Manchester.'

Alex Ferguson had once described Elland Road as 'the most intimidating venue in Europe'. You could see him rapidly changing his mind down there on the pitch. Of the players only Schmeichel, bounding around waving, looked as if he were enjoying the reception. Perhaps he believed they really were pleased to see him.

We still hadn't had word as to who was being left out. But as Ferguson, Kidd and Jimmy McGregor trotted over to their dugout, sited just in front of the directors' ornamental garden, Hughes, still in his day clothes, scowled slowly in their wake.

'Christ,' said Joe Lovejoy. 'That I do not believe.'

Hughes, the man, according to Gordon Milne the then manager of Besiktas, Galatasaray's neighbours, who worried the Turks the most. Hughes, not a great goal-scorer, according to David Lacey, but a scorer of great goals. Ferguson later said that he was worried about Robson's fitness, and couldn't afford to drop Keane. So Hughes, the man you would want next to you in a trench, was on the bench.

It would have been no consolation to Hughesie, brooding on the touchline, that immediately behind him sat Turkey's beleaguered Prime Minister Mrs Ciller, rosetted in yellow and red, milking the opportunity to associate herself with Turkish success. For this was what it was: beating the English champions at their own game would not just be good news in the Galatasaray district of Istanbul, it would chuff up an entire country. That was why the home team players had added the Turkish crest to their shirts, they were carrying some heady aspirations on their shoulders. Compared to that, United's motivation of a few million quid to be spun in the mini-league was small beer.

When it finally started the noise was unceasing, as if chanting alone would bear the Turks to victory. United, though, never began. It was one of those games when a greasy lump of depression settles in the stomach from the kickoff and stays there, immovable, for ninety minutes. From the way they played, the United players were carrying a similar lump in their boots. Cantona, uneasy up front as the solo target man, spent the evening re-enacting the Franco-Prussian war with his marker, the German, Stumpf. Robson snapped around in frustration, yelling at linesmen, yelling at Keane, yelling at Bruce. As if anyone could hear him. Giggs and Sharpe looked as though they wanted to get the hell out of Hell as quickly as possible.

Despite Ferguson's prediction, the Turks seemed delighted to sit on 0–0. They had one chance: Hakan drawing a double save from Schmeichel, tumbling and scooping to his right, a block to match the best of Banks. That apart, they spent most of the game spread-eagled on the turf: drilled with German tricks, they would go down in the tackle as if hit by a high-velocity bullet, roll around and then bounce up and trot away once a couple of minutes had been wasted.

With no more than three minutes left, and United looking as though three hours wouldn't have been enough, the ball went off for a throw-in. It disappeared into an unseemly melee of the over-wrought: photographers, policemen, Turkish substitutes, anyone who could do their bit by wasting a second. Cantona, seeing the ball in the arms of someone who had little intention of throwing it back, ran twenty yards and executing a drop kick which would have thrilled Bruce Lee, knocked it out of the man's grasp. At that, everyone was up and flapping. Cantona stood, as is his way, in the middle of it, arms spread, palms upward, as if bemused at the fuss.

No more than a minute later, the final whistle blew. It signalled chaos. They could probably hear the roar in Athens. Tugay, carrying three men on his back, raced to their supporters to conduct the celebrations. The pitch was invaded by the very people who should have been protecting it from invasion. Policemen losing any sense of discipline charged around high-fiving, skipping like five-year-olds. Our favourite son of a peach ran to the referee, shook him by the hand and made a zero sign with his thumb and forefinger. I watched him closely and he clearly didn't say anything. Unfortunately in German, the zero sign carries a different message. And the referee was a German-speaking Swiss. As Cantona turned to walk to the dressing room, with Robson wrapping a protective arm around him, the ref showed the red card to his departing back. Robson needed to be protective, the police enveloped the pair, jostling, shoving, thrusting them towards the tunnel. In the tunnel, a policeman, in full view of Robson and Bruce, punched Cantona on the back of the head.

On the pitch behind them the Turkish players wept, television cameramen wept, police dogs wept, the Prime Minister wept. What, you thought, would they have done had they lost. I wandered outside. The whole city was already out on the streets. A lorry drove over the flyover which skirted the ground. On its bonnet, four youths balanced, struggling with an air horn. I grabbed people leaving the ground to join the party and, with the help of Hugh

Pope, *The Independent*'s Turkish correspondent, who had sat next to me during the game and spoke the lingo, asked them why it meant so much.

'It means we get rid of all the problems on our agenda,' said Onur Arifglou, who claimed he was twenty-five but looked forty, hoarse with the roaring. 'It's wonderful especially as Manchester United are the best team in the world. Everywhere you go tonight in Turkey is a party.'

Probably the same in Moss Side.

Ayhan Cadlay, a twenty-year-old shoemaker, added his ten pennyworth of cobblers: 'Everyone says Turks are bad people,' he yelled. 'We are good people and Cim Bom will be champions of the world. Your hooligans are a shameful thing. We are friendly to guests, but they burn our flag. Let them show how good they are on the field. No good.'

As he spoke, his friends began to surround us, jostling, chanting and mocking: 'Fuck you, fuck you, fuck you, Manchester.'

A man grabbed my elbow.

'Please ignore them,' he said, introducing himself as Ardem Serezli. He explained he had travelled to the first leg in Manchester and took his ticket stub from his pocket to prove it. 'Manchester people were really friendly to me. Manchester people are my friends. So please, my friend, I suggest you go back inside now.'

We took his advice. I made my way across the pitch down to United's subterranean dressing room. It was, as was now par for the course, chaos down there. At least fifty policemen filled the corridor, holding back the press. You could hear the party above ground, percolating down through the ventilation shafts, the horns, the hoots, the yells. Not a sound came from the dressing room. No one looked happy, Hugh McIlvanney, the *Sunday Times*'s great reporter and an old pal of Fergie's looked particularly thoughtful. Eventually Fergie appeared, standing with his back to the closed door, and the bruiser of a security man United had brought with them protecting him from the cops. McIlvanney offered a consoling hand.

'Alex . . .'

'We just didn't play well enough,' Ferguson said, dignified in his club blazer, anger spent.

'It was desperation in the end, a shambles.'

Why was Cantona shown the red card? someone asked.

'He complained about the lack of time added on. I think the guy overreacted. It was sheer desperation on Eric's part. The lad was desperate.'

It had looked chaos.

'Aye, a policeman hit Robson with his riot shield, he's having two stitches in his hand just now. But we can't use that as an excuse.'

Cantona, too, had been struck. Did the club intend to protest to UEFA about the treatment of the players? someone asked.

'I don't intend to look for any excuses whatsoever. I think the biggest loss tonight is our European experience. OK?'

He turned back into the dressing room. The minder, who wore the disappointed gaze and sandy moustache of a founder of the Afrikaner resistance movement, put a large palm in the lens of a cameraman who tried to follow him in.

I went back up on the pitch. The ground was now empty except for a cat, picking its way across the terraces looking for titbits. And in the corner, the United fans, the most defeated bunch of Brits abroad since Dunkirk, were still surrounded by police twenty deep, as if a threat to national security.

'They nicked the film from my camera,' a woman yelled down at me. 'Bastard police, just pulled it out for the hell of it. Put that in the paper for a change.'

Outside the ground I stood next to a police dog with a red-and-yellow scarf tied round its neck and watched the United players climb aboard their coach. They looked straight ahead, none of them staring at the carnival around them, the people lining the streets for ten miles to the airport, the women holding their children up to the windows to show them what losers looked like.

'We couldn't,' said Giggsy later, 'get out of there fast enough.'

On the way out of town someone chucked a brick at the coach window; it shattered just where Bruce had been leaning his head.

'If it had smashed through I'd've been dead,' he said. 'That would have just about summed it up.'

Outgunned, outplayed, outthought, outsung: it was one of those nights for United. But the omen had been there on the plane on the way out. The in-flight movie was *Last of the Mohicans*. Halfway through the action came a scene in which a regiment of scarlet-coated, English soldiers marching through a wood is set upon by howling Mohawks, who proceed to kebab the lot. When you're up against it on foreign soil and the natives get uppity, being English and wearing red isn't enough.

When we got back to Manchester there was another reception committee at the airport. The place, as you might expect at four in the morning, was empty, apart from four television crews, waiting outside customs, two cleaners and a lone fan in an anorak. As Fergie appeared, head down, pushing his luggage trolley, the fan started yelling out at him.

'Alex, Alex,' he shouted. Fergie, thinking it was perhaps one of the television reporters, looked up, blinking, into the arc lights. 'Alex, it's your fault. You fucking blew it. You should've played Sparky. He'd have won it for us. It's your fault we're out, Alex, and you know it.'

5

Cold Turkey

*The worst part of it was the plane on the way
home. That, my friend, was the real hell.*
John Cunningham, jailed in Istanbul for
twenty-six days

There were some sore heads in Istanbul the next day: two people were killed by falling bullets as armed locals fired their guns in the air in celebration. Another man died tumbling drunk under a train. Dozens were injured by fearsome pyrotechnics. They know how to enjoy their football in Turkey.

'The Turkey mounted the English,' roared the headline in the mass-circulation daily, *Sabah*, the next morning. 'When they want to criticise us they say they will cut these turkeys to pieces. But Manchester United got the lesson of their lives. Be proud, Turkey.'

The sorest heads of all belonged to the United fans who had travelled to Istanbul to follow their team. Two days after I got home, I was listening to David Mellor's '606 Show' on Radio 5. Calls began to come in and a story began to emerge. We had been led to believe when we were in Istanbul that some United supporters had smashed up their hotel and, in the one-for-all, all-for-one way in which police forces dealt with outbreaks of hooliganism these days, everyone at the place had been deported. The callers to '606' had a different story to tell, a story of a mass denial of basic rights and of the not untypical way in which British football supporters abroad are treated these days – the inevitable knockback of twenty years of hooliganism.

Over the next few months of the season I met several people who were there. These are the stories of three of them.

Jon Shine is an accountant from north London in his forties. He has been a United fan since 1963, a dedicated Cockney red. He travelled to Istanbul with his friend Paul, also from north London, another long-distance fanatic whose BMW is registered A10 UTD.

'Paul and I have been to loads of European games; we drove to St Étienne in a Mini that broke down. I'm well used to what happens on them, I know no one protects the innocent fan and that over most of Europe the police forces haven't a clue. I went with that attitude of mind. But what happened in Istanbul appalled me.

'We travelled with the London Supporters Branch and stayed in the Holiday Inn, all nice and civilised. I had combined the trip with a business meeting in the city, which was scheduled at 4 p.m. on the day of the game, the same time, as it happens, all the other lot in the hotel were going to the game. I said to them, "do yourselves a favour, what you going so early for, I'll see you there". So Paul and I went off, did our business and we hired a cab after the meeting. We got to the ground about 6.20 p.m., a good hour and a half before kickoff.

'Well, there's not a bugger outside the ground, they're all packed in already. So we walked around the place following signs in English saying: "ManU supporters this way". We get to this big gate and all I can see is United, about a hundred of them, just milling. We bump into this geezer we know, a tout, and he says: "They're not going to let you in, they're taking the piss." I said, "Behave," and walked up to the gate, where I showed my ticket, but this Turkish toe-rag just shrugged his shoulders and said: "No room."

'Then some geezer appeared and said that if we queued up, they'd let us in, so we did. But they didn't. Instead the gate opened and all these police came out, batons raised, just pushing us back, back, back. They didn't care. There were dogs there too, snapping and barking. Didn't care. One bloke fell over, they smacked him about with truncheons. Didn't care. We ended up well away from the ground, no one knowing what to do.

'I said to Paul: "Look, I've never not got into a game in my life, come on." So we walked round the ground and we found this geezer who looked like George Graham and spoke English. "I'll get you in," he says. Bollocks. By now the game had started. I found another policeman who was sympathetic, he said he'd get us in. So we followed him. This is the third time I've been round the ground, I know the place better than I know Old Trafford. We are told to wait by a gate and we will be let in at half-time. We weren't. Instead more police emerge from the ground and we get hit about the legs by truncheons and told to fuck off, which by now I'm beginning to suspect is the limit of their English in the Istanbul police. So I said to Paul: "Look we're not going to get in." He said: "It's your fault, you and your bloody meeting."

'So we went to a bar, where there were about forty other United supporters all with tickets, none of whom got in. We watched for a bit, but I sensed it was going to get ugly. So I said to Paul: "This is going off." And the moment the final whistle went, we dashed out and flagged a cab. I looked back out of the cab and I saw about fifty of the bastard police piling into the bar, truncheons up.

'We drove back to the hotel, and the scene is incredible. Everywhere the city has gone mad; our hotel was thirty miles outside town and it was mental out there. We sat in the bar for about an hour before the minibus arrived with the other lads. They said: "Where were you?" We told them. They said: "Ah, we're not surprised. The entire United section was filled with police, sitting in your seats."

'When I got back home, I wrote to everyone: to UEFA, to United, to the Turkish embassy. United were the only ones to reply, they wrote me a formal letter saying they were collating information. And that was it. I've written time and again, official letters, on company paper, I've driven my colleagues mad. Nothing. No one else even gave me the courtesy of a reply. And to this day [it was five months later] I have yet to receive an apology or a refund on my unused ticket from anyone. Nor did I get the business.'

Jon Shine was lucky.

Andy Mitten is a twenty-year-old journalism student from Urmston who edits the fanzine *United We Stand*. His great-uncle is Charlie Mitten. This is his story.

'I went on the UF Tours trip, organised without the official sanction of the club. I went with UF because, to be honest, they give better value for money, and the official tours tend to be a bit overrun with librarians. We arrived at midday the day before the game. That afternoon, we were given a guided tour of the city, treated like wealthy tourists, taken to belly dancing. It was sound. When we arrived at the hotel, The Tansa, later on that afternoon, I thought: Hold on, trouble here. It was in a right rough area of town, at the end of a cul-de-sac with blocks of flats canyoning up around it and this big flight of steps leading up to the city facing its front door. Get trapped there and you're well trapped.

'That evening about thirty of us went to a bar to watch the Cup Winners Cup game between Besiktas and Ajax on the telly. Others went their own way to different parts of the city. In the bar we were pretty raucous and thirsty, but we were getting on really well with the locals. But towards the end of the game, I could sense that the atmosphere towards us had changed. I think what had happened was people were in bars watching and, as it became obvious that Besiktas were losing, they went on to the street. Then word had got round where we were.

'The bar got surrounded, and some Turkish lad chucked a glass inside. Well, there were some reds in there who were all for going out there and kicking off. I said: "I don't believe you lot, don't you know where we are? Haven't you seen *Midnight Express*?"

'Anyhow, the police arrived, about twenty of them and suggested to us we'd be best to go back to our hotel. So we did as we were told, and as we got out on the street we found ourselves surrounded by a line of police. And behind them there was a chanting mob of locals, about a hundred and fifty of them. Some daft twat said: "C'mon let's do 'em." But most of us just said: "You've got to be mental. You can't win this one."

'So we walked back, followed by the police, who I don't think could cope. They certainly did nothing to stop all this stuff being chucked at us. It was coming down at us from the flats, shopkeepers were coming out of their shops and chucking stuff and the police just kind of let them. Everyone was chanting "Cim Bom, Cim Bom," and to be honest I was crapping myself, because at the other end of the alley, I could see a big gang of them at the top of the steps and I thought we were going to get pincered. Then I got this fucking great whack on the back of the head which turned out to be a watermelon.

'We got back to the hotel, and it was madness in there. People were arriving back from their evenings out in other parts of the city saying they had to run a gauntlet to get back, saying that they'd been smacked all over the place. Then the bricks and bottles started to come into the hotel lobby. We were surrounded by now by most of the lot who had followed us and a load more. The hotel was soon a wreck, an absolute state and everyone was hyper. A few United burst out of the hotel and into them. There was fighting, the hooligans were buzzing like it was the old days. I saw a lad wading into them wielding a chair. But then this lad came in with blood all over him, and his girlfriend screaming he was dead. Some reds managed to get him out and into a police car, and that seemed to calm things down. The police managed to get rid of all the Turks, and it just stopped.

'About two in the morning, I went to bed. I had to brush the glass of my bed first from where the window had shattered from someone chucking a brick through it, and I sparked out. I don't know what time it was, say three-thirty, I got woken up by someone kicking my feet. There were these policemen in my room and they said: "We move you to another hotel!" which I thought seemed reasonable. But they took us to a police station. I got put in a cell with about six others, and then they breathalysed us. About six in the morning I looked up through the cell window and I saw the crack of dawn in the sky and I said to myself: This is going to be a long day. Gradually more people came in and we were getting the picture that everyone had been lifted from the hotel, floor by floor. Didn't matter who you were, what age, whether you'd gone to bed at nine: if you were United, you were lifted. I was one of the first because I was in a lower floor. About ten o'clock the police started producing these bits of paper, saying: "You sign statement, you see match." I didn't want to sign nowt I couldn't understand, but some did. They didn't get to the match.

'It was getting a bit crowded by now in the cell, and we hadn't had any food, drink or access to anyone who spoke English. Then they said they were going to move us to another police station. What this meant was that one by one we had to walk out of the station into a police van parked about twenty yards away. There was hundreds of media there, forming a line. We were, in effect, paraded in front of them, like a show trial. I thought: Christ, if my mum sees me.

'At the next police station, there were loads of us, all in cells – no food, no drink. By now we're resigned to not seeing the match. About seven o'clock they said: "We take you to airport." What this meant was: We put you in coaches, leave you there unattended for an hour while a big crowd forms and intimidates the shit out of you.

'When we got to the airport, all the police lined up and we had to walk, one by one, through them, getting jostled and laughed at, because by now the news had come through of the result. We got on the plane, and the pilot was brilliant, he wouldn't take off until we all had our passports returned. They came to us shoved in a bin liner. They all had "Deporte" stamped on them. We realised we weren't all there; then news came through that six of the lads were still in prison, so we had a whip-round.

'When we got back to Manchester there were loads of media there, and we were just yobbos besmirching the good name of England abroad once more. I just said to the reporters: "No, you've got it all wrong, this isn't the usual, this is an outrage." I think if the party had just been lads my age, hoolies and that, there wouldn't have been much sympathy. But there were middle-aged people, doctors, respectable people, a woman in her fifties who's deaf. And you could see on the faces of the reporters: Bloody hell, what's been going on here?

'Because of a campaign worked through the Football Supporters Association, Tom Pendry, David Mellor and the club, we got the deportee status revoked – which I'm bloody pleased about. But I got no compensation.'

Andy Mitten was lucky.

John Cunningham, known as Scotty, is in his thirties. He runs UF Tours, a travel agency specialising in arrangements for football supporters in Europe. Once a member of United's main hoolie firm – he gets a name-check in Bill Buford's book *Among the Thugs* – he is a poacher turned gamekeeper and, from knowledge of how to start it, is now an expert in how to avoid trouble on trips. He didn't manage it in Istanbul.

'Sometimes it happens too quick in football. I spoke to people before the trip, and I knew that the Turks like to gather round the hotels of visiting supporters. I don't know if they mean to be provocative, or what, but it's their way: another country. What I wanted was a hotel out of town, nice and secluded. But there wasn't time to recce. The geezer assured me that The Tansa was fine, but when we got there, I thought: I'm not too happy. I was in the bar all afternoon, and at about five there was a bit of a commotion in the lobby – I honestly don't know what about. I went out, calmed it all down, and I said to the owner. "I want a police car on the door now." He said fine. We then got a routine visit from the football liaison officer, you know, a British policeman, from Manchester United. I gave him a list of names and passport numbers of those on the trip and I said to him: "Make sure we get a police car on the door, I'm worried about tonight." He said fine.

'Well, none came.

'I went out to a bar for the evening, a cab ride away. I wanted to meet people; it's nice to find out about the city you're visiting, find out where the women are, what the good nightclubs are and that. We were sitting out on the pavement and within minutes of the Besiktas game finishing, the street is full of blokes, a lot of them pulling blades. They're Muslim brothers, they're a race unknown, attack one and you attack them all. All that shit in the English press about them, it had got back and they were insulted, no doubt about that. Well, the Englishman's a fighting man. It's in his blood, why do you think we won two world wars? We're brought up to bundle. And I reckon, had it been anywhere else in the world, it would have gone off. But being Turkey, none of us wants to get locked up, so when the bar owner says, come inside, go upstairs, we do, all of us. Then a police van arrives and they take us back to the hotel in it.

'We were the first back. Slowly but surely people start coming back, and everyone has been attacked, a lot of them hammered, absolutely hammered. When the lot come back who've been in the bar round the corner, it all goes off. I tried to calm things, but it was a lost cause. I thought: Fuck this, I want none of it. And I went to the hotel bar. The next thing I know they're all shouting: "Someone's dead." I got out into the foyer and there's this lad on the floor, blue in the face, blood everywhere and his girlfriend's hysterical. We manage to get him out into a police car and just say "Get him to hospital." And suddenly it's all stopped. We drink in the hotel bar and it's fine. About two they shut the bar and I decided to go out to see what was what in Istanbul. I was just getting into a cab, when I got lifted.

'I got taken to a police station and there's already about six there, including the lad who I thought was dead, lifted from hospital. During the night everyone started coming in. There was no food, no drink, it wasn't fun. But I never thought for one minute I had a problem. I was deffo not involved, I had tried to calm things.

'Then suddenly they arrive with a list of names and I'm on it. We're taken, we don't know where, in a van. Then, we walk into this building, into this room which might, comfortably, hold twenty and there's two hundred in there – press, cameras. You'd think they'd caught Jack the Ripper there was that much snapping going on. We're sat down and there's this bloke with a typewriter typing I know not what. Finally the British ambassador turns up: two minutes of civilisation. He hadn't a clue what was going on. I said: "I'm innocent."

He shrugged and said: "What can I do? This is Turkey."

'This Is Turkey. TIT. I heard that a few times.

'Then they said we were going before a judge. I was first in. I had no representation except an interpreter who didn't speak English. The ambassador's not allowed in. I had no idea what was going on, but I honestly thought: It's a show, prove they can handle hoolies, kick us out. One by one we were all, I suppose, charged. I knew I'd done nothing, and even if some of the others had, they was provoked like I've never experienced. Then they said they were letting one of us go. Well, obviously, I thought it was me. But it wasn't. Suddenly we're told that the rest of us would appear in court in twenty-six days. It's then that I took control of the situation. I organised a letter, gave it to the kid who was being let out. I had to get a message to my girlfriend, tell her what's what and to pay the rent. We'd only just moved in. Everyone's mind's on *Midnight Express*, obviously, so on the way to the jail I laid out some ground rules. I said: "Whatever happens stick together. If one fights, we all fight. Otherwise we're gone." We got to the jail and all the prisoners were looking at us like we were Martians. We had four searches, got spat on, kicked. I was scared to death. But when we got to the actual cell bit, the first bloke we see starts talking English. So straightaway I'm on him, to find out the score.

'And the score was: it was all right. To be perfectly honest the jail was a piece of piss. The foreigners looked after themselves in one part. Because we were English, we were treated with the utmost respect, no one touched us. The British consul came about twice a week with food and money and clothes, and one of the lads managed, through his brother, to get hold of a Turkish lawyer called Nadir, who also came to see us. Without this Nadir, I reckon we'd still be in there.

'I learnt a lot in there. It was packed with people who'd lived amazing lives. Real lives, not football-in-Manchester lives. I'd sleep during the day and stay up all night talking. Amazing. About the beginning of the third week, through the consul and Nadir we heard that the tide had turned back home, that there was a lot of political pressure to get us out.

'The twenty-sixth day we were back in court. This Nadir pulled strings, got himself into court as our interpreter. He was brilliant. It was a charade, cameras everywhere. The court was adjourned, still no charges, and we were remanded to appear at another date. But in the meantime we could go home. We got our stuff from the jail and we got clapped out by the prisoners. It was a pretty moving experience.

'Then we had a night in what they called immigration, which was basically this cage, about the size of the goalie's box in a penalty area, with hundreds in there, some of whom had been in for months, poor sods. The stink. The next morning we got on the plane. The worse part of it all was that plane home. That, my friend, was the real hell.

'We'd been so tight, such a group in the prison, the Turkey Six. But as soon as we were out we were superstars for a minute. There was going to be money on the table, so we made some rules: we'd split whatever was earned six ways and we wouldn't tell lies. Well, I could see it in some of their eyes, like them cartoon characters, the fruit machine coming up jackpot. They'd sniffed money.

'We got back and there's a great reception, and a party organised by the Birmingham Branch of the United Supporters Club which most of the others were from. And at this party there's talk about telling the story to the papers.

'But I didn't want to deal with them yet, I wanted to talk to my family first. But everyone was saying that it wouldn't be news if we didn't tell all immediately. Also there's this talk at the party that if we said we were brutalised in prison, one paper would give us fifty thousand pounds. I said: "No bloody way." But you could see it, some of them, thinking: Hey. Pitiful, really. The papers wanted all of us, but I refused to be railroaded, and another lad did too. But one lad in particular, he went off and tried to do his own deal. It ended up with a fight, a fist fight. And in the end, nobody got nothing and the story has remained untold until I'm telling you – which I'm quite glad about.

Scotty was lucky. I had to go to the match. And this book, it became a domestic issue.

6

Back To Basics

Respect . . .

               Paul Ince, on Eric Cantona

In the *Sun* two days after the Galatasaray match, John Sadler wrote that Eric Cantona was now a spent force at Old Trafford; his ill discipline in Turkey proved he was a liability. The columnist advised Alex Ferguson to off-load him immediately to whoever would take him, while there was still a chance of getting a cash return.

Fortunately for Eric, fortunately for all of us, of the many influences Fergie draws upon, of the many people he turns to for advice, he does not count John Sadler among them. Cantona was in the team which faced Manchester City at Maine Road the following Sunday. Giggsy though – once again the fall guy, once again being educated in football the harsh way – wasn't. He was on the bench.

'At the moment he reminds me of a lad who knows all these card tricks,' Ferguson told Hugh McIlvanney in the *Sunday Times* the morning of the game, 'but has still to learn how to play cards.'

The City fans were in good voice. They didn't have much to cheer about at the time: their team was languishing, their manager had just been sacked, and they hated their chairman. Not in the routine, down-with-the-bosses way United fans disliked Martin Edwards, but with a virulence. Peter Swales, the man with the hair like he's spilt a pot of gloss paint over his head, they saw as the personification of all their problems, the reason why they lived forever in the shadow of United.

'Swales Out,' they chanted after every game, led by a vicar who was featured in the *Mirror* (which appeared to have spotted a sales opportunity coordinating the campaign) saying unchristian things about his chairman. They had cast their old forward Francis Lee, the man who used to dive so frequently in opposition penalty areas he should have been fitted with an aqualung, as their saviour. For the moment, Swales was still there, under police protection as he took his place in the directors' box.

'Swales In,' United fans would chant occasionally, to amuse themselves.

But for this game, the Blues – the 'bitters', in United-speak – had cheered up enormously. Someone had just put one over on United, which is what cheers them up most of all. The chants of 'five–one', the memory of that November day in 1989 which was Alex Ferguson's lowest, were full in their throats. Bars of Turkish Delight flew over the gap between the two sets of supporters in the Kippax stand. To the tune of the 'Camptown Races' they sang: 'Galatasaray, Galatasaray, two–nil up and you fucked it up, Galatasaray.'

And by half-time they were on 'Blue Moon', 'Cloud Nine' and 'Seventh Heaven' all rolled into one. Two raking crosses, two firm and tidy headers from Niall Quinn, 2–0 up.

Afterwards, Roy Keane was asked what Alex Ferguson had said in the United dressing room during the interval. Showing an admirable grasp of the footballer's understatement, Keane said: 'Well, basically he said, "Keep playing your game. Keep patient and it'll come." '

If that's what Fergie said, he must have said it while inserting what remained of the Guy Fawkes night fireworks between his players well-muscled buttocks. They came out into the second half a different team; they played electric football.

Cantona started to do things. Wonderful things. Finding, after the first half, that the ball was not coming to him, he dropped back to collect it for himself, to spray the passes around, to be the puppet-master pulling the strings of the Captain Scarlets round him. He started slipping astutely weighted passes out to the wing, where

Sharpe and Kanchelskis gathered them in full stride. And when they crossed, he drifted into the area, unseen, when it counted.

Cantona was there first to pick up a misplaced back-header by Vonk and pop it away with panache. He was there when Giggs, off the bench and with almost his first touch, supplied a killer cross, arcing away from the defender and into his path for the equaliser. He was there to feed Sharpe for the cross which Roy Keane, running in at the far post, coverted into the winner. And when Keane belly-flopped into the corner of the pitch in celebration, he was there to congratulate him.

The United fans nearly burst with excitement, with pride, with relief that the Turkish debacle could be forgotten.

'City is your name, City is your name,' they sang. 'Two–nil up and you lost three–two/City is your name.'

Some time later Paul Ince told me: 'Cantona is someone you want on your team. The very fact that's he's playing, his presence on the field, his awareness of where everyone is on the field, it sets you up. You want that beside you. He can take it all in straightaway, what's happening. Whereas it takes me two or three seconds to work out who's where, he knows it straightaway and he can pick them out: the right players, in the right positions, at the right time. Cantona, man. Respect. Bona fide respect.'

It was a significant win. When Alex Ferguson came down from Aberdeen to Old Trafford, the first thing he was keen to do was to instil some backbone into a club which traditionally had the spinal consistency of a jellyfish. Resilience to come back from disappointment; the ability to fight back from a position apparently lost: those were the qualities of winners as Ferguson understood them. Cantona had them. After a cockup like Turkey, in the old days it would have been a month before United recovered. But Ferguson is a man in a hurry, he doesn't have time to wait for a bounce-back.

At the same time, in Paris, the Gatt talks were stumbling over the question of subsidies to the French film industry: the size of Gérard Depardieu's salary about to bring down the world's trading system. At Old Trafford, there was one French export that no one objected to seeing inflate the local wage system. For the rest of November, back to basics in the domestic mixer, Cantona was majestic: 'the sporting God of the season', the *Sun* called him. Led by him United cantered through wins against Wimbledon and Coventry in the league and Everton in the League Cup, breaking stride only once: when they failed to break down the eleven-man defence of Ipswich in a dull, dull, dull 0–0. By the end of the month they had forty-four points from seventeen games, fourteen ahead of Leeds in second place.

That was a nice irony to greet the first anniversary of his signing from Elland Road. *Red Issue*, the United fanzine, printed a full page 'Thank You' card to Howard Wilkinson, the Leeds manager, for selling him, together with the Elland Road fax number. Our rivals across the Pennines were not amused when their fax jammed.

Meanwhile Ferguson set to work in the background. At The Cliff, Brian Kidd was trying out new training methods involving more shooting: Cantona, Ince, Giggs, Keane and Kanchelskis were staying on in the afternoons just pumping shots at Schmeichel. It sometimes got heated in these sessions and, after concerted efforts to remove his head with the ball, Schmeichel was regularly to be seen tramping back to the changing room like a schoolboy taking his ball home with him from the park, grumbling, muttering, swearing.

A nutritionist was brought in to sort out the players' eating habits. Diet sheets were supplied for wives, mums and landladies explaining that garibaldis and Jaffa Cakes were good, chocolate gâteaux bad. Giggs and Sharpe, the bachelor boys, were sent on cookery lessons. Body fat was measured: Cantona's was the lowest; Bruce was told to lay off the puddings.

Also, the need for experienced cover not quite so desperate now that they were out of Europe, the manager began to do a bit of gentle dead-heading. Some of his older reserves found themselves out of the fantasy league into the real world: Wallace went to Birmingham, Martin went to Celtic, his son Darren was soon to go to Wolves. The idea was to release some of the log jam building up in the lower reaches of the club, a pile-up of talent as the youth conveyor belt was beginning to churn out graduates of promise. Ferguson had signed up eight of the previous year's youth team – David Beckham, Keith Gillespie, Ben Thornley, Colin McKee, Nicky Butt, Gary Neville, Paul Scoles and Chris Casper – boys of frightening potential, and sometimes they couldn't even get a game in the reserves, never mind the first team.

'I feel sorry for them sometimes, the kids,' Ince told me. 'There's Giggsy, twenty, Sharpie twenty-two, Roy twenty-two, me I'm only twenty-six, and I've no intention of packing it in yet. They must think, Christ, I'm not waiting seven, eight years for my chance. I'll try my hand elsewhere.'

It is not possible to ask the kids if that's what they do think. Just as Giggs was protected by Ferguson from speaking to the press when he first emerged, so the new boys, the eight who hope to make it, are out of bounds.

But I was allowed to talk to Eric Harrison, the youth coach, for an article for the *Manchester United Magazine*.

'Think about it,' Giggs said to me. 'The youth coach has got to be the best in the club. The first-team coach, he's got world-class players to work with. The youth-team geezer, he's got kids who haven't got a clue. For my money, Eric Harrison is the best coach in the world.'

It was bitter the day I went to see Harrison, a wind was whipping over the Salford plains cold enough to freeze the handles of a brass trophy. Out on Littleton Road, at the juniors' training pitch about two miles from The Cliff, more than thirty young lads, with French crops and pastry skin, were belting around, sweating in the chill, playing a practice game.

'Irv, Irv, you don't need so many touches there,' Eric Harrison, on the touchline, was shouting. 'Johnno, Johnno, no, no. You're fiddling around in the wrong areas. All that work went out the window then.'

On the other side of the field, Harrison's assistant, Bryan Robson (the other one, the one who used to play for Newcastle and West

Ham) was equally attentive, peering from underneath a woolly hat at the pitch.

I stood next to Harrison and watched them, these prodigies, some of whom will be earning £6,000 a week in three years' time, some of whom will be playing for Rochdale, some of whom will be cleaning windows. As I watched them chesting, juggling, showing skills that would turn heads on Copacabana, there was one player who stood out. Not so much for his ability (they were all so brilliant I wouldn't know who was better than whom), but for the fact that among the adolescent spots and bum-fluff he was wearing a beard. He looked like one of those players the Mexicans tried to pass off as youth-teamers in the World Junior Cup who turn out to be twenty-seven. When he had the ball and several lads started shouting, 'Jules, Jules,' I clicked.

It was Guiliano Maiorana. He'd been one of Fergie's fledglings, the youth lads thrown in in the dark days of 1989. Of them only Lee Sharpe had made it. The others – Russell Beardsmore, Tony Gill and Deniol Graham – were no more. Maiorano, now well into his twenties, had suffered a terrible time with Gazza knee: Ferguson kept him on as a debt of honour. As he ran around, I thought of what Ince had said: 'What kept him going?'

After the session was over, and the kids trotted into the changing rooms, faces pinked from exertion, I asked Harrison if he ever had any difficulty motivating his boys, when their chances of making the first team were so remote.

'Are you kidding?' he said, looking at me as though he thought I was. 'What could be a better motivation for a young lad than knowing that if he impresses everyone here he will become a Manchester United player? These boys are seventeen, eighteen, they're convinced in their hearts that they'll make it. They think they're the best players in the world. Besides, I'm absolutely certain that there will be half a dozen of these boys in the first team in five years' time. There's no question of that.'

Seven or eight years ago, Harrison would not have dared make a statement like that. When Alex Ferguson arrived, the youth policy was a mess. Ron Atkinson preferred to buy ready-made, off the peg from other clubs. He gave starts to Whiteside, Hughes and Blackmore, but they were the exceptions. What's worse, Manchester City were very active locally in the eighties, developing north-west talent like White, Redmond, Lake, Hinchcliffe and Brightwell.

'It's no secret we were losing out to City,' said Harrison. 'To be honest, we were floundering. The Boss called everyone together, all the scouts, and basically told us we weren't doing our job to his satisfaction. We hadn't really addressed the fact that schools weren't so important any more, after the teachers' strikes it was all junior clubs. But then he sent Brian Kidd, who was a youth liaison officer, out into the field to sort things out. He knew what was going on, Kiddo, had great contacts with the clubs. He did a brilliant job. And gradually I started to get the best talent around to work with. Instead of two or three handy lads, I was getting seven or eight a year. You can work with that, make something of it. The big turning point for me was when they got Giggs, snapped him away from under City's nose. That meant they meant business. That was Kiddo's doing.'

And now, in a way that is characteristic of the new imperial United, they have schools of excellence established in Birmingham, Durham and Belfast, geographically poised to cream off the best throughout the country. Once a boy has been targeted as United material, Kidd and Ferguson move in to encourage them to sign for the reds instead of any other club which might be sniffing. When Ferguson knocked on the Giggses' door in Swinton, for instance, and asked Lynne Giggs for permission to sign up her son, it sent a ripple of excitement even through a household where there was never any doubt that their offspring would become a professional footballer.

'Its very flattering when you're fourteen and Alex Ferguson comes in for you,' Giggs told me. 'You tend to think: yeah.'

For two years the newly signed play part time, while still at school. At sixteen, some will be let go, but others will sign on as YTS juniors. It is then that the schooling begins: Harrison teaches them how to play the game. Not just the rules and how to read what's going on, but how to play.

'At sixteen, boys don't know anything like enough to play professional football. I know old folk like me would say this sort of thing,' Harrison said (he's in his forties). 'But kids aren't as good technically as they used to be twenty years ago. I do honestly believe that. When I was a kid, we used to be outside on the streets all the time doing nothing but playing football, that's where we did our learning, our practising. For various perfectly understandable reasons, parents don't let their children do that any more, stay out all hours on their tod. It's getting better now with all the schools of excellence, but we still have to work on it.'

And then, when they get to seventeen, after a year or two on YTS and all that work, Harrison, Ferguson and Kidd have to decide whether to take them on or lose them. They don't always get it right. Harrison, who discovered David Platt, saw him go to Crewe.

'The real reason Platt went has never been revealed and I don't suppose it ever will be,' said Harrison.

Sounds like a whodunnit.

'No, no, I don't mean there was any skulduggery involved. It is simply that some lads do that: they look ordinary at seventeen and end up world class at twenty-three. And others look world class at seventeen and end up ordinary at twenty-three. What I will say is, if there is a Platt among this lot, we'll make sure we don't lose him.'

Harrison's boys earn £29.50 YTS plus £10 expenses a week, another fiver when they turn seventeen – which means it must have taken several weeks to save up for the stack-heeled work boots at £75 a pair and the Replay jeans at £65, which most of them changed into when training was over. It is an odd world they live in. There they are on subsistence wages while workmates a couple of years older than them are filling their wardrobes with Armani and Valentino and driving around in the best German machinery money can buy. There are their non-footballing contemporaries at all-nighters, experimenting with pharmaceuticals and large quantities of expensive bottled water, while they are tucked up early readying themselves for training. There is the average seventeen-year-old lying in bed until midday, while they are up and running laps. And when they've finished working on the training pitch, they are working inside, cleaning the first team's boots. There is no room for adolescent rebellion, no opportunity for individualism in their world: it is like being in the army.

'It's changed a bit since the old days,' said Eric Harrison. 'There is more emphasis on education. Everyone spends a day a week at college. But yes, we still expect them to undertake chores, clean out the showers, do the boots, serve in the souvenir shop, that sort of thing. You should see the state of that dressing room after they've been in it, when they've chucked kit all over the place. You've got to get them to clear that up, even though later on at United someone else will do it for them. You see, they've got to learn that if they end up at Rochdale it won't be like this. They'll be lucky to have any training kit at all, so they better have respect for it.'

Like senior consultants making junior hospital doctors work days on end because they did it when they were young, the system of using the juniors as skivvies, of billeting them with a directory of trusted motherly landladies if they are not local boys who can stay at home, perpetuates because it is reckoned that is the way to build professional footballers, to instil in them the discipline they will require if they are to make it. Oddly, the boys seem not to resent the graft. One I spoke to said: 'Yeah, it's a pain and you whinge about it, but you do it, because you know Giggsy and Sparky and Sharpie did it. That's what you got to do if you want to play for ManU.'

And these boys know who they play for. They hold themselves in a way which exhibits differentness. I saw a group of them out for a drink one night at a pub in a Manchester suburb. It was more than arrogance, as they stood there in their long, fishermen's jerseys and the drop-dead girlies silent on their arms. No one knew their faces, but they were still the centre of attention as they stood there in the middle of the crowded pub, telling in-jokes in in-language and laughing about Garry Pallister's dress sense. They were elevated, oozing a youthful, scrubbed sense of satisfaction, a sense of arrival, which was entirely absent from the normal run of Mancunian youth surrounding them. They looked about three inches taller than anyone else in the place.

'Everyone we play against thinks we think we're the business,' my youth contact told me. 'They think because we turn up in a nice coach, because we've got good kit, because we get crowds showing up to A team games, we reckon ourselves. So they kick shite out of us. It's because we're ManU.'

I went to watch some of these boys, Harrison's talent, play in a reserve match a couple of weeks later, to see if there were any Platts there, to see if the shite was kicked out of them. Old Trafford's a strange place during a reserve match. Only one section of the main stand is open, the rest of the ground is unoccupied – cavernous, eerie. Those who go to watch, the three thousand who show up, the players' friends and relatives apart, are a different breed. There were three Wolves fans at this game. Imagine having so little to do with your life on a Wednesday evening that you will follow your club's reserves to an away match. These three, they wore old gold bobble hats and gaberdines with belts and carried Radio Rentals plastic carrier bags. I asked them whey they had bothered, and they said it was because they watched every Wolves game. As if that was a plausible explanation.

Behind me sat a dozen ten-year-olds, junior lads, learning their craft at a reserve fixture in the same way the juniors on the pitch were learning theirs. They smoked eagerly, quickly, hiding their cigs between puffs, passing them one to another. They tried out a few chants, their voices so high, it sounded like the Three Little Maids echoing through the main stand.

'What the fuckin' 'ell was that?' they piped when a Wolves player fell over the ball.

'Do you mind?' an elderly man nearby asked them. 'There are ladies present.'

'They should be at home knitting,' chirruped one back.

'Awfully sorry,' said his mate, in a mock posh accent. 'What the flipping heck was that' – which made them almost choke with laughter.

It was a godawful night – freezing, wind swirling. But you could see there was football being played. Marshalled by the unlikely old head of Clayton Blackmore (the Frank Hayes of football: thirty and full of potential), they played better than most premiership first teams. David Beckham, tall and elegant, cutting diagonal passes; Paul Scoles, laying off passes to the wing with Cantona panache; Ben Thornley, with Tom Cruise girl-catching grin flashing, tying defenders' and sometimes his own legs up; Chris Casper, cool, Hansen-like at sweeper.

'Ooh-aah Cas-pah, say ooh-ah Cas-pah,' squeaked the dusk chorus as he dispossessed some Wolves player ten years his senior. In front of me, his mum and his dad (Frank, the former Burnley player) swapped proud looks.

It was settled by one goal, from Richard Irving – Irv, who had needed too many touches on the training ground. Here he only needed one, sticking away a rebound off the bar, kicked there by a helpless, flapping defender.

'Well in, Irv, lad,' said the man sitting next to me. 'Who needs Cantona, eh?'

Well, I wouldn't go that far.

Ryan Giggs had a different theory about the young reserve players, about Irv and Johnno, and Nicky Butt who, to reinforce a reputation as the new Cantona, was sent off in successive reserve matches – in the second one he punched Jan Molby (lost his fist in the flab for several minutes, apparently).

'You can feel them there, on your shoulder,' Giggs said. 'You can sense that queue behind you. The Boss is always asking us if we are hungry enough. If we're not he knows plenty who are. And we know they're there, definitely. His theory is that if you're good enough you're old enough. When I was a kid I never thought I'd get in. Now I'm worried they're going to replace me. You motivate each other really.'

Guiliano Maiorana, incidentally, who I wasn't allowed to ask what it was like being perpetually on the shoulder of the first team, was released at the end of the season.

7

The Folk Hero

Sealey we love you, Sealey we do
Although you don't play any games, we still love you
And one day when we're older we'll look back and say
There's no one quite like Les Sealey
He helped us in his way.
Terrace chant, to the tune of 'Grandma We Love You'

Cantona is the King among reds: more songs are sung in his honour, more T-shirts sold. My colleague Andy, by day a sober, even respected, art critic, bought one during the season which simply said '*Dieu*' on it. Not only that, he wore it to work. Next in line is Mark Hughes, whose every rigorous challenge is greeted by the chant: 'You-zee, You-zee,' making his name sound, appropriately, like a brand of machine gun. Giggs and Sharpe are followed by the younger elements in the crowd with jean-dampening adulation; and towards the end of the season I saw more and more people with 'Kanchelskis, 14' ironed on to the back of their United replica shirts – which, at 75p a letter and £5.50 for the number, is a more economically significant act of devotion than, say, 'Ince, 8'.

But the man who inspired the most unexpected affection among the faithful only played twice all season. He was there every game, though, worrying on the bench, yelling, covering his eyes, fretting for the cause. When he trotted along the touchline for a warm-up, the chant of 'Seee-leh, Seee-leh' echoed round the stadium. He replied with a military click of the heels and a salute. Les Sealey: Mad Les, the folk hero of Old Trafford.

Sealey holds a record at United, the only player to have been signed four times. First he arrived from Luton on loan, then was signed permanently, then was sold to Villa, then re-signed on loan, then finally, when the rule changed to allow substitute goalkeepers, he was signed full-time again. United fans, though, prefer to remember him for another reason. He is the man who changed our luck.

The hero lived in a mock-Georgian town house in Wilmslow, the poshest of Cheshire suburbs, where the neighbours are all lawyers. Or footballers. He was out when I got there, but his wife let me in, then disappeared to make tea. While she was gone, I looked round the room. Standard footballer's place: expensive furnishings, no clutter, no books, a lot of electronics. Like a hotel room. Through the French windows I could see bulldozers, churning away at the end of his garden. The parkland which the house was built to overlook was being modernised into a bypass.

Les arrived about five minutes later, full of apologies for being out, on an errand. He is a tall man with a big chin and bandy legs, a big Cockney voice and a big handshake. I noticed there was a hint of overhang at the waist, pressing against the cream polo neck he was wearing. No more than you might expect for a thirty-seven-year-old, but a surprise for an athlete. He must have noticed me looking and slapped his stomach.

'Can't get the hang of this new diet they give you,' he said.

'That's a pisser,' I said, pointing out of the window, when he came back with two mugs of tea.

'Not a problem, mate,' he said, moving a copy of the *Sun* and a car magazine on the coffee table to accommodate the teas which his wife had just brought in to the room. 'Not my house. Rented, innit.'

Is it expensive, I asked.

'Dunno, club done it,' he said, and I thought that's a goalkeeper's coordination: talking, drinking tea and chewing gum all at the same time. 'That's the thing about ManU. Sort you out. Make you feel wanted. When I was at Villa, I was expected to travel up every day from my house in London. None of that with United. No, it was: here's a hotel room, then here's a house, then here's school for your kids. We'll sort you.'

They look after players, then.

'Do they,' he said. 'I'll give you a for instance. End of last year,

I was out on loan to Birmingham from Villa and I was just about to sign for them when United phoned to say they wanted me back here for a second spell. Well, there was no choice. I rang Terry Cooper, who was boss there then, on the Friday, and said: "I ain't playing tomorrow." I came straight back up here without discussing money or anything and they put me straight up in the Holiday Inn. I thought: that's it, I'm back in the swing. These things count for a player. I mean at Birmingham I went to get my petrol money and you got a two-hour quiz: "Can't you get a smaller-engined car?" I know they got money problems, but it makes a player feel they don't care if they act like that. It amazes me when some of them who've grown up here talk about going somewhere else. I tell them, the grass is not greener. I've been around, I left here and came back. I tell them it's an anti-climax going anywhere else. I mean, I'm reserve here, and people say: "Don't you miss playing first-team football? You could be number one somewhere else." Well, maybe I could, maybe I couldn't. But I'd rather be reserve at ManU than play number one at a lesser club.'

That's what Gordon McQueen reckoned, I said. He always maintained that 99 per cent of professional footballers when questioned would say they want to play for Manchester United. And the other 1 per cent, who said they didn't, were lying.

'Well, he's right. Spot on, that.'

Les Sealey arrived for the first time at Old Trafford in the dark days of 1989, as understudy for Jim Leighton. Leighton was not a folk hero; he was abused viciously not just by a section of the crowd but by almost everyone. *Red Issue*, when it was first launched, was stocked in the United superstore, but when Alex Ferguson saw a copy which included a cartoon of Leighton receiving a giant phallus from a man in black tie, with the caption, 'Cockup of the Year Award Winner for the third season running', he had the magazine banned from the premises immediately.

Leighton knew he was a target. Just before the 1990 Cup final against Palace he was quoted in the *News of the World* saying he was determined to show the idiots who barracked him what he was made of. Unfortunately, he did. He was held responsible for two of Palace's goals in the 3–3 draw. Before the replay, Ferguson took what he said was the hardest decision of his career: he dropped Leighton and promoted Sealey. United won the Cup, and the new man's arrival seemed to precipitate the great revival.

I asked Sealey if he sensed Leighton's discomfort when he first arrived at Old Trafford. 'If they don't like you, it's the loneliest place in the world out there,' he said. 'They can destroy you. When I got here, a lot of people were getting stick, but one or two, it was affecting their lives. In front of you, you've got eleven men physically trying to stop you and kick your head in and you've got forty-four thousand people behind you screaming they hate you. It takes a very big man to survive that. And with goalkeeping, it's all about confidence.'

So, was he nervous that it might happen to him when he took over?

'No. I always loved it at Old Trafford. Even as a member of the oppo, I didn't find it intimidating. Now I'm here, I've found everyone wants to beat you, and if you've got that thing inside you that likes confrontation, you'll thrive on it. Also, technically, I'm not a very good goalkeeper. Look at Shilton, he had everything in line, neat as you like. Me, I'm all over the place. I stop shots with me feet, me head, me bum. Because I wasn't that technically good, I had to play with enthusiasm and venom to make my mark. And I think that rubs off on fans. I've always played the game emotionally charged and fans always seem to respond well to that.'

Ah, Mad Les. Our bonkers keeper, the man who once ran fifty yards from his goal to attack the referee. No wonder the fans love him. He's even less sober than they are.

'I'm not like that in real life,' he said. 'People seem to think I'm Mr Angry, go into the pub and start on five geezers. I'm not. The last time I had a fight was years ago, and I mean years ago. No, I tend to come home, have a cup of tea, watch the telly. I've no special interests, just football. It's my life. Even when I'm on the bench I kick every ball, and the fans, they sort of see that, see you as one of them.'

What's more he seems to have a talismanic effect: Lucky Les. In just fifty-five games with United he collected an FA Cup-winner's medal, a European Cup Winners Cup-winner's medal and two League Cup-finalist's medals. You don't barrack the good-luck charm.

'Yeah, I think I'm the manager's lucky mascot. I believe in all that, superstitions. I've got me own way of doing things, right down to the order I take my clothes off and put on my kit. I had this accident once on my way to a game, bumper ripped off the front of the car. I played a blinder that day, and didn't want to get the car repaired. I got slaughtered, everyone saying: "Look at the state of your car." But I wouldn't get it repaired, would I. Ask her, she'll tell you.'

His wife could be heard in the adjoining room, cleaning.

'What's that?' she said.

'About the car, tell him.'

'Yeah,' his wife said. 'That's right.'

According to other players, there is a code at United by which players are expected to live, a way in which they are expected to conduct themselves in public. I asked Sealey if the standards of presumed behaviour were fiercer at United than at other clubs he had played at. 'It's down to the manager,' he said. 'There is a code you live by, but it's unsaid. You don't get a list of rules, you take the lead from the Boss. You know he has standards, and you respect that. I've got a bit of a reputation as being a troublemaker with managers, but you ask Ferguson or Ron Atkinson if I gave them problems. I think they'll say no, because if I respect a man's ability, I'll run my legs off for the geezer. And if I don't I'll tell him he's a prat. But with the Boss, you know he wants you to stay in three nights before a game, so you do. Only silly people break that rule. Because in this town, someone will ring up, probably a City supporter, and say they saw you in a bar or whatever. They'll probably do that anyway even if you're not. They'll get the hump with you because you get paid fantastic money.'

How fantastic?

'Well,' he said, 'put it this way, you'll miss it when it stops. The thing is, for me, it's not enough to retire on. Well, I could if I wanted to like live in a flat with one bedroom and drive a Reliant Robin. I'll have to work afterwards, but it'll never be as well paid as this. I'm lucky being a goalkeeper, I can go on longer, and you're less prone to injury. That's why players get worried sick about injury, they see all this coming to a stop.'

Not that Sealey had not been injured in United's cause. In the 1991 Rumbelows Cup final, he collided with a Sheffield Wednesday player, and quite a drama followed.

'With it being Wembley, where the grass is a bit longer, everyone had long metal studs,' he remembered. 'Anyway, so I collided with this feller, accidental, like, and I felt like this cut. Clean, like a blade. I remember looking down and seeing this big flap of skin. Then I could see I was cut right through to the bone. And what struck me was how white the bone looked. Not white like paint, but a pure white, like ivory. A white I'd never seen before.'

If most of us had been given such an impromptu anatomy lesson, our response would have been to go straight off the pitch and head for the nearest hospital. But when Jimmy McGregor, United's physio, suggested Sealey do just that, he responded in a manner which made it plain he did not agree. Not so much Mr Angry as Mr Absolutely Apoplectic. Why on earth did he insist on playing on?

'It's odd, but it didn't hurt at the time,' he said. 'The cut was clean, like it was done with a razor, a pure knife cut. And it wasn't restricting movement. We were playing really badly, worse than we had all year and I thought the last thing we needed was to put an outfield player in goal. This was in the days before substitute keepers, remember. So I refused to go off. Mind you if I'd known what was going to happen afterwards, I wouldn't have been so keen to stay on.'

Which was?

'On the bus on the way to the airport after the game, the knee blew up. The idea had been: put temporary stitches in, get back to Manchester quick, see a doctor when we got back. But on the bus you could see it ballooning up, pushing against the material of my trousers. And the pain, God. You know some pain you can fight, but this was unbelievable. Anyhow, I collapsed. I got taken to Middlesex Hospital and I had emergency surgery. They needed a gallon and a half of saline solution to flush it out, the wound, and half fucking Wembley was in there. I woke up after the anaesthetic had worn off and the doctor's standing over me saying: "Who's a lucky boy, then?" And I looked at my leg and I thought: Christ, it's the Cup Winners Cup final in five weeks' time. So I said to the doc: "What chances have I got of making the big one?" And the doc says: "Playing? You're lucky to be alive." Apparently, if I'd got on the plane the pressure in the cabin would have accelerated the poisoning. He said I could easily have lost a leg, if not died. That's what he said, I mean he's the doctor.'

By now, Mrs Sealey had abandoned her chores and was sitting in on the conversation, enjoying all the medical details.

'But you played in Rotterdam, didn't you,' she said. 'You weren't going to miss out on a medal and that, were you?'

'I was not fit,' he said. 'No way. I was nowhere near their goal, which I should've got. Anyway after the presentation, I was the one chosen for the drug test, wasn't I. So I went into this room to do the business, and I'd taken the bandage off I'd worn during the game. And Barcelona's two players were in there. Koeman and what's his name? Salinas, I think it was. Anyway they took one look at my leg where it was all bald from being shaved for the op and this great line of stitches across the knee and they looked at each other. And you could see them thinking: is this geezer off his trolley playing like that or what?'

There is an answer to that.

Two months later, in an act which demonstrates the ruthlessness of football, Peter Schmeichel was signed and United had an offer to sell Sealey on to Aston Villa.

'Problem was,' he said, 'the knee hadn't healed. Playing in Rotterdam had really done for it. It was all swollen, and I knew I wasn't going to pass a medical. I said to the wife, basically, I'm done. Then I was talking to Robbo about it – he's had some, hasn't he, Robbo?

And he slipped me this number on a piece of paper, and says: "Ring it." And it's this medium in Blackpool, Olga Stringfellow's her name. Basically, I'm the biggest sceptic in the world, I thought this was a load of old rubbish. But it's getting close to the medical by now and I went, like, as the last chance.

'I took the two boys and the wife. It was about eleven o'clock in the morning, and she got out a bottle of vodka, and said: "I've got to drink all this, otherwise it won't work." And I thought: I've let myself in for a right handful here. The wife was there, she'll tell you.'

His wife just raised her eyes.

I said, did you laugh?

'No, it was too important to laugh,' he said. 'Anyway this Olga, she's about ninety, puts my legs on her lap and she put her hand on my knee. And it was like someone's put a red-hot iron on me and there's this clicking noise like them toy frogs you used to get, remember, coming out of her hand. Honestly. And she says: "You've got a problem with your ankle." I says: "Hold up, it's my knee." She says: "No, it's your ankle."

'Anyway she kept her hand on my knee for an hour and a half while she drinks her way through the bottle of vodka. Never offered me any. Then she said: "That's it, you can go home now. You'll be all right in three days." So I got dressed and went home.

'On the Monday I did a lap round the park and it was agony. On the Wednesday I had to go to Villa for training. We played five-a-side and I wore a tracksuit so they couldn't see the knee, but I've dived about a bit and banged it and it's got bigger. After the five-a-side we agreed a contract and Big Ron says: "Come back tomorrow for your medical. You can sign up on condition you pass."

'I went home, had a cup of tea, two bacon sandwiches, took my trousers off – and the knee? The knee was bigger than ever. I lay on the settee and said to the wife, for want of a better word, "I'm fucked. Completely fucking fucked. There's no way I'll pass." She goes out and I fall asleep in the settee. I woke up about two hours later and, fuck me, the knee's normal size. I go down to Villa, I pass the medical, sign and haven't had a moment's problem since.'

I must have looked sceptical.

'True story,' he said, looking insistent. 'God's honest. On my kids' lives. And our eldest, he had a graze on his arm, she touched that and it went. Tell him, it did, didn't it!'

'She just touched it,' said his wife. 'By the time we got back home, it had gone.'

'Disappeared.'

'All you could see was a slight mark.'

'Gone. I never believed in it before, but now I do, totally,' said Sealey. 'It would have been all right in time, but how long? Six months, seven months? Too long. She literally saved my career. But I never found out what she meant about the ankle.'

After that, there wasn't a lot to say. Sealey gave me a lift to the station. He had a brand new car, provided by the club, a Golf convertible ('not bad, eh? I like the new shape better than the old one') which, I noticed, had a full set of bumpers. As we drove through the roadworks bespoiling the best of Cheshire, I asked him whether he found it hard motivating himself for a life on the bench.

'You're joking. Listen, at this club you get sleepless nights if you play badly in the reserves. Honest, there's always someone watching you, and if you slack, word will get back. To him. You'll find yourself making the tea. If all it takes is a bit of sweat and graft to stay here, then I'll put in a bit of sweat and graft. Besides you've got to prepare yourself as if you're going out there. You never know, Peter might get injured or sent off and you've got to be ready.'

'Unlikely,' I said.

'You've not seen him in five-a-sides,' he said. And I caught the train.

8

Tickets Please

Anyone need tickets? Buy or sell.
Sales cry on Warwick Road, once a fortnight

The third round of the FA Cup. The glamour, the heart-warming, tear-forming collision of David and Goliath; the glorious Corinthian achievement; the legendary giant-killing conducted through stud-swallowing mud; the after-match interviews with Gerald Sinstadt. The most thrilling Saturday of the English season. Yes, we'd drawn Sheffield United away, and, because it was a live match, it was on a Sunday, which meant engineering works north of Peterborough.

After three hours, I eventually reached my brother-in-law in Doncaster, who was coming with me, and we drove to Sheffield to find the town *en fête* for the great occasion: someone had attached three balloons to the door frame of the tobacconist opposite Bramhall Lane. Our tickets were for the main stand, and we were surrounded by Sheffield followers with faces which suggested they had celebrated the start of the FA Cup by sucking lemons.

'Come on Sheffield,' shouted one of them as the teams lined up for the kickoff. 'Watch out for the ref. You'll get nowt from him against this lot of prima donnas.'

'Aye,' added the woman sitting next to me. 'It were the same against Oldham.'

Oldham: those sophisticated, metropolitan fancy pants.

At the kickoff Sheffield passed the ball back to their centre back who kicked it as hard and as high as possible. Time seemed to stand still as the ball went up and up. You could see the look on Steve

Bruce's face as he prepared himself for its arrival on his forehead, the hint of trepidation that the thing might actually have combusted on its way back into the lower atmosphere.

That was the limit of Sheffield's attacking effort: hoof. A month earlier in the league fixture here, they had given Sharpe, Giggs and Cantona too much space and had lost 3–0. This time they spent the entire match as if magnetically attracted to the centre circle, squeezing the playing surface down to less than ten yards, determined to clutter up United's scope for endeavour.

It was appalling. No wonder of all the grounds I visited in the season, this was the only one not full. They don't really set the city's pulse racing, Dave Bassett's tactics. The United end was packed enough, the reds taking their mind off the game in front of them by singing their way through their new song, 'The Twelve Days of Cantona'. But the newly seated home end was only two-thirds occupied. After forty-five minutes of nonsense, you expected to see the empty bucket seats lining up at the exits trying to get out of the place.

In the second half, a pearl emerged from the seaweed. At the end of a sequence of keep-ball short passes, Cantona laid the ball off to Hughes, who burst into purposefulness. He carried it diagonally across the pitch, exchanging as he went three intricate, high-speed one-twos with Ince, leaving the Sheffield defence leaden-footed in his wash. He then slotted the ball, precisely, from the edge of the area into the corner of the net. Dave, my brother-in-law, neutral at best towards United, turned to me in blinking disbelief.

'That's absolutely brilliant,' he said.

The mark of a great side: how to score a perfect team goal against an outfit determined to suffocate any flash of enterprise. The Sheffield folk around me were quiet, not certain how to react to the unexpected sight of good football at Bramhall Lane.

They cheered up five minutes later, though. Hughes, in an act a schoolboy might have considered immature, chased his marker into the corner and kicked him up the backside. He had already been booked, so off he went. As he came towards us (we were sitting immediately above the tunnel to the dressing rooms), the woman next to me stood up and wagged her finger.

'Oi, Hughes,' she shouted. He looked up at her as he made his way towards his early bath. 'Yeah, you, you think you're clever, don't you? Well let me tell you summat. You're not.' Hughes rolled his eyes at her as he disappeared.

'I think I made myself clear,' she said, sitting down.

'Aye,' said her neighbour.

After the game someone asked Alex Ferguson if Hughes had not spoilt his wonder goal with his petulance.

'The lad knows he was silly to retaliate,' said Fergie. 'But, well, it's no surprising he reacted as he did. He spent the entire game being kicked. It's about time referees gave him some protection.'

Sending off? It was a theme to which he would return in press conferences to follow.

The goal apart, that was the worst game I was to see United play. All the more unexpected because three days earlier they had been involved in a classic. Not that I was there to see it. I was on my way out of the house one day, just into the New Year, when the phone rang. It was a polite woman, with a Scouse accent, who introduced herself as 'the Anfield ticket office'.

'We just wanted to know,' she said, 'now the game has been rearranged for Sky, whether you are still able to come.'

Nice of her to be so thoughtful. I had applied for a ticket to stand in the Kop for United's game at Anfield. Unfortunately, after they sent me the letter saying there were no tickets available, I had accepted an assignment from a magazine to go to Los Angeles and I was just on my way to the airport. Now there was a ticket. It was some dilemma: Liverpool v. United or a trip to LA. I wavered for a moment. Then I said no, thanks, but I couldn't go. I went to Los Angeles instead. A big mistake.

If you want to follow Manchester United, you live in this uncertainty, never quite able to make plans. When I first started going to games in the seventies, I used to turn up an hour before kickoff, home or away, queue up, pay my money at the turnstile and go in. If you arrived too late, you got locked out.

Now, post the *Taylor Report*, with capacity 15,000 lower than it was in those days, demand means every game at Old Trafford is all-ticket. Most of the tickets are pre-sold as season and corporate packages, leaving only about 14,000 a game to be distributed among an army of the interested. To apply for one of these you have to be a member; it costs over £10 a year and there are over 100,000 others in the tombola (a pleasant little dividend spinner). The chances of landing one are about as high as sitting next to Andie MacDowell on the plane to Los Angeles and her asking if you fancied a quickie in the loo.

For away matches, the process is even more exasperating. In order to justify the huge cost of the annual club-class tickets and the executive boxes, holders of these privileges are guaranteed tickets to away matches, up to six in the case of box-holders. And this means that ever more Byzantine ways have been invented by the club to allocate the remainder. For instance, this was the instruction as to how the ordinary fan might apply for a ticket to one big fixture:

'Members presenting voucher QQ fully completed, together with their book and not less than twenty-two match vouchers properly affixed to the official sheet, can apply by post.'

Thus, if you want to watch United regularly, you have to do one of several things. You can mortgage the house and buy club class; you can spend your free time queueing up and sticking vouchers to official sheets; you can cultivate influential friends who can accommodate you in their box (not easy if you have MUFC tattooed on your knuckles); or you can make a Faustian deal with the men in the American designer sportswear who hover round Old Trafford like pilot fish round a shark, feeding off the scraps.

'I haven't paid face value for a ticket for five years,' Jon Shine told me. 'I reckon I could have bought the entire Stretford End on the amount I've poured into the black economy over the years.'

Every match day the roads to Old Trafford are full of those who can help alleviate the nostalgic urge to gain entry to a United game by paying cash on the day. The drawback is, it tends to be slightly more than the 80p I used to pay to stand in the Stretford Paddock. How much more depends, as this is the most brutal of free markets, on the popularity of the game. You can tell how much you are going to have to pay by the geographical spread of the touts. The further away from the ground you encounter them, the cheaper it will be to negotiate. For the game against Ipswich last season, for instance, I was jostled on the platform of Old Trafford station as I got off the tram by a lad in a beanie hat flourishing a wad of tickets.

'Anyone need tickets?' he said.

How much did he want, I asked him.

'Thirt-eh,' he said. This is for a £14 seat.

I said I wasn't interested and walked away.

'Arright then, mate,' he said, chasing after me. 'Twent-eh.'

'No,' I said, and carried on down the disabled access slope from the platform.

'Come 'ere,' he shouted. 'Talk to meh. How much do you want to pay, fifteen pounds? Face value. Just tell meh. Go on mate, yer arright.'

I said it didn't really matter, as I had a ticket.

'Time waster,' he sneered.

For the game against Manchester City later in the season, on the other hand, I didn't see evidence of a tout until I got to the car park in front of the stadium. There was one wearing a Ralph Lauren blouson, jabbing at the keys of a mobile phone. He was surrounded by a dozen anxious faces, and occasionally switching attention from his phone, he would conduct negotiations. His price was rising faster than a Tory politician's at an arms trade fair. 'What can I do, mate,' he said to one fan who had objected to his price of £60. 'I'm not a charity.'

From this season, touting in the street is illegal. The club has said it is delighted with the new law. Perhaps it does not appreciate how its own ticket distribution system has, by default, helped the black marketeers' business thrive.

I know of a solicitor in Manchester, a mad United fan, who runs a box, in which he entertains clients. For away matches, most of which he attends himself, he rings round a few friends he knows to be dedicated fans, takes orders, applies for tickets. He then passes on the tickets to his friends at face value, sometimes he doesn't charge at all, sometimes he doesn't take up his full allocation. Now if I ran a box, or if I sponsored a match and, as part of the package, was given a hundred tickets but had only forty clients I wanted to entertain, I'm not sure I would be so scrupulous. I think I might try to recoup some of my costs by selling on my spares, at a pre-mium, to a man in American sportswear. And I don't think I am being unduly cynical to suggest I might not be the first to think of that idea. In the end, such tickets eventually filter their way through to people who have a good use for them: full-time reds like Jon Shine. But it means for them to support their chosen club they have to finance the habits and mobile-phone bills of Mancunian wannabe-gangsters in the process.

Nevertheless, this does not explain why I was doing business direct with the smooth-talking 'Anfield ticket office'. I discovered a while ago that not every club has such a demand for tickets as United. In fact, no other club does. What I do is write at the beginning of the season to every club in the Premiership, asking for two seats for the game against Manchester United, whenever it might be scheduled, quoting my credit card number and enclosing a stamped addressed envelope. Last season every single club I applied to sent me a pair, except Wimbledon (who sent me four) and Norwich who sent me a letter apologising, but explaining they operated a members-only policy. This approach means you are always placed with the opposition supporters like the happy bunch at Bramhall Lane. But this is only occasionally a problem (at West Ham or Leeds) and, in some instances, there are so many reds doing the same you feel as though you are in the away end anyway.

But I turned down Liverpool's kind offer and when I bought a paper the morning I got back from America I knew I was wrong to do it. Joe Lovejoy, almost salivating over his word processor, pronounced it the game of the season. United went 3–0 up within twenty minutes and then Liverpool, playing better than they did for the rest of the campaign, pulled it back to 3–3.

'I came out of that panting,' Jon Daniels, editor of *Red Issue* told me. 'And you know what, there were people on the coach whinging about it. Complaining that we had let slip three–nil. I mean, what do they want, some people. That was an absolute great, and to be honest, with Liverpool in that mood, we were lucky to get away with a draw.'

Later in the season, Alex Ferguson, looking back on the game, told me: 'I thought at the time that Liverpool had knackered themselves that night. The look in their eyes, they were so charged, so determined to prove to us that they were still the top dogs. I feared for them, I really did, I thought they would go flat after that display. They were due to play Bristol City in the Cup and I said to Brian Kidd after the game, look out for an upset there.'

He was right. After a postponed match due to a floodlight failure, Liverpool were knocked out in the third round in ignominy. It precipitated the departure of Graeme Souness. Not many tears were shed on Merseyside at that news.

In Manchester, meanwhile, we had fifty-eight points, were top of the Premiership, unbeaten since September and were thirteen points clear of Blackburn who, through the pack, had emerged as the only ones with the wherewithal to stop us. We were in the fourth round of the Cup, and were in the quarter-finals of the Coca-Cola Cup. A new word started to be uttered around the stands of Old Trafford: the treble, the clean sweep, the one thing the Scousers had never done.

9

Busby

*I remember my father telling me as a young
boy that you don't meet more than three
great people in your life. I know I met one.*
                    Alex Ferguson, 22 February 1994

Never mind the sinking Gatt talks. Never mind the government
slipping on yet another skid-pan of its own making. Never mind
further revelations about President Clinton's serial philandering.
On the evening of Thursday, 20 January there was no question
which was the most appropriate item to lead 'News at Ten'. Earlier
that day, at the Alexandra Hospital in Cheadle, Sir Matt Busby, the
greatest of Manchester United's managers, died peacefully in his
sleep. He was eighty-four. As with John Smith four months later,
the death of a dignified, passionate, honourable Scotsman made the
nation pause for a moment.

In Manchester, the pause lasted slightly longer. Almost immediately,
underneath the clock at Old Trafford which commemorates the
Munich air crash in which Busby nearly perished almost thirty-six
years previously, a shrine began to grow. Fans went along and laid
out items they cherished: United shirts, scarves, and hats often with
verses of home-penned doggerel pinned on to them. Within hours
an ocean of artificial fibre was advancing across the stadium fore-
court, ten thousand personal tributes to the man who had built
Manchester United merging into one, tracking his career through
the triumph of the Busby Babes, through disaster and rebuilding
to the final fulfilment of the European Cup. It was all the more
poignant because it was so spontaneous. No one planned it or

oversaw it. No announcement was made to bring your scrapbook, or newspaper cutting or framed picture. The mourners wanted to show their appreciation for the man who had not simply created a good football team, he had engendered self-esteem in anyone who called themselves a follower of Manchester United.

The Saturday after Sir Matt died, United were at home to Everton and Manchester was in full mourning. Everywhere, as I made my way to Old Trafford, people were doing their best to show they were touched by his passing. On the tram from the city centre, three boys not born when Sir Matt's teams were playing, not born when he retired, not born when United were relegated three managers later, looked serious as they pored over the tributes in the papers and speculated on how the minute's silence would be observed across the country.

'Liverpool and City will be interesting,' one said.

'Best we're not playing Leeds,' his mate said.

Outside Old Trafford cricket ground I overtook a man and his son negotiating with a tout. I watched them pay £80 for two £8 standing tickets, and when their business was completed, I asked them why they considered it worth paying so much.

'I first came in nineteen fifty-eight when I was thirteen, his age,' the man said, indicating his son. 'I gave up in the seventies, when Sir Matt did. Wasn't the same. I was watching the telly last night and it just hit me. I had to get down here, had to make sure that the lad was here too. Important he understands these things.'

I asked him what his name was.

'I'm not going to tell you,' he said. 'I don't think the wife would appreciate it, me paying eighty pounds for two tickets. She doesn't realise what it means.'

The commercial circus of Old Trafford knew what it meant, though. There were, apparently, dozens of forged tickets abroad. I saw two touts outside Stretford town hall, celebrating a sale with giggling relish.

'It's great this,' said one. 'Wish he died every week.'

Just into Sir Matt Busby Way a man was selling 'Matt Busby:

The Legend Lives On' T-shirts for a fiver a piece. How many had he sold, I asked him?

''bout thirty so far,' he said, breaking off to deal with a Scotsman who had clearly taken to alcohol to deaden his pain. 'That kid's done better,' he added, indicating a man in the middle of the road selling sprays of red and white carnations to be laid at the shrine. This entrepreneurial florist looked not a bit embarrassed when I asked him if he considered it tasteless to make money on this day, in that way.

'Not really,' he said. 'Fellers stand outside hospital and that, doing it.'

I left him to it and pushed my way through the heave towards the flowers' destination. There was a silence both profound and catching as I approached the shrine. People stood ten deep behind crush barriers erected to protect the offerings, which were lying soggy after a Mancunian soaking. Everywhere there were tributes, along the wall of the stadium, newspaper cuttings pasted on to the front of the entrance to the executive boxes, washing lines of banners and scarves growing along the telephone cabling. I stood against the barrier and looked at the tidal wave of sentimentality washing across the tarmac: teddy bears holding the European Cup, shirts of every merchandising generation, tributes from the fans of other clubs.

Overhead, a steady rain fell of more scarves, hats and flowers thrown by people who couldn't get near enough to lay them down. A bunch of roses landed a foot in front of me: 'Sir Matt, you was Heaven sent to turn Old Trafford into Mecca', read the note attached. To my left a man held his camcorder unsteadily over each item in reach. To my right, a man in his sixties, red-faced, head down, had a moment's contemplation before tossing an untidy knot of flowers on to the shrine. I felt I was talking in church when I asked him where he was from.

'Belfast,' he whispered back. 'Set off the moment I heard that yer man had died. I had to be here. To give me condolences, like, to the city.'

I asked him if he had a ticket.

'No, and I not seen sight of one,' he said. 'I'll do me best, but it doesn't matter if I don't get one. The game's not the big thing today.'

Inside the stadium, it was quieter still, a cathedral rather than a church. Outside were left 14,000 people, their hopes of a ticket thwarted. But a huge wad of photographers had been let in. They stood on the pitch, corralled into a rope enclosure, telephoto lenses threading in on the seat which Busby used to occupy in the directors' box, which was to remain empty for the rest of the season. Around the empty place the great and the good gathered: Law, Best, Michel Platini, Mick Hucknall, Peter Brooke the Heritage Secretary, everyone consoling each other. Angus Deayton wore a black tie.

The public address announcer asked everyone to remain silent as the teams came on to the pitch. He was five minutes premature. It was a strange thing, standing there silent among so many people, for so long, like watching a game at Burnden Park, the only noise a radio reporter behind me whispering his commentary of the nothingness. The silence was finally cut by a piper leading the teams slowly from the tunnel. The two groups of players lined up from the centre circle, the directors of each club tagging on to the lines, including Bobby Charlton, the one who had been through most with Busby. They shuffled into place in the silence, then stood, heads down, faced by the battery of photographers. The minute's silence itself finally began, with a parp from the ref's whistle. In the press box in front of me, Pat Crerand, Busby's elegant midfield stroller, bit his knuckles, a tear slowly working its way down his face.

At the end of the time, the referee blew his whistle: 44,750 people had been absolutely quiet for nearly six minutes. A huge cheer broke to mark its end. Then applause, most of it directed at the Everton fans, uncomfortable interlopers who had kept a total and honourable silence through someone else's grief.

'I've been through some minutes' silence before,' Les Sealey told me afterwards. 'But never anything like that. I remember we did one for some anniversary of Munich which fell on a Saturday. We walked out there, and as we stood silent, snow began to fall. Absolutely at that moment, not just a bit, but chucking it down. I thought that was the ultimate, but this topped it. Busby was that important round the place. It's all Busby's, this place.'

Five years earlier, the place was less comfortable with Busby. Before Ferguson sorted it out, the great former manager was a living indictment in the Old Trafford corridors; a still eye of achievement, restraint and calm in the middle of a maelstrom of inadequacy, greed and panic. Physically, he appeared to age very little; he was always there, an unchanging reminder of the days when it seemed so easy to do things properly. So when finally, so recently, Ferguson had achieved the title, and the twenty-six-year gap was bridged, Busby's presence became a celebration: you could look back with pride, not with pain. And Busby himself clearly preferred it that way.

'You remember the pictures of him the night against Blackburn after we won the title,' Ferguson said to me. 'His eyes were completely lit up. He was delighted. All the more so because I think it was achieved in a style he would have recognised and appreciated. The players were at last capturing some of the standards he set.'

The standard Busby set was not just winning five championships, not just rebuilding the club after the war, not just winning the European Cup ten years after a plane crash had destroyed his team, but doing it all with style. His philosophy was articulated by the Bishop of Chester, preaching after the Munich disaster, a sermon Busby committed to heart: 'The ultimate discharge of any Manchester United team is a duty to become a byword for those who play a good game wherever in the world football is played.'

With Ferguson, Busby was an inspiration rather than the intimidation he had been for lesser managers.

'Oh aye,' Ferguson said. 'Everyone of us was inspired by him, by the challenge he set for Manchester United. Right till the end he was in every day, sitting there with his soup and his cheese and his pipe, with time for a quiet word with everybody. Even towards the end when the memory was mebbe going a little and he couldn't remember everyone's names, he'd have a "hello, son" or "hello, dear, how are you?" He had time for everyone and an ability to make everyone seem special and that's some gift. I used to watch the players when Sir Matt came on the team bus to away matches, they'd nudge each other when he walked past and go: "Hey, that's Sir Matt." '

Somehow, in the celebratory air at the end of the 1993 season, the two Scots' reigns became telescoped together; the sixteen years between Busby retiring and Ferguson arriving forgotten as an unfortunate interregnum. On most match days round the club, Busby's men were to be seen enjoying the achievements of Ferguson's team. Law, Best and Charlton were the VIPS. But Crerand, McGuinness and Willie Morgan (Busby's last signing and great confidant) were no less frequent visitors – commentating, analysing, relishing the reflected glory.

Ferguson's new team seemed to provide continuity with the Busby era: Cantona, Hughes and Giggs the natural heirs of Law, Best and Charlton rather than Davenport, Gibson and Olsen. The Boss was dead, long live the Boss.

It was lucky it was that team and not some of their predecessors who were playing on Busby's memorial day. United were stylish, flamboyant, quick, eager, magnificent: everything you might hope for in a football team. They won 1–0, a Giggs goal. It was one of those 1–0s when you imagine there must have been a printing error. It should have been 10. At the end of it, United were top, with sixty-four points, sixteen ahead of Blackburn: the proper tribute to Busby.

After it, in the press conference in United's plush press lounge with pictures of Busby times and Ferguson times on the wall, the new Boss looked like a man relieved to have acquitted himself well.

'As I said to them yesterday, just go out and enjoy yourselves,' he said. 'And they did. The chances they missed. It was a difficult day for everyone. A difficult day for Everton, a difficult day for their fans, who were brilliant. I think our players were taken aback by the atmosphere. When we walked into the tunnel it hit us, the

absolute silence. It was very, very moving, so I was delighted
the players responded in the manner they did.'

Had it been a difficult time for the manager too? someone asked.

'Aye, well. A difficult two or three days, handling the media. It
had to be done. Sir Matt was a worldwide figure and it had to be
acknowledged in the proper way. It's easy for me to do that because
he was such a great man who meant so much to me.'

After he went, Mark Hughes came into the press room.

'I've been here since I was fourteen,' he said. 'Sir Matt was always
here, always in his office. He'd give you a wave and that big smile
of his. He'll be missed. Badly, badly missed.'

The minute's silence was generally well observed across the country.
At Highbury someone broke it with a shout of 'Pick Merson'. An
Arsenal supporter I know said this was fair enough: Sir Matt would
have picked Merson. At Anfield, a few Manchester City fans
chanted throughout. They were booed roundly afterwards by the
Liverpool followers. On Merseyside, they know how to behave
about death: they have had plenty of recent practice. I would like
to think all United fans would have done the same had it been the
other way round. I'd like to think it, but since some elements
thought it amusing to chant through the silence for one of the
Hillsborough victims a couple of years ago, I'm not so sure. And I
can remember standing in the Clock End at Highbury once when,
as the rest of the ground observed a minute for some FA official, a
couple of dozen of my fellow reds couldn't wait to deliver the news
that 'Nicholas is a wanker'.

During the televised match on the Sunday, though, the Leeds
diplomatic corps went one worse. At Ewood Park they held a
premeditated chant-in about Don Revie, flourishing banners, while
all around the Blackburn followers were solid in their tribute. There
were pictures in the papers the following day of the Leeds players
McAllister, Strachan and Newsome looking anguished in the centre
circle, flapping their arms in quieten-down gestures.

Leeds played ineptly that day, as if ashamed to show themselves
after that performance by their fans.

'I could use every adjective I know but what would it matter,' Howard Wilkinson said of the incident. 'All I know is I abhor it.'

It added an extra dash of poison to the relations between United and Leeds fans. The next home game there were T-shirts on sale outside Old Trafford with a photograph of Strachan and his colleagues and the legend: 'Leeds Scum, even your players are ashamed of you', and I soon heard the chant, to the tune of the old Club biscuit commercial: 'If you follow Leeds United, then you must be fuckin' scum.' The lad on the tram was right, it was a lucky coincidence that United played a team like Everton on the day. If it had been Leeds, and some of their supporters had done that at Old Trafford, there would have been murder afterwards.

After Busby was buried in the Catholic church in the modest suburb of Chorlton where he had lived and worshipped all his illustrious career, there was another minor commotion. One of the pallbearers had taken pictures of him in his coffin, and had tried to sell them to the *Sun*. After its front page in the aftermath of Hillsborough, when it had blamed Liverpool's fans under the headline 'The Truth' and copies were burned on Merseyside streets, the paper was too chastened to fall for that. Instead, with a flourish of self-righteousness, they exposed the ill-advised pallbearer. A day later, he was in hiding on police advice.

10

We All Live In A Ryan Giggs World

If I had to choose an all-time United team,
Giggs would be in it. And he'd be wearing
Reebok boots.
>   The voice of Bobby Charlton, Reebok
>   television commercial, May 1994

After the Busby memorial game, in the discussion which took place
in the press box, as copy was being prepared and words spun down
the telephone wires, a theme emerged: wasn't it appropriate that,
on the day we remembered the great man, Ryan Giggs should be
the scorer of the goal, the best player on a convocation of brilli-
ance, the man of the match. Giggs, more than anyone since Sir
Matt's time, embodied the Busby vision of Manchester United: a
talent in love with the ball, a talent clean of cynicism, most of all
a talent discovered not purchased.

'Aye, Sir Matt would've loved the boy today,' said Alex Ferguson,
when the theory was put to him in the press room.

Sentiment may have been obstructing objectivity at that moment,
but there is no question Giggs can play with the unencumbered
spirit that was reckoned as greatness in Busby's philosophy. He can
do things on a football pitch that should qualify for an Arts Council
grant; among the concrete house-builders of British football, he
stands out like Michelangelo. Against Arsenal in September, for
instance, I sat there, in the Old Trafford press box, staggered as he
did this:

He was standing, not quite still, down by the corner flag, facing
the Arsenal goal, with two of their defenders within shin-stamping
range. The ball was between his feet, not quite stationary. He rolled
his left foot over it three times. He repeated the process with his

right foot, this time nudging the ball forwards with his heel. The Arsenal defenders, in their daffodil-yellow shirts, waited and waited, eyes on the ball, shoulders cramped, not wanting to commit until something happened. When it did, they were mesmerised. Flicking his hips as he went, Giggs stepped over the ball and, whipping his right foot around behind his left, kicked it crisply with his toe between the daffodil shirts and out into open space. Then he ran after it at full pelt, as his opponents stood with eyes rooted to the turf, as if demanding confirmation from an action replay that it had actually happened before responding. Except I didn't see him doing that. I saw a blur and a swivel and Winterburn looking embarrassed and trying to cut at Giggsy's heels a couple of moments later to get over his humiliation. It took me five plays of the video'd evidence to work out that's what he did. It is hard enough to do this in front of the bedroom mirror: try it and you'll fall over. But in front of 44,009 people, when confronted by defenders, one of whom, at the start of the game had said he would kick your lights out if you tried to get past him, it was an act of stunning audacity.

'Ryan's powers of control at speed are due to his incredible balance,' explained Alex Ferguson. 'He can wrong-foot anybody just by a movement and when you think a tackler is going to get a foot to the ball, he seems to float or ride or roll over the challenge. The defender always seems to go down, while the lad stays on his feet.'

Giggs himself saw it all much more succinctly. 'Sometimes,' he said to me when I asked him about that Arsenal incident, 'you've got to take the piss.'

It is possible, in the analysis of the temperaments of the great British players, to identify three distinct types of character.

One is the Gary: the lad who raises his game above even the limits suggested by his talent, who excels because of his clear understanding of what can be achieved. On the field, his brain acts faster than his feet, he knows how to exploit his abilities to cause maximum damage. Off the field, he makes a conscious decision to do whatever is necessary: he trains, he resists temptation, he develops his media skills, he is a model of self-discipline. He makes lucrative moves to difficult new terrain and emerges triumphant, his bank balance in clover. When his career finishes, though he has enough to live on for the rest of his life, he finds he is much in demand in the game's hinterland. He is the head boy of football: Lineker, Keegan, Platt.

The second is the Gazza: the secondary modern boy, overendowed in skill and underfunded in the brain. Childishly unaware from where his talent comes, he just does it, which makes him profoundly more attractive than the Gary. But though capable of periods of sustained success, he cannot take in the broader picture, place himself in context and exploit the possibilities offered. Often, off the field, he finds himself driven by boredom into bad habits: booze and gambling, say, or ice cream and hair extensions. When the Gazza finishes playing, the obituaries of his career often conclude: 'if only . . .' Gascoigne, Bowles, Jim Baxter are Gazzas. Best is a sort of semi-detached Gazza, one not through lack of brain but almost through surfeit of it. Bestie saw beyond the everyday and glimpsed the absurdity of possessing so much more than his peers, and that terrified him. He ran away and hid.

The third category is the Glenn. Unnaturally blessed with both skill and intelligence, he is potentially capable of combining the two to world-beating effect. But he doesn't. Never quite dominating as he should, he is prone to the most irrational and irritating disappearing acts. His problem is he has none of the selfish ruthlessness of the Gary; and he can be subject to the kind of debilitating nerves and self-doubt which would not occur to the Gazza. John Barnes is the ultimate Glenn.

Ryan Giggs is twenty. And the question which exercises we reds in the stands is, which of these three is Ryan Giggs?

When Giggsy first appeared, we were told he was the new George Best – which means in twenty-five years from now, we know what he'll be doing. He'll be at the Tameside Hippodrome, Ashton-under-Lyne, a dinner suit stretched across his barrel chest, developing a career cracking gags about how he buggered up his first career. He'll be speaking to an audience of the middle-aged and the nostalgic, telling them stories about his life with the candour of one who has been exposed so profoundly that there is really nothing worth hiding any more.

I saw Best do that one depressing night during the season, looking like Robert De Niro in *Raging Bull*, glass in hand, cracking jokes about scoring at Old Trafford and scóring with Miss World. Afterwards, as he sat in his dressing room, with a bottle of chardonnay and his then girlfriend, who was also his manager, he told me he had an idea how Ryan Giggs would develop. He said he thought the lad wouldn't do what he did (not, you understand, that he regretted what he had done for a moment) because times had changed and Ryan was a sensible lad, feet on the ground and all that. And besides, Alex Ferguson wouldn't bloody let him.

For three years, Alex Ferguson put a total media exclusion zone round his most precious charge: it was easier to talk to Lord Lucan than Ryan Giggs. The football writing pack respected the restrictions absolutely. They knew Fergie's ire, they knew he would happily throw them off the gravy train of reporting United if they didn't do as he told them: it was not worth their while to test his resolve with a snatched word at a training ground or an airport. When Giggs played for Wales, there seemed a chance to get him while on another territory. But Fergie obviously had had a word with Terry Yorath.

'One last thing,' Yorath told the assembled pack before Giggs made his international debut, 'any of you trying to get an interview with Ryan, forget it.'

Ferguson's restrictions were not unique to Giggs. It is the same with any player under twenty at United. And it's a canny move. Despite the media presentation, young footballers are not the same as young pop stars. Unlike members of Take That, they do not set out to be in the public eye. Their intention is to play football; if they are good at it, the public eye comes as part of the excess baggage. But, unlike the extrovert pop star, they are often ill-equipped to handle it. The eighteen-, nineteen-year-old working-class boy is unlikely, with a microphone and arc light thrust into his face, to say anything worthwhile. If he is incoherent, he is dismissed; if he is prattish, he is pilloried. It takes time to learn the rudiments of media presentability, and during his period of enforced silence Giggs, along with all the other young lads at Old Trafford, was given lessons in how to address a camera, how to spot a leading question. But the media forgot that Lee Sharpe, too, when he broke into the first team was strictly off limits. Giggs was presented as a special case; Des Lynam whinged about the lack of access every week on 'Match of the Day', as if United were contractually obliged to serve up their young stars to the BBC. The protection of Giggs was interpreted by some commentators as evidence that there was something to hide. The non-football reporting wing of the tabloids took up the challenge: never has a young player had his upbringing, his relationships with his parents, his very genetic and racial make-up so constantly analysed. At the end of the 1993 season, Alex Ferguson decided to relax the muzzle. Unusually for him, Fergie was responding to press criticism when he did it. He read some-where that he had created a monster with Giggs: that the very lack of access, the silence, had, rather in the manner of the royal family, spawned a Ryan Giggs character analysis operation which bore little relation to the truth.

The thing that may have sparked Fergie's change of mind was a piece in the *Today* newspaper which particularly upset Giggs and his mum. In a lengthy unauthorised biography, it was suggested that the club's protectiveness of its new boy was given extra incentive because, to use the north Manchester vernacular, Giggs's father was a 'wrong un'.

Now, Danny Wilson was a Gazza. A supremely gifted fly-half for Cardiff, then Swinton, it was Wilson who bequeathed to his son his blinding pace and balance. But he had problems off the pitch, with drink, with the police, and he walked out on the family when Ryan was twelve. Going off the rails, *Today* suggested, was in the lad's blood, that's why such care was being taken – one slip and they'd have a Gazza. The tale was presented like the script of an Oliver

Stone movie: the story of a boy faced with a choice between two fathers. The bad father, Danny Wilson; the good, Alex Ferguson.

'I must admit,' Ferguson said, 'there has always been a seed of doubt in my mind about the way I've handled him. I have been in complete control of Ryan Giggs, and by doing that I may have created a monster. I can certainly see the problem, but basically I believe I have done right. My responsibility is to the parents of the youngsters at the club and that's what I've always tried to do. I first allowed him to speak to the press after the last game of last [1993] season against Blackburn Rovers, but I was being clever there as we had won the championship and there wasn't much Ryan could say.'

Nor indeed, that the rest of us could understand. The young genius catapulted into the media with a virtually incomprehensible mumble. As the chains were loosened and some press were allowed limited access, so Ferguson allowed Giggs to make some financial gain from his increasing fame, to take on some of the commercial opportunities which were queueing up for his photogenic services. Of course, Ferguson knew the two were linked: if Giggs was to take financial advantage of his position, he would have to be available for comment. No sponsor is going to pay big money to be endorsed by a Trappist.

But even then Ferguson was careful about it. He recommended to Giggs an agent to handle his business called Harry Swales, who had had Kevin Keegan on his books when he was a player, and latterly had worked with Bryan Robson. Swales is in his sixties, a man who has about as much in common with the modern wheeler-dealer, agent *provocateur* as Nelson Mandela has with Eugene Terre Blanche. Steve Bruce had recently taken his agent to court, but you could not imagine any relationship with Swales, with his RAF handlebar moustache and his house in the Yorkshire countryside, ending like that. Importantly too for Fergie's peace of mind, he is not the sort to agitate for a transfer on Giggs's behalf (agents receive a cut of a transfer fee). Swales, in short, is clearly terrified of Alex Ferguson.

'I've had one heart attack,' he told me *apropos* his dealings with Giggs. 'I don't want to have another.'

At the end of the day, the Giggs that emerged from the gagging order, not surprisingly for someone who had grown up a professional footballer, was imbued in the linguistic culture of the dressing room, keen to take every interview as it came. He was, despite the mystique, apparently normal. Behind the clichés, though, there appeared to be a careful brain at work, aware that anything he said might be taken down and used in tabloid evidence against him. He learnt well from those media training sessions. The first rule of the Gary: better bland than misquoted.

Though not incapable of the wry, he gives little away, fielding leading questions with a 'you might say that but I can't possibly comment' smile. He has been particularly careful about his love life, since kiss-and-tell stories about footballers of the most modest celebrity are now buoyant currency in the Sunday tabloids. In a Radio 4 interview during the season, Stuart Hall asked him if he had a girlfriend.

'I like to take every day as it comes, really,' said Giggs, with a Geoffrey Boycott block.

'What a different girl every day?' spluttered a well-impressed Hall.

'No,' said Giggs, in a way which pre-empted any follow-up.

I went to see him at the cheerful cottage in Swinton that his mum and stepfather had done up. I really liked his mum. The parents of sporting prodigies are often monsters, living vicariously through their offspring, pushing with an ugly force which does not brook compassion. Ask Mary Pierce. Lynne Giggs is the opposite of that. Proud, obviously, the front room of her house is a Ryan shrine, full of pictures, trophies and pottery figures of him that look more like Will Carling. But not pushy. Protective, defensive, gently deprecating, she is the reason, I think, her son has stayed sane beneath the avalanche.

When I met her, a television documentary had just been screened about a five-year-old who had attracted the interest of the top footballing sides. The boy's father said he wasn't putting any pressure on his son: he could choose whatever career he wanted when the time came. But he had put a bet on with his local bookies that the lad would sign professional before he was eighteen. And yes, he would land a pretty decent sum should that happen. Lynne Giggs had found the programme horrifying: 'How can anyone do that to their own child?' she said, astonished.

Just like Jennifer Capriati or Andrea Jaeger or all those other girl tennis players, Giggs is a child prodigy. He could walk at seven months, run at a year, run fast at two. He has, to all intents and purposes, been a full-time sportsman since he was fourteen, when his secondary school let him bunk off because he was captaining England Schoolboys. He has grown up in a strange and restrictive environment, where decision-making and risk-taking is removed from every part of life except the playing field. From the age of fourteen he has been told what to do, at what time and what he can eat on the way, which makes him oddly dependent for a twenty-year-old. Before he moved into his grand, newly built house down the road from his mum's, for instance, he got her to go out and do the shopping for him, to stock him up with essentials.

And while other players grow up and make their mistakes away from the public, and arrive in the first team at twenty, twenty-one or twenty-two, Giggs had eager red eyes on him from the age of sixteen. Everyone knew about the wizard on the wing. They were desperate for him to succeed – the weight of expectation was there from the off. It is no wonder that, faced with a pressure like that, Giggsy's predecessors in the role of United boy wonders – Best and Whiteside – had sought the refuge of the Gazza in a bottle. And no wonder that Alex Ferguson took measures to cushion him from it.

So far Ryan Giggs has stayed the course. So far he hasn't cracked, done everything right, shown no hint of Gazza. And his mum, she keeps his ego grounded.

'He's supposed to be living at his own place now,' she said when

I arrived at her house. 'But he's always round here at meal-times. Funny that.'

She, characteristically, suggests others are equally responsible for the boy genius's cockup-free development: 'Mr Ferguson', as she calls him, and Ryan's mates. Where Giggs is luckier than Whiteside or Best is that he plays for his home-town team. He has kept in touch with the lads he grew up with, and has not become subject, through the loneliness of being a young player away from home with a wallet full of cash, to platoons of hangers-on.

His mates, too, understand the discipline required to be a sportsman. Now salesmen or shop managers, they were all football aspirants once: good enough to be Giggs's team-mates in the youth teams of their teens, but not possessing that edge of athleticism to make it as professionals. They respect the restrictions on his life, he trusts them, and they throw a protective cordon around him in return.

A red I know told me a story of how the mates operate.

'I see Giggsy all the time in that Home nightclub in town,' he said. 'I seen a lot of them there, Incey, Sharpie, but mostly Giggsy. They don't get mithered there. I think people are trying too hard to look cool to let on to them. But a lad I know did offer Giggsy a joint one night when I was there. He worshipped him, just wanted to share everything he had with him, like. Giggsy refused and his mates, seeing what had happened, quickly moved in and suggested to my mate it wasn't the best idea he ever had. Not heavy, like, but just making it plain.'

When he came into his mum's front room from training, Giggsy had a couple of mates with him. Hair slicked back in a style which was informing a whole Mancunian generation's sartorial approach in the way Willie Morgan's once did, he nodded, flashed a welcoming smile and said 'Arright?'

He was wearing training gear: sweat shirt, sweat pants, trainers. It's what he favours most of the time, head-to-toe-Reebok. Though not always head. He was once spotted in a photo by a Reebok executive wearing a plain old New York Mets baseball cap. The next morning by special delivery he received thirty-five Reebok caps: a windfall for the mates. He obviously passes a lot round: the mates with him were wearing Reebok too – the walking endorsement team. I found myself jumping up from my seat when he came in, holding out my hand to be shaken, uttering meaningless platitudes about his performances this season. He took it in his stride, well experienced in surfing the sycophancy wave, shook hands firmly, and engaged in direct and unswerving eye contact. As he sat on one of the sofas, spinning his trainers off and dispatching a mate into the kitchen to make tea ('you're under a lot of pressure to make it right,' he shouted), I noticed his feet. He never wears socks, so the £5 million apiece objects were on full display, there on his mum's lush front-room carpet. They are unnaturally long and thin, with finger-length prehensile toes he curls constantly while talking. An atlas of bruises and nicks, each foot tells a story: here's the place where he kicked Steve MacMahon's studs, there's the scar where Vinny Jones clipped him, this is the ankle he's been feeling for a while.

'I've been lucky though, up till now, touch wood,' he said, and he touched the head of a mate sitting next to him on the sofa. 'I mean you see these on my feet, but the longest I've been out with injury is two weeks. Talk to some lads, and that's just a joke.'

Injuries. There are more pressing things you might want to ask Ryan Giggs, like if he could turn out for your scratch team next Sunday. But he had a way of steering conversations to talk about what he wants to. He does this by not answering at all when you ask him something he doesn't want to talk about, like what he thought of the appointment of John Toshack as Wales manager, for instance. So I asked him how come people don't seem to kick him. How come he is not seen flying, Maradona-style through the Mancunian air, launched by an opponent's boot and wearing a comedy face of pain? Do opponents like him too much much to kick him?

'You know when it's coming. You can sense it. If you're quick you can get out of the way.'

Who is the full back in the Premiership that has given him the hardest time?

'The old players, like Earl Barrett, who close you down and use their experience against you, they're the hardest, really.'

What about Gary Kelly of Leeds who, at Old Trafford on New Year's day, had – many commentators reckoned – smothered him.

'He did all right. He's quick,' he said. And the edges of the smile turned down.

His mum had said he was a bad loser.

'Terrible. I hate it. If I have a bad game, or we've lost, I'm last in the shower, just sit there thinking over where I went wrong, where I should've scored or laid the ball off better. I hate it.'

Is he particularly bad compared to the others in the United dressing room?

'The worst. But we all hate it. That's what drives us forward. If you hate losing, you make sure you win.'

I asked him, then, if he hates losing and likes winning so much, why does he look so miserable when he scores? A radio commentator said, when he moped off after scoring a blistering goal, that his lack of joy showed he had fallen out of love with the game.

He smiled a lot at that observation, a big, full face-break of a smile that was more and more in evidence as he relaxed.

'Celebrations have got well out of hand,' he said. 'The best celebrations are the simple ones, cool ones. Cole, Shearer, Ian Wright – you've got to have respect for Ian Wright. I'm trying to do a celebration which isn't.'

And which goal had he most enjoyed not celebrating? That free kick against Belgium he scored on his Welsh debut? Or the mazy run through Spurs's defence the previous season?

'They were all right,' he said. 'But I've scored some this year like I wasn't scoring before. Like the one against Everton, a header. I'm happier with them than I am with the spectacular ones, because I'm getting into the positions I wasn't in the past, the positions that hurt. Brian Kidd gave me some videos of the great goal-scorers to study. They got knock-ins, tap-ins, got in and did damage.'

I asked him who the best player he had ever encountered on a football field was, and he said Hagi, the Romanian, who had been masterful when Wales had lost in Bucharest in a World Cup qualifier.

'I only came on as sub, but we never got a kick. He was different class. But then when we played them in Cardiff, he disappeared. I couldn't believe it, we got a goal and were going right at them, and he just bottled it, went and stood on the touchline sulking. A player of his class, I'd never seen it before, I couldn't believe it. It's not like that at our club. Take Eric, even when he's having a quiet game, he wants the ball all the time, wants to play his way out of it.'

Cantona is a recurring theme in Giggs's conversation, as being the apex of style, the kind of geezer he would like to be. Not just in his off-field attire, but also in his attitude to his craft. An attitude Giggs finds wholly attractive.

'He's always out there after training, doing his extra bit and that. When you see someone like Eric Cantona out there training, you know you can never rest on what you've got. A few of us, we've taken to staying on and doing extra in the afternoons, but Eric, he's always the last one off.'

Gary-talk, that.

What with Fergie, his mum, his mates and his minder at the club, Paul Ince, all keen to shield him from predators, you might think that we have a frail bird here, an eggshell ego. The stuff of the Glenn. He can, after all, be inconsistent to the point of infuriation: for every piece of Arsenal trickery there are two occasions when he shoots at the keeper's legs after being put clean through.

But he says he is never struck by nerves or worries about his own ability.

'I'm lucky really, because I was brought up at the club I never found Old Trafford frightening.'

He says he knows where he is going and what he wants to do. Ambition, you sense, cuts through him. There is none of that scared bird vulnerability that Best exhibits in Hugh McIlvanney's film about him. None of that off-field deference that so contrasts with the on-field self-confidence. It's not that he is cocky, it's just that he is aware of his potential. I asked him, for instance, since he is motivated by victory, what he felt he had left to win. Before the age of twenty-one, he had totted up more than most achieve in a career. He looked at me as if I clearly didn't understand.

'Where do you want me to start?' he said. 'I want to win the European Cup with United. It was horrible losing in Turkey, horrible. I don't want that to happen again. I want to go to a major championship with Wales. We didn't get to the World Cup and we've only ourselves to blame, we reckon we could have done well out there. I don't want to miss out again. And I want to score twenty-five goals in a season. I've got a lot to learn, too.'

A lot to learn. As anyone who has sat within earshot of the dugout at Old Trafford will confirm, Alex Ferguson is never slow during matches to point out quite how much. Does he, I wondered, notice how much he is shouted at.

'Oh yeah. I think it's because I play nearest to him, he can have a right go at me. I'm listening to what he's shouting sometimes and the ball comes towards me and I let it go, because I'm concentrating on what he's saying and he'll yell, "Watch the ball!" '

But the hard taskmaster had this to say of his pupil's capacity for learning.

'He has such a wonderful attitude, such a desire to realise the greatest that is within him and it's up to us at the club to assist his development. He is a thinker about the game and a listener, no question about that. Ryan has a shit disposal unit in his head and much of what he hears goes into that. But if something is useful or valid, he'll store it away for the future.'

And there is some shit that surrounds Ryan Giggs. If there is a monster at large here, it is not the quiet, careful player himself, but the juggernaut of Giggs-mania. The comparisons with Best are at their most apt in the presentation. Best was the first footballer to be cast as pop star; Giggs has become the dream-boat of the prepubescent girl, a demographic group not generally attracted to football. At the *Manchester United Magazine*, for instance, they get phone calls everyday from mothers saying: 'It's my daughter's birthday tomorrow and we were wondering if Ryan Giggs could pop round to say Happy Birthday, and if so does he charge for this service?'

'No,' they say.

'You mean he does it for free?'

At times during last season, as the Giggs industry developed a momentum of its own, it was easy to forget he was a footballer, the purveyor of foot-shimmies to the red hordes. Press coverage of him put him in the Princess Di league of column inches. Everything he did came under scrutiny. He steps out with a girl and *Today* devotes a whole page to pictures of her from a modelling assignment; the week before his television commercial for Reebok boots is launched and the *Sun* runs a three-page sneak preview of the thing, presenting it with all the fanfare of a Hollywood hypebuster. He has become a staple of the teen market – seen as frequently on the pages of *Smash Hits* (favourite food: pasta; favourite pastime: buying clothes) as in *Ninety Minutes* (favourite player: Roberto Baggio; favourite away ground: Elland Road). He is up there, this young lad with the Salford accent, with the stars of Australian beach soaps.

Why? Because he sells. And the more he is seen, the more he seems to sell. *GQ* magazine asked me to do an interview with him, so they could put his picture on the cover: when the rival publication *FHM* had done the same, circulation of that issue had gone up 40 per cent.

How he reacts to the fame, that's what's crucial to his development. At the moment he regards it as a joke, a laugh to share with his mates.

'It can get a bit mental,' he said. 'I had to do this appearance for Reebok in the centre of Swansea and the whole town came out, fifteen thousand people. Girls were getting crushed and that. It was mad.'

The thing is, it will get more intrusive. And while Ferguson might have realised this when he limited the number of commercial engagements he could take on to six a year, other parts of the club are not entirely innocent of hyping up the ante. In the superstore, Giggs is their biggest brand: pictures of him looking doe-eyed and lovely in civilian clothes are promoted more rigorously than snaps of him looking determined in playing kit; the merchandise catalogue includes a picture of a naked girl wrapped in a Giggs beach towel.

On the day I went to see him, the *Mirror* printed a piece headlined 'The £15 million player'. Flagged with a prominent picture on the front page, it was a series of interviews with image-builders, asking them how they could maximise Ryan Giggs's earnings, make him £15 million in three years. Eric Hall, the football agent, said he would take him away from football altogether, turn him into a 'media celebrity'; Max Clifford said he would keep him on the football field, but use the close seasons to cut a pop record, do a tour to promote it: 'You don't have to be able to sing to be a pop star these days.'

'I'd like to see what the Boss had to say about that idea,' he said, when I told him about the piece. 'These people, they think being a footballer only entails getting up on a Saturday morning and kicking a ball around. They make me laugh.'

I asked him how he responded to the fame, to the fact that he has reached the point where his picture on the cover of a magazine is regarded as a weapon in the circulation war.

'Funnily enough, it was always my ambition to appear on the cover of *GQ* when I was a kid.'

It's not any more?

He smiled his what-do-you-think smile.

Indeed he didn't appear to be someone who courted celebrity (as opposed to courting celebrities). About his days of silence, he said he didn't find it the most onerous of restrictions not being allowed to talk to John Motson. And perhaps it was just me, but when I spoke to him I didn't get the feeling conversations with members of the press were all he had ever lived for.

'All the pictures and that, it bothers my mum more than it bothers me,' he said. 'She comes home and she says: "Everywhere I go I see pictures of you and you don't get any better looking." At The Cliff during school holidays, you've seen it, it gets mad. But when

I'm out I don't get mithered that much, because I tend to stick with my mates, go to places where they know me.'

And what about the press?

'It's not a lot of fun having mike and pens and stuff shoved in your face and some of what they wrote about the family was out of order. That's why I think the Boss has been brilliant with me. I owe him a lot, really. He knew what was going to happen and he tried to let me in slowly. Now I can take it or leave it. It's part and parcel of the game.'

How did he feel though, when he read some of that stuff that was written during his days of silence? Didn't he feel like making sure his version of events was aired?

'Some of the stuff about my family was not on,' he said. 'Now it doesn't bother me. Because I know whatever they write about me isn't true. How can it be? They've no idea what I'm like. They've never met me.'

Even now, though, that access was granted, the press seemed desperate to create an image for him as a playboy, which seemed at odds with the present reality. I had read, for instance, in *Today*, that he had picked up a girlfriend from her house in a £30,000 BMW. But he drove a red Golf. One of the mates smiled.

'Well, I have got a BMW, and a jeep me mum uses,' he said. 'But I don't drive them to the club.'

Why not? Frightened of them being damaged in The Cliff crush?

'No it's not that. It's, you know. The Boss.'

It may be he says all these things because they are learnt responses, and that never mind the gorgeous pouting clotheshorse, the image that really sells is that of the dedicated worker bee, whose only ambition in life is to do his best for the common cause. If he is lynx-eyed enough to have learnt that game, then he is a Gary indeed. But you get the feeling that he's naturally like that: modest, single-minded, the opposite of flash, not the kind to say to a waiter, 'Do you know who I am?'

We had been talking for about an hour when he said, polite but firm, that he had to go. He was picking his car up from the garage and it shut at five. In which case, one last thing: Italy, what about Italy, the ultimate challenge of the Gary? When's he off to Italy?

He smiled a weary smile as he showed me to his mum's front door.

'I've still got three years on my contract to run, so I'm not even contemplating it,' he said. 'To be honest, in this game, three years ahead is so long, it's like saying it will never happen. I mean, at Man United, you don't even know if you'll be playing next week.'

11

Caution: Genius At Work

*Well, I thought we got close to them in the
warm-up.*

Vinny Jones, 20 February 1994

In January and February 1994, I saw United give three of the
best performances I have ever seen on a football pitch. It was no
coincidence that, at the same time, with Sharpe injured, Ferguson
at last gave a sustained run to Andrei Kanchelskis.

'With me choosing him all the time, it's confirmed in his own
mind that he's the best right-sided player in the club,' Ferguson said
of his Ukranian. 'Now he's more sure of himself, he's playing better.
He's given us better balance for it.'

Giggs was back on the left, and appeared to be happier for it, too.
Left-footed players are often described by commentators as having
a 'cultured' left foot. Giggsy, on the other hand, has a cultured right
foot: it has mould growing on it from lack of use.

Now with the balance properly restored, United were simply
unstoppable, a potent and productive mixture of skill, resolve and
arrogant certainty in their own abilities.

It began, this barnstormer of a spell, at Norwich City, in the fourth
round of the FA Cup. Pulling strings like a chemically stimulated
Jim Henson, I managed to land a ticket for the United section at
Carrow Road through a friend of a friend. I travelled to East Anglia
with Jon Shine and his friend Paul, in the BMW with the registration
A10 UTD. They, too, had secured their tickets in a similar fashion.

Except their friend of a friend charged three times face value for each item.

In the car park in the shadow of Carrow Road's smart new stands, the attendant waved us through, and, as we got out of the car, I noticed everyone kept looking at us.

'Happens all the time,' said Jon. 'They see the number plate, reckon we must be directors.'

'Directors would find it easier to get tickets,' I said.

'Are you sure?' he said. 'No one finds it easy to get United tickets.'

Inside the ground, the red fans were squashed into the one bit of Carrow Road which had not been recently freshened up. They were noisy in there. Norwich had just lost their manager to Everton, an event the United fans commemorated by singing 'Where's your Walker gone?' (perhaps the only instance in twenty years that the tune of Middle of the Road's seventies hit, 'Chirpy Chirpy Cheep Cheep', has been put to useful purpose).

I found myself sitting four rows from the touchline and when the players trotted out to warm up, the middle-aged man in a duffel coat and thick woollen gloves next to me began, as if this was the most natural thing in the world, to engage them in conversation.

'Gary, Gary,' he called to Pallister, the nearest player to us, 'is Sparky playing?'

Pallister raised a thumb in confirmation that Hughes, missing for a game, was back.

'Thank Christ for that,' my neighbour shouted. 'Tell Ferguson thank Christ for that.'

Then, when Kanchelskis came near, he shouted:

'Andrei, Andrei, how yer doing, mate?'

Kanchelskis, as he does in most situations, just smiled.

Seeing Les Sealey trot over, I was tempted to beggar my neighbour. I thought I might ask how the bypass was going, and he might lean across the front few rows and tell me he had his faith healer on the case, thinking the bulldozers away. But I didn't get the chance. As I weighed up the social niceties of making contact, the know-everyone next to me yelled:

'All right, Les. Give that bastard Schmeichel a kick from me, Les.'

Sealey replied with a grin and a gum-chew. I don't think he spotted me.

Norwich had lost their manager, but they had lost none of their enterprise. As they had proved in the better of a 2–2 draw at Old Trafford, they were a crisp, sharp, incisive team. United, though, that cold January Sunday, were on another plane. They swept Norwich away. The speed of Kanchelskis and Giggs as they latched on to Cantona's passes, sprayed with a draughtsman's awareness of angles and degrees, found no answer in the City defence. It was all over as a contest, Cantona and Keane having scored without reply, when, with ten minutes to go Eric chased a through ball into the area, shadowed by their man Polston. There was some contact – arms and shirts were pulled as they ran. Then Polston fell; Cantona started to creak at the knees, but stayed upright. The momentum of the chase carried the two of them into the advertising hoarding close to where we were sitting. It seemed from my vantage point that Polston didn't appear to do anything more provocative in the exchange than be a Norwich player. But Cantona seemed to harbour a grudge from the fixtures at Old Trafford and had already been booked earlier in this game for attempting on-pitch surgery on Goss. For Eric, the very existence of a Norwich player was enough. As Polston lay on the ground, he adopted some of his rugby-playing compatriots' rucking technique and applied studs to the prone man's shoulder with a sharp, downward back heel. I blinked in astonishment. Gunn, the Norwich keeper and owner of the least impressive pony tail in football, looked as surprised as me as he piled in to remonstrate. Eric, in the pose we had seen on the touchline in Istanbul, stood aside from the ensuing handbags, shoulders round his ears, arms spread, palms upward, a look of infantile insouciance on his face, as if wondering what the fuss was about.

Ryan Giggs, at the Charity Shield, auditioning for the role of Mr Red in
Reservoir Dogs II.
Allsport

'Moi?'
Peter Jay / *Independent*

Cantona celebrates a 30-yard chip at Southampton: nobody does it better.
Action Images

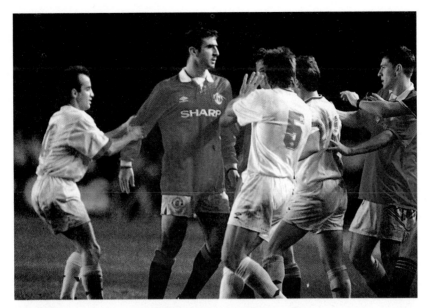

November in Istanbul: Eric fails to breech the Dardanelles.
Action Images

Roy Keane, not unhappy about scoring the winner in his first Derby.
Empics Ltd

To get a better view of Paul Ince's equaliser against Blackburn at Old Trafford, Peter Schmeichel would require a season ticket in K Stand.

Action Images

Giggs begins his goal of the season run at Loftus Road. QPR's Ray Wilkins is already prone in worship; Darren Peacock is about to trip over his own hair.
Action Images

Les Sealey, shy and retiring on the touchline, seeks support during a game from Brian Kidd. Sealey, the hero of Rotterdam, is now a rock at Blackpool.
John Peters

Mark Hughes, raging all season like something let loose on the streets of
Pamplona, swaps notes on coiffure with QPR's Peacock.
Peter Jay / *Independent*

A good old East End knees-up of a welcome for Paul Ince on his first return to
West Ham.
Sportsview

Cantona sees yellow at Highbury. Red was soon to follow. Tony Adams casts
an intelligent eye over proceedings.
Peter Jay / *Independent*

The fizz goes out of the Treble. Dalien Atkinson skids the first of Villa's three
goals past Les Sealey at the Coca-Cola Cup Final.
David Ashdown / *Independent*

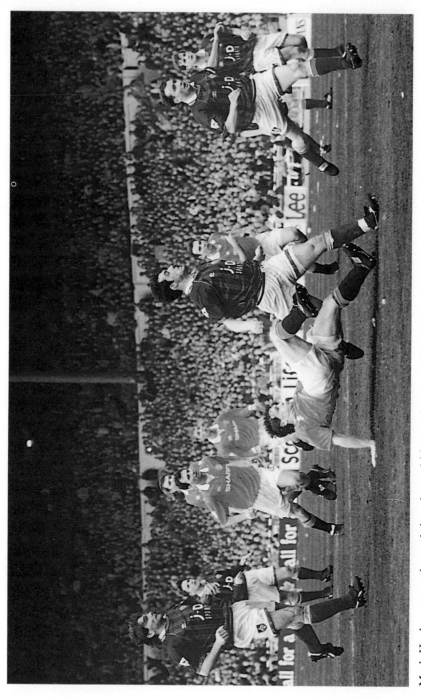

Mark Hughes scores the goal that changed history. Against Oldham Athletic, FA Cup semi-final, Wembley.
Action Images

'Horrible pitch, horrible game, horrible team. Horrible.' Ryan Giggs sees another chance disappear at Wimbledon.

Adam Scott / *Independent*

According to George Graham, Eric Cantona is 'a cry baby who will let you down at the highest level.' Here the King is, letting United down at the highest level again, as he scores his first penalty in the Cup Final.
David Ashdown / *Independent*

Back home in Manchester and, oddly, it is raining. Note for Manchester City fans: the bright metal things at the front of the bus are trophies.
Action Images

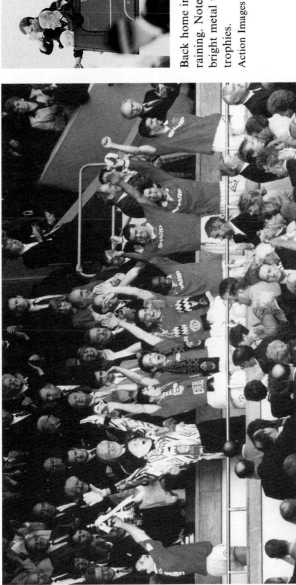

Behind the double winners, Chelsea's chairman Ken Bates (pictured between Peter Schmeichel's arms) is a model of good cheer in defeat. Meanwhile, Chancellor Kenneth Clark (above Mark Hughes) ponders new ways to tax silverware.
David Ashdown / *Independent*

Alex Ferguson celebrates becoming the only manager to achieve the double north and south of the border in headgear on loan from Kevin Keegan.
Sportsview

'Christ,' I said turning to my neighbour, the man on first-name terms with the team. 'He'll have to go for that.'

Clearly a student of post-match managerial interviews, he replied: 'I didn't see the incident, so I can't comment.'

The referee, too, apparently had a blind spot for that corner of the pitch: Cantona was not even booked. Jimmy Hill, though, sitting in a glass-fronted gantry box just above us and afforded much the same view, had been more attentive. I have since watched a recording of what Hill said about Cantona's behaviour and I have to say, however much it may pain me to do so, that what he said was moderate and appropriate. He said that given the lad's skill, given the fact that he had scored in the game, given how much pleasure he had spread around the football grounds of Britain, stamping on an opponent was not on. Whoever you are. There was a dark side to the genius, Hill said, and such an action as this was 'despicable'.

After the game, as we in the stands indulged in that great FA Cup tradition of listening communally to the draw for the next round transmitted over the PA ('Wimbledon away? Wooooo. Dodgy, dodgy'), the reporter from the Press Association collared Ferguson outside the United dressing room and asked what he thought about Hill's 'despicable' comment. And Fergie said:

'Jimmy Hill is verbal when it suits him. If there's a prat going about in this world, he's the prat. I am not interested in Jimmy Hill. Four years ago he wrote us off in the warm-up, that's how much he knows about the game. The BBC are dying for us to lose. Everyone is from Liverpool with a Liverpool supporter's flag. They'll be here every time until we lose, that mob – Barry, Bob, Hansen, the lot of them. Liverpool Supporters Association. You can quote me if you like.'

And he did.

I thought, as I read the papers the next day, that Ferguson must have gone bonkers. Here was a player of his behaving badly, despicably in fact, and instead of condemning him, he assaulted the reputation of a media pundit who had. He said of Cantona: 'Eric probably reacted to a bit of off-the-ball intimidation. He knows he doesn't have to get involved in things like that. You can't take the law into your own hands, but at least some of his passing was incredible.' As whitewashes went it may not have been in the 'Death of the Rock' class, but it was close. Everyone in the papers thought he was bonkers, too. Old Hill was generally gaga, everyone said, but on this occasion even Ferguson must see he was right. The columnists and pontificators all wondered why, when his team were playing so well, that the old Fergie paranoia, the chip of Aberdeen granite on his shoulder which we hadn't seen for a year or so, was resurfacing. Perhaps he was so in love with Cantona he was blind to his faults. Perhaps, the more sophisticated speculation ran, he was so terrified that Cantona would leave for home the moment he was criticised that he was prepared to soften the discipline for which he was so famed for a special case. That was Rob Hughes's view in *The Times*.

It took me a month to work out Ferguson's game here, a month during which I would have plenty of opportunity to see it in action.

Oh well, I thought, as United went to Queens Park Rangers the following Saturday, at least Eric won't try anything like that again: there can't be two blind refs in the Premiership. And on a warm, early spring afternoon, standing among a group of noisy reds in the heart of the Queens Park Rangers end, my mates Nigel, Simon and I saw another cracker – a game which took our minds entirely off Fergie's rants and Eric's misdemeanours.

The first goal of United's three took precisely nine seconds to accomplish, from the moment it left Schmeichel's quarter-back bowl, to the moment Kanchelskis, receiving the ball on the halfway line, had run to the box and popped it away. Nine seconds, about the time it would have taken local boy Linford Christie to run the pitch. The most dynamic of route one goals. Cantona scored a sweet second, but it was left to Giggs to lift the game above the merely majestic to the spiritual.

He did what he had been threatening to do for several games now, but never quite managed: he scored a wonder goal. Taking the ball on the halfway line, he skipped past a sliding sideways challenge from Wilkins, leaving him on his back. He then skipped away from the sliding Peacock, leaving him also on his back. Then, as he arced a parabola through the Rangers defence, Bardsley, who had patrolled him all afternoon, lost his balance in the confusion, tumbled over, and Yates fell over him. Behind the single-minded Giggs as he glided goalwards across the turf, Hughes, running into space, collided into Holloway and they both fell over. As they did so, Giggs then slipped the ball off his left foot, past Steyskal's flounder, into the net. As he walked towards the corner flag, a funereal expression on his face, marking a circle in the air with his raised index finger, the scene he had left behind him looked like something from a Roy-of-the-Rovers comic strip: six Rangers players and one United man lying on the ground; you could almost see the dotted line marking Giggsy's maze-like course through the breached defence.

A few days later, I asked the boy wonder if it was the best goal he had ever scored.

'Not really,' he said. 'To be honest I had no idea when I scored it that I'd beaten so many men.'

I looked incredulous.

'No, honest, really. When I got the ball, I honestly thought I had a free run at goal. I just put my head down and went for it. It was only when I watched "Match of the Day" that night that I saw what I'd done. I thought: where'd he come from?'

His mum, though, thought it was 'just brilliant'.

Me, I was on his mum's side. I thought I wouldn't see a better goal all season. Then I went to Wimbledon for the fifth round of the Cup.

In a paradigm of the way commercial forces are squeezing the tradition from the game, this one, because of live television coverage, kicked off at five on a Sunday afternoon. Worse, because Wimbledon's new dark-blue kit, colour-coded to blend nicely with referees' pastel-green outfits in the Premiership, was too much of a clash with the black the officials wore in the Cup, they were decked in their change strip. So, for a game between the blues and the reds, the blues wore red and the reds wore yellow and green. Confused? No, just resigned to it.

As my mate Eugen, 24,998 other United fans and I pushed our way into Selhurst Park, I spotted a workmate, one of the 2511 Wimbledon die-hards at the game. He said he hated games against United. He said he liked to swap seats at half-time, move to the end that the Dons were attacking. And he said when United came, the place was a sellout and he couldn't do it, he had to stick where he was. A big, ambitious club, Wimbledon.

To compound his misery, stuck in the same seat all game, he was obliged to watch United score three goals from heaven. First Cantona, lurking outside the box received a weak headed clearance. He received it on his thigh. With one smooth golf-swing of his leg he killed the force of the ball, flicked it up and volleyed it over Segers into the goal before the keeper could move. Then, early in the second half, Ince leapt ahead of the Wimbledon defence to pop home Gigg's corner, the perfect set-piece strike.

But it was all a prelude to the big one. Midway through the second half, United were enjoying a spell of total possession domination. As the ball travelled across the pitch, skidding and spinning from United player to United player, the red-shirted Wimbledon men were no more capable of having a foot in the course of this game than us in the stands. Then United constructed a move which went like this:

Pallister, in defence, headed a stray Wimbledon cross out to Giggs on the left wing. Giggs chipped the ball forward to Hughes, whose deft lay-off header fell into the path of Cantona. Cantona strode forward to just outside the Wimbledon box and found Kanchelskis on the right wing. Kanchelskis then passed inside to Parker, Parker moved it on to Keane, Keane then on to Ince. By now, each touch was greeted with an eager 'olé' from the United followers. Then Ince passed to Cantona, who passed it back. Ince then threaded the ball across the pitch to Giggs, who passed to Irwin, who passed it back. Apparently unwilling to be landed with the thing, Giggs passed it back to Irwin again. Irwin passed inside to Ince, and then suddenly, as if bored by the foreplay, Irwin ran into the penalty area to pick up Ince's return pass. He then skipped past Scales and Barton, Wimbledon defenders, as if they were bollards put by Brian Kidd on The Cliff training pitch, and scuffed his shot into the corner of the goal.

I once interviewed Peter Roebuck, the cricketer, and he said that taking on the fastest bowling, thrashing a boundary against the quickest around, made you feel more of a man. Not simply because you had overcome your fear, but because you had won a power struggle: you had humiliated an opponent expected to intimidate you. Denis Irwin must have felt like a man at that moment, destroying a team which has become a synonym for intimidatory play.

As Eugen and I celebrated that rare moment for an English football supporter, when the team you follow repay your uncritical loyalty with football of unimpeachable quality, I noticed that the quintet of Wimbledon fans in front of me, perhaps the only five home fans in the main stand of their own home during a home fixture, looked less happy. They had that same look of silent, sullen, depressed resignation that had been in evidence at Bramhall Lane when Hughes had scored, that had been on faces at Loftus Road when Giggs scored, that I could see in the stands at Carrow Road when Cantona scored. Everywhere they went in January and February, this United side were inflicting misery on the locals.

12

The Prodigal Returns

I thought it would be bad, but nothing like that.

Paul Ince, 26 February 1994

'Do you reckon,' the youth in front of me said. 'Do you reckon I could hit the fucking Munich monkey from here?'

'What wiv?' asked his mate.

'This,' he said, removing from his pocket a banana.

The East End of London. Nigel and I had negotiated the one-way labyrinth of the Stratford urban motorway interchange and made our way down a street of small, crumbling Victorian terraces. In the doorway of the house outside which we parked, five Asian children were watching with big eyes as, by the gate of the house next door, a young black couple argued in an impenetrable patois. We walked down the street, passing Asian families in colourful trousers, passing black youths working on car stereos turned up so loud that the plastic spoilers on their cars were humming to the beat. We walked out on to a high-street market thrumming with activity. Asian traders and black shoppers haggled over goods – yams, akis, spangly jogging pants – on stalls set so close to the pavement edge that strollers had to spill into the traffic. At a household-goods stall a white youth was shouting out his wares.

'Get your bin liners, ten for a pahnd.'

As we approached him, three large black women in African garb, headdresses and bustles, were coming towards us. When they were

level with the lad, he yelled hard into the face of the woman nearest
to him.

'Fucking great big black bags.'

The woman nearly jumped out of her costume.

'Ten for a pahnd, darlin'.'

We thought we might have a pint before the game and jostled
our way through the clutter to an ugly sixties-built pub, abutting an
ugly sixties-built covered market. Three weeks previously we had
been in Shepherd's Bush where United fans had taken over the
pubs, singing, chanting, dancing on the tables, mingling beerily with
the QPR followers. It was different out East. I walked into the pub
first, colliding with a man in a beard, a red United shirt visible
beneath his jacket, on his way out, his face bleached of colour.

'You're taking the piss incha,' a man by the door shouted to him
as he left.

Walking in, it was as if the cosmopolitan jumble on the street
was in another country. The place was packed with men thumping
fists on tables, on the bar, on the pub ceiling as they chanted over
and over and over again: 'Billy Bonds' clarenbloo army.' Every one
of them was white. Every one of them looked angry. We had a
drink, a very quick drink, and headed for Upton Park.

I had purchased tickets direct from West Ham and we were to
stand on the North Bank terrace. Among the home fans. The first
person we saw as we came through the turnstiles, though, was
Michael Crick. And we decided, as we stood among the necks and
the shoulders and the surly faces of this last redoubt of the white
East End, that it might be wise for us three reds to keep our
counsel. There was anger in the air, anger which left an uncomfortable feeling in the root of the stomach, an anger which would not
have taken kindly to the enamel club crest I wore under my jacket;
a badge which could not be removed whatever the circumstances
because of the devastating ill-fortune that would consequently befall
United.

They were angry, these West Ham lads, because one of their own
had defected. Paul Ince, once the hero of the 'Chicken Run', had
moved up north. It was his first trip back, the first time he had played

there since he was photographed in the tabloids wearing a United shirt while still a West Ham player. Not the most tactful thing in the world, that photo opportunity. That was five years ago, but in the stands at Upton Park they have a memory for a slight which would serve them well in Bosnia or Northern Ireland. And what's more, now he was at United, the Hammer boys had noticed that Incey was never quite as much one of them as they had first thought. He was black.

On to the best playing surface in the Premiership, United came out of the tunnel first. After them came one or two West Ham players. As Miklosko, their keeper, trotted towards the North Bank, his arms skyward in greeting, he looked more than a little perplexed when almost as one the terrace responded with a roar of malice: 'Judas, Judas.' What he didn't realise was that behind him Ince, by superstition always the last man out for United, had arrived.

It is always verbal at Upton Park. The pitch is close to the stands and the crowd do their bit, intimidating. The Chicken Run, the paddock which runs down one touchline, is so named because chickens don't last long in front of it. Pat Van Den Hauwe, playing there once for Spurs, suddenly, while taking a throw-in, turned round and piled into the Run, seeking retribution for one too many insults about Mandy Smith, his new love.

But what happened when United visited in the spring of 1994 was not a bit of isolated intimidation. For ninety minutes Paul Ince was subjected to the worst barracking I have ever heard at a football ground. It went on and on and monotonously on: shouts, chants, monkey grunts, fruit chucking. Once, he put in a robust sliding tackle on a West Ham player that carried him over the touchline to within handshaking distance of the crowd. To a man, the stand stood up and threatened him with death, at least. Ince can never have moved as quickly as he did then, back to the calm of the centre circle.

That night on 'Match of the Day', Des and Trevor made the usual noises about a minority of fans behaving badly. Minority? All round us they were at it, the racist bollocks. Well, not quite all round us.

When Hughes scored within ten minutes, it was clear there were reds dotted throughout the terrace (Andy the art critic was in there somewhere). While the West Ham followers looked as though they had just been bereaved at this goal, the United fans were the ones turning to their neighbours and raising a quizzical eyebrow, Roger Moore style. And when West Ham equalised, they were the ones who, instead of jumping around as if someone had suddenly inserted a squadron of soldier ants into their underpants, held their ground and nodded. And at half-time, instead of talking about games watched and goals seen, like everyone around them, they were the ones discussing the weather. In fact, it was bloody obvious who *we* were.

In the second half West Ham took the lead, cue for the only light-hearted insult of the afternoon when the inquiry was made: 'Incey, Incey, what's the score?' With three minutes remaining, United's thirty-three-match unbeaten run looked about to end. West Ham, as they usually do against us, had raised their game: they played neat, clever football. United were never quite on song; Giggs was injured and the balance that had served them so well against Wimbledon was disrupted.

But then there was a scramble in their area, the ball bobbled, and steaming through the melee to slam in the equaliser, as if scripted by Ian Botham, was Paul Ince. I felt so moved by the poetic justice of it all, I let out a yelp of triumph. A hundred eyes spun angrily round to confront me. Fortunately it is not hard to convert a yelp of triumph into a snort of pain.

'Had to be him, dinnit,' I said in terrible Mockney to the youth with the banana in front of me.

'Fucking streaky Manc cant,' he answered.

When I asked him about that reception, it was clear Ince felt aggrieved. Not for him football's standard bland dismissal about not really noticing it.

'I was disappointed,' he said. 'I was there as a kid. I thought perhaps they should be proud of me, going on to lead my country, bettering myself and that. I went on to bigger things, you've got to further your career. You think at one time I was the hero, there. I only played two seasons, but I got Hammer of the Year in the second season. And to come back to that. You think perhaps it should be like the prodigal son and that. But it wasn't. It wasn't the booing, that doesn't bother you, you expect that. It was the fact that bananas were thrown, that kind of thing, which has gone out of the game. And to think that fans who maybe used to rave about me would go to that extent, bring that back into the game, was very disappointing.'

Why, I asked him, since he had been at United for four years, had it taken so long for him to play at his former home ground?

'I got injured before the game in ninety-two,' he said. 'And there were quotes I'd chickened out, particularly as I played at Liverpool a couple of days later. But I'd never do that. I wasn't up to it, physically. Then they were down last year, so this was my first return. The fact it was so long and they'd been waiting made it worse.'

I asked him if the crowd reaction, which had clearly upset him, had affected his play.

'I just thought do it simple, don't make mistakes, you'll get slaughtered if you do. I was quite pleased with the way I handled the situation. When I scored I could've gone to their fans, but I didn't. And the United fans were absolutely brilliant to me. It helped me to get through the game. If it's the same next year, I'll be ready. But hopefully it will be without the racial taunts. You don't mind the booing, see, you don't mind that.'

And then he smiled.

'Something else about that game,' he said. 'That was the best goal I scored all year. Well happy with that one.'

The next week, the unbeaten record did go west. To west London. Chelsea won 1–0 at Old Trafford. With Cantona injured, Peacock took full advantage, repeating his trick of September and popping the only goal of the game. Fergie was philosophical afterwards:

'Perhaps it has come as a reminder at the right time.' He didn't look convinced.

There was nothing else worth recording about the match except this: that night I had my first anxiety attack. About Blackburn. I lay awake working out how many points each team could gather over the run-in, comparing the fixture list, seeing who could do us a favour. Doing, in fact, what you do in a normal season – which was odd, because up until now, this had not been a normal season. On the day of the Cheltenham Gold Cup the week before, my local bookies were so convinced of United's domination that they were quoting evens on the treble. You shouldn't have anxiety spins over odds like that. Yet here I was, a study of insomnia. The things was, for two months between 26 January and 16 March, time and energy engaged in qualifying for the final of the Coca-Cola Cup and the quarter-final of the FA Cup, we played just three league games. And acquired just four points from them. In the same period Blackburn, concentrating on the league now they were out of everything else, were winning their games in hand and gathering thirteen. They had appeared on our shoulder as quickly and unexpectedly as a police car in a speeder's rear-view mirror. The unassailable thirteen points gap at the top of the premiership was developing anorexia: United had sixty-eight points from thirty games; Blackburn had sixty-four from thirty-one. And their man Alan Shearer, he was scoring more frequently than Alan Clark.

The following weekend, we could forget about the league for an afternoon. It was the FA Cup quarter-final against Charlton Athletic, a game which, presumably by some administrative solecism, was scheduled for the quaint and half-forgotten time of 3 p.m. on a Saturday. This meant travelling up on the train from London at the same time as the rest of the football communion. On the train there were reds and Charlton followers, there were City fans on their way to see the home game with Wimbledon, there were Stoke and Forest fans on their way to Stoke, and at Stoke station I even saw a man in an Ipswich shirt, looking a little confused. I didn't see any Wimbledon fans, but then you don't see many of them at

Selhurst Park. The tram I caught to the ground was called Sparky: which made me wonder, are there trams called Choccy, Incey and Giggsy?

Charlton, a team which, I assumed when I first discovered United, had named themselves in honour of Bobby, had beaten Blackburn in the previous round. They were no mugs. They had brought with them ten thousand followers (Michael Grade was there, attached to a mammoth fedora and foot-long Havana, every inch the football fan). As was the habit these days at Old Trafford, the visitors embarrassed the home supporters with their noise. For forty-four minutes as their team outplayed United on the pitch, so they out-sung us in the stands – until something not entirely unexpected happened.

Peter Schmeichel had been flappy and windy all game. He had made a grotesque error in the first minute, almost letting their man in. He had shouted constantly at Bruce in a way which was frantic even by his noisy standards. Then Kim Grant, their pacey winger, knocked the ball past Bruce on the right wing and into space. Parker was covering, but Schmeichel decided to ignore him. He ran thirty yards from his area and slid like a medallist in the Olympic luge. Grant shot at goal at precisely the moment Schmeichel arrived at his shins. As Grant was afforded a close inspection of the flags brimming the top of the stands, the ball thwacked against the keeper's outstretched arms.

Referee Robbie Hart sent Schmeichel straight off. He could have gone for any one of three offences: deliberate hand-ball; fouling an opponent in a goal-scoring position; or leaving his brain in the dressing room. It was clear his team-mates felt it was the last.

'What the fuck were you doing?' you could see Bruce yelling at his keeper in the immediate aftermath. For once, Schmeichel had nothing to say in response. He was sent on his mournful trudge back to the tunnel past a blast of ear-melt from Bryan Robson, pacing the touchline.

To huge roars of welcome, Sealey the hero came on for his first game in the United first team since the European Cup Winners

Cup final three years previously. There was then an inordinate delay before Parker was selected as the man to be replaced.

Meanwhile, something remarkable had happened in the ground. The United crowd had woken up. Everyone was on their feet, baying with indignation. As the half-time whistle blew, they cheered every player to the echo as they returned to the dressing room, urging them, with clenched fist, to win the thing.

'It was brilliant,' Giggs told me. 'You could see it in their faces, how much it meant to them that we win. The Boss didn't have to say anything in the dressing room at half-time. We were that fired up.'

In the second half, driven by a blistering volume of noise from the stands, United were unstoppable. Hughes gave a stamping, snorting display of bullish power. Dropped back into midfield while Keane covered for Parker at right back, he was everywhere, tackling, running, and within in a minute of the re-start, scoring. As Charlton pushed forward looking for an equaliser, he was there to mop up in front of his back four and coordinate the counter-attacks. Giggs and Cantona went close, but it was Kanchelskis who snapped the opposition twice on the break; his second goal, as he rounded their keeper to tuck it home, looked like something from a park game it was so easy. Sealey was untroubled until the end, and made pretend-scared, wobbly leg movements to the crowd to show how untroubled he was.

'Ten men, we've only got ten men,' chanted the Stretford End in mocking triumph. They would get used to such numerical inferiority over the next few weeks.

Afterwards in the press room, as the media boys were still chewing away at their plates of complimentary sandwiches, Ferguson marched in and said:

'On the Schmeichel incident, we're going to appeal. Having looked at the video there was no way it was intentional. I think when the referee sees it he'll be embarrassed with his decision.'

The noise to be heard was the thump of the press corps' chins hitting the floor. The ref embarrassed? Fergie's defence of his players' indiscretions was getting odder by the game. 'He'll be suspended now from the Coca-Cola Cup final,' he continued, ignoring the stares of amazement. 'For a lad to miss a Cup final for that is a tragedy. But on the positive side, honestly, the determination in the dressing room at half-time was fabulous. The lads were all determined to do it for Peter. They felt the injustice of it. I'm very, very proud of the boys, I must say.'

David Lacey managed to contain his astonishment at Fergie's reading of Schmeichel's dismissal long enough to say he thought Hughes's performance in midfield was the key to the win.

'Ah, aye, Sparky, what can you say,' said Ferguson, pulling the face of awed wonder he generally reserved for describing Cantona's play. 'And you know I was going to take him off to bring Sealey on. But Brian Kidd persuaded me to bring off Paul Parker instead. He pointed out we needed to score a goal and, after all, wee Paul's not got the best scoring record in the club.'

After Ferguson left, as Steve Gritt, the Charlton manager, was saying he wished the ref hadn't sent Schmeichel off ('seemed to inspire them, even with ten men they were awesome'), the United press secretary stuck his head round the door to announce that Les Sealey would be available in the lounge next door in five minutes. I waited a polite moment or two before walking out on Gritt (no one was asking the poor bloke any questions; after what Fergie had said, they didn't need to, they had their story) and wandering through to see Sealey. Unless Ferguson's appeal was successful, Sealey would make his first start of the season in the League Cup final: Lucky Les, indeed.

But when I got into the lounge he was nowhere to be seen. There was just one journalist in there, tapping away at his lap-top.

'Sealey been in?' I asked.

'He's fucked off,' the lap-topper said. 'He came in here, I asked him a question and he said he didn't talk to the press. So I asked him why he'd come up here then. He said: "Because I was told to." '

On the train on the way home I sat with a crowd of Charlton fans.

Except they weren't Charlton fans. With an average gate of 8000, and 10,000 tickets available, Charlton had contrived to infuriate a lot of die-hards by putting the tickets on unrestricted sale. Their contingent filled up with trippers, anyone who fancied a day out up to Manchester to see the best stadium in the country. At my table there was a Millwall supporter and a West Ham fan keeping their Charlton-following mate company.

'Good ground and all that,' said the West Ham fan. 'But you lot don't half expect everything to go your way. I mean, did you see Robson on the touchline, all the second half, having a go at the linesman. He's meant to be the sub, but he's just standing there making sure the linesman does as he's told. I never seen intimidation like it at a football match.'

It was hard to argue with what he said. It wasn't just Robson – Ince and Keane were at the referee throughout: there was a disposition abroad to complain. But I couldn't tell him I agreed. I said if he thought that was intimidation, he obviously had not been at his home ground the previous week.

'What wiv Ince?' he said. 'Shouldn't take it to heart, mate. That was just a good, old-fashioned East End welcome. For a Judas.'

13

The Pilgrims

United are my team. Ireland's an accident of birth.

Paul, from the Cork branch of the
Manchester United Supporters Association

In May 1993, when the tug of war between United, Arsenal and
Blackburn over Roy Keane's contract was at its most fierce, I was
in Cork, to cover the Eurovision Song Contest. After the storm of
boom-banga-banging had abated, I took a taxi to the airport to
catch a flight home. The driver looked at me in his mirror, and
asked me whereabouts in England I came from. I told him. A happy
look flashed across his mirror.

'Do you, by any chance, follow football?'

I told him I did.

'And is it, by any chance, United you'll be following?'

I told him it was.

'Then this,' he said, 'is my lucky day. I can talk United with a fan
from Manchester.'

It turned out he was a stalwart of the Cork branch of the United
Supporters Association, had followed the reds since before I was
born.

'You'll find United are big in Cork,' he said. 'Everyone with any
sense follows United.'

And he was right. I couldn't vouch for their sense, but almost
every other car we passed had a United sticker in the window,
almost every other street we drove through contained a youth in a
replica shirt. There were bars in County Cork called things like the
Stretford End and Bestie's, he told me; there was a chip shop called

Sharpe's with, in a display case securely fastened to the wall, a ball signed by all the European Cup-winning side ('including Sir Matt').

'There's a feller in Killarney owns a bar,' he said. 'Sure, he's an alcoholic, but he always has something on him that's red and white.'

Was it possible, he wanted to know, that they could be more fanatical about United in Manchester than they were in County Cork?

I didn't get much chance to answer.

His most fervent wish, he continued, was that Roy Keane, the Cork bad boy made good, would join the other local hero Denis Irwin and sign for United. Not content to leave it to chance, he added, he was doing something practical about it.

'Every night,' he lowered his voice conspiratorially, 'I pray on my rosary that it will happen, God willing.'

God (with some help from Alex Ferguson and Roy's agent) willed it. And every home game last season, pilgrims flew over from Cork to Manchester to celebrate the happy coincidence of two of the city's finest turning out for the boys.

There is something of an ambivalent attitude among the Old Trafford hard core towards fans who hail from outside Manchester. Leeds fans don't show any apparent animosity towards their supporters on the south coast (the 'Hampshire whites'); Arsenal appear to be rather proud of a cosmopolitan following which includes a congregation of 'gooners' in Devizes; at Rangers they take the fact that folk make trips to Glasgow from Canada as a compliment. But at United, the club with far and away the biggest worldwide network of supporters, there is an element which takes all those 'you-don't-come-from-Manchester' tauntings from opposition mobs to heart. Despite the fact it is clearly not true that United have no local support (sales of replica United shirts outnumber those of City by 20–1 in Greater Manchester), some fans have succumbed to the old canard, started to believe that outside support somehow dilutes the authenticity of their club. In the fanzine *Red Issue*, a correspondent called J. Reeve set off a heated debate in the letters column about out-of-towners, suggesting that the seventies fashion for ambushes of Cockney reds at Piccadilly Station might be profitably revived. Not perhaps sensing the irony, he gave his address as Cheadle Hulme: for those unfamiliar with this Cheshire suburb, it is not the Mancunian equivalent of being born within earshot of Bow Bells.

Nevertheless, his plea for birthplace purity was picked up.

'Can these people honestly understand what the Manchester derby means?' said one subsequent correspondent, railing against the foreigners. 'Can they honestly understand the Manchester–Merseyside rivalry?'

The non-Manc reds responded predictably, strenuously defending their loyalty and their integrity.

'I believe we are all now quite familiar with the letter from J. Reeve,' wrote someone calling himself Drum: 'a Bielefeld Red from BFPO 39, Germany'. 'Who the fuck is this twat? . . . The best thing for Mr Reeve would be to go to Maine Road. At least there he'd be assured that all the fans would be from Manchester, the whole capacity has only to walk from the housing estate on the other side of the road.'

Me, I share the view of *Red Issue*'s editor who prefaced the screeds of Reeve-led correspondence with an apology: 'We're sorry to say that the rest of this month's letters pages are being taken up with the ongoing, fruitless feud between Manchester and out-of-town supporters.'

I think we should be happy to share the gospel according to Sir Alex with the world, provided everyone brings something to the party. And few bring as much to the party as the Irish.

In the bar of a hotel at the bottom of Market Street, the Cork branch of the United Supporters Association had been enjoying their Saturday in Manchester so much on the occasion I met up with them, that they had decided to extend it until well past three on Sunday morning. There were about seventy of them – men, women and children – sitting round tables singing red songs, talking through the game they had just seen, drooling about Cantona, articulating their affection for an organisation which did its business three thousand miles from their homes.

'This Manchester United thing, it's huge,' said Martin O'Neill, the branch secretary, and a Cork shopowner in his forties. 'Wherever you go you meet people who support United. Or hate them. Back home we always get it, you know, "ah, but Blackburn they'll be catching you." People know who you are because you support United.'

It would be hard for people to miss the fact that Martin supported United: he had named his shop Trafford Park and he had named his two-year-old son after Giggsy (Ryan O'Neill: familiar name that). Much of his life was centred around United. His branch has three hundred and fifty members spread across County Cork. They have monthly meetings, their own eleven-a-side teams competing in leagues in United kit, and every week they gather to watch the games on the telly ('I've heard people complaining about Sky, but for us, it's been a godsend'). Also, every year, they invite players over as guest of honour to their annual dinner.

'United are tremendous at helping us with that,' he said. 'We've had Denis Irwin, of course, and Steve Bruce. He took one look at Callum, our most fanatical supporter, and he sees Callum's a heavy feller. So he says to Callum, "You know Gazza's mate Five Bellies? Well you must be Ten Bellies." So that's what Callum's become just now, Ten Bellies.'

The player who has been most frequently to the Cork branch jollies, is Lee Sharpe.

'He loves it,' said Martin. 'Really gets into the spirit. Stays up and parties all night with us.'

No change there, if Sharpe is enjoying a party.

Cantona, they were desperate to invite over, but as yet he had not taken up the offer. They had been to see him, though: one day, after training at The Cliff, Callum and Martin presented him with the Cork branch's Player of the Year trophy. It was an interesting culture clash that, written plain in the snapshots Martin produced of the scene: the large-girthed out-of-towners with red faces and the hyper-cool metropolitan aesthete shaking hands over a little alloy trophy.

The thing, however, that the branch members liked best of all, was the trips over to see games in England: to Manchester, the place Martin said he would prefer to visit over London any day of the week. Sitting around the bar, over enough lager to flood Old Trafford, they told tales of games seen and journeys made. There was the time in the sixties when they travelled by train and ferry and train again on the worst day of the winter – thirty-six hours of delays and discomfort only to discover, when they finally made it to Manchester, that the match had been abandoned. There was the time more recently when two Cork lads had got tickets for the League Cup final and, because it was the only way they could make a flight back, had left at half-time. There was the time, too, when Billy O'Sullivan, now in his fifties, was lifted while standing on the United terrace during a match against Birmingham and was interrogated by the police for six hours because there had been a pub bomb in the city and he was Irish.

'I was lucky,' said Billy, white-haired and red-faced. 'I might not have got home from that game for seventeen years.'

Now, although communications had improved, trips still took planning. This one had been arranged months in advance.

'Everyone put fifty pounds down last autumn,' said Martin. 'For me, that's a genuine supporter.'

Whole families had flown in to pay homage at the distant shrine. They had arrived in Manchester on Friday morning, spent the day shopping and the night in Chinatown. Then it was off early to the ground, round the souvenir shop, buying up print-runs of the match programme. It was a costly operation, 'a dear do'.

'For the other long-distance United supporters – from Newport or London – they can just hire a coach,' said Martin. 'For us it gets expensive with plane fares and that. It costs a man two hundred and forty pounds just for travel and hotels. Now if the man has a fourteen-year-old son he's wanting to bring, you're looking at five hundred pounds before you start.'

Alan, a draughtsman in his twenties, who had worn a French national football shirt to the match and was now propped up against the bar by an unsteady elbow, chipped in.

'And then there's this to buy,' he said, waving his pint pot around. 'It cost me two hundred and forty pounds to come, and I've spent about another two hundred pounds on dis stuff. It's murder.'

United themselves, with their usual marketing verve, have not been slow to exploit the opportunity presented by their Irish support. Particularly Cork support, stuck as it is in the middle of a local economy bloated by EC agricultural subsidy money.

'We had these Irish fans coming over for a match and arriving at the ground at quarter to ten on a Saturday morning to savour the atmosphere and they had nothing to do,' Danny McGregor told me when I saw him in his office. 'They just hung around, mooching. So we got involved with travel agents from Cork, Belfast and Dublin – Norway and Finland, too – and produced this.'

He handed over a glossy leaflet detailing match-ticket-inclusive weekend breaks. There were three kinds: executive, club and budget. Prices were determined, it seemed from the brochure, on whether you took a trip round Granada Studios and had dinner at Harry Ramsden's Largest Fish and Chip Shop in the World or not.

'VFM, typical United: value for money,' McGregor said. 'We pick them up from the airport on a coach, take them to their hotel, then on to Old Trafford where we give them a buffet lunch where an old player will perhaps give a funny introductory speech, and they can meet one or two members of the current squad.'

Usually Les Sealey, as it happens. Pinned to the wall in the dressing room at Old Trafford there is a chart listing players' names against a score, which reveals how often they have 'been upstairs' to meet the patrons of travel packages like this. When I scrutinised it three-quarters of the way through the 1993–94 season, while Giggsy had been twice and Roy Keane not at all, Lucky Les had done the business eight times. 'Someone's got to,' he said of the task.

'The evening of match day they have to themselves, to enjoy Manchester,' continued McGregor. 'Then, on the Sunday morning, we give them a tour of the museum and a chance to visit the souvenir shop.'

A chance to spend some money? I said.

'A chance to enjoy their weekend to the full,' he corrected me. 'And the demand's there. I have been limited to two hundred people a game this season. Next year I'll double it.'

The Irish were not unaware of the strategy United were involved in here.

'By Christ,' said Martin O'Neill, 'do they see us coming. I reckon we spend about ten minutes more in that superstore than anyone local. I come here with a list of things to buy for folk as long as your arm, and of course United know I do. They love me coming.'

But most of the Cork branch had not taken advantage of one of Danny McGregor's packages. Martin had worked it out, how to play the game. If he applied for seats in the usual members' lottery, and arranged his own travel, it cost him about £100 less.

'You can't rely on tickets, but we done all right so far,' he said. 'And why do you think we Irish always do better than you lot in the ticket draw?'

I said I didn't know: the luck of the Irish?

'Don't be naive,' said Paul, an accountant in his thirties sitting at the table next to ours.

'Because they see our address, they know we'll make more of a trip of it. Spend more money.'

As the morning drew on, as the tills expanded with foreign exchange, as pilgrims fell out of consciousness around the bar, the big question remained unanswered: why United? Why not Liverpool? Why not Celtic? Why not Barcelona? It wasn't much further away. Why was Cork such a dedicated pocket of red?

'You'll find in Ireland that everyone supports an English team,' explained Martin. 'With me it was United because of the nineteen fifty-seven Cup final. My Da was Villa, but I'd always sort of looked to United before, what with Johnny Carey being Ireland captain and all, so we had a fight about that final and that made me more determined.'

'It's odd,' added Paul, 'but in Ireland what they do is follow whoever is big when they are about eight and stick with them. Roddy Doyle, he's Chelsea, a lot of lads my age are Leeds. The Sultans of Ping, that pop group, they're from Cork and they're Notts Forest.'

'I've seen Derby County holdalls in Cork,' added Martin.

'United have always picked up fans,' continued Paul. 'But now they're so successful, it's just snowballed.'

I wondered if there was anything in the Catholic connection: United, the traditionally left-footed organisation, picking up similarly inclined Irishmen.

'Not really,' said Martin. 'Though sure when Matt was here, I used to be in the Stretford End and the whole main stand was priests, thick with the cloth it was. But you don't think about which is a Catholic club, you support who turns your fancy.'

'That said,' said Paul, 'you won't be finding many following Rangers down our way.'

Another thing, I suggested, was the Keane connection. Like the taxi driver I met, they must have been delighted that he had signed.

'Sure, but I feel ashamed of Cork's attitude to him, sometimes,' said Martin. 'When Roy comes home, there's a lot of jealousy, a lot of folk are bitter about him. There's fellers saying he's got too big for his boots. Everyone's making up stories about him behaving like the big feller in bars. There's that many stories and that many bars, he would have to have been Superman to have done all the things he's supposed to have done.'

'I heard,' said Alan, 'he went in a bar and by accident he brushed against a feller's pint and knocked it over. Before he could say I'll buy you another, feller'd planted him one in the face.'

'Me, I'm different,' said Paul. 'I wouldn't really care if Roy played for someone else. I don't support the reds just because they have local lads in the team. I'm not into Ireland. I mean I'd rather United won the league than Ireland won the World Cup. United are my team, Ireland are an accident of birth. Sure we love them, but it doesn't hurt when they lose like it does when United lose.'

About four o'clock, with the strained top notes of 'Danny Boy' crescendoing in the background, with the empty glasses rising like the mountains of Mourne on our table, I decided to leave them to it. They had to catch a plane home early the next morning, and it looked as though they might drink on through. As I got up to leave, Martin, seeing the world with the clear eyes of a drinker at four in the morning, said he had a story which summed it all up.

'A fourteen-year-old girl,' he said, 'she's coming into my shop the day before I'm on my way here and she's asking for a poster of Giggs. So I ask why she's wanting a picture of him, and not some pop star. "Why," she said, "but he's a fine flarr." '

'That's a Cork word for a ride,' translated Paul.

I looked blank.

'You know, a shag.'

'Sure, and her not knowing whether a football is stuffed or pumped, and yet she loves them,' said Martin. 'There. That's United for you. Something for everyone.'

As I walked out of the hotel, the man on the door said he hoped to see me again.

'The Irish are always welcome here, mate,' he said.

And their wallets.

14

A Little National Difficulty

*I was the first to stand up and be counted, to
attack the great Manchester United side. But
I don't want to sound as though I'm gloating.*
                    Jimmy Hill, March 1994

On the evening of 16 March, Alex Ferguson didn't have to worry
about defending his players. He sat accepting the plaudits of an
appreciative pack in the press room at Old Trafford, eyes glittering
with pride, smile broader than Jan Molby's behind. He had much
to be cheerful about. We had just seen United demolish Sheffield
Wednesday with a display of ferociously destructive football, the
like of which I had not witnessed at Old Trafford since Forest won
4–0 there in 1978. Wednesday were lucky to escape without scorch
marks. Trevor Francis, returning over the Pennines after his fourth
defeat of the season at red hands, said: 'Thank God we don't have
to play them again.'

Cantona was at the centre of everything – full of flicks and fancy,
scoring twice, involved in the other three. When asked what he
thought of the King's performance, Ferguson said nothing. Just shut
his eyes, shook his head, pursed his lips and exhaled in wonder. He
had the look a teenage girl might wear if asked by her dad why she
liked East 17: did he really need to explain?

'Bravura Cantona the Conductor in United Cantata' was *The
Independent*'s headline the next day. The only thing more certain
than United winning the title now, every paper concluded, was that
Eric would be crowned player of the Year by the PFA, the Football
Writers' Association, and probably the College of Cardinals. The

next day, the odds the bookies were offering on United winning the treble were evens.

Three days later, United travelled to Wiltshire for their first-ever league game with Swindon Town at the County Ground. In this insubstantial setting, the team sank from their Wednesday high with a speed sufficient to induce a mass attack of the bends in K stand. It is one of the mysteries of form that a team who have played like gods can, within seventy-two hours, play as if their boots were sponsored by Evercrete.

It started as it meant to go on. In the first ten minutes, chasing the ball into touch, Hughes collided with an advertising hoarding and made close contact with the crowd. As he tried to right himself, he suddenly got very angry, pointing into the terraces, pointing at the referee, pointing at his cheek, thrusting aside a consoling arm offered by a Swindon defender.

'I didn't know what he was on about,' Giggs told me later. 'It wasn't till I saw "Match of the Day" that I realised a feller'd smacked him. You can't have that.'

Elsewhere, niggled by a team who seemed to have snorted grams of powdered determination before the game, determined as much to do down the leaders as to stop going down themselves, the United whinge tendency that had first surfaced against Charlton was on militant form. Keane behaved like a child denied access to the television remote-control unit; Ince wore a snarl; Schmeichel, apparently not inhibited by his sending off the previous week, warred constantly with his back four. Half the team were trying to moan the ref into submission. They managed to stop complaining long enough to score though – twice – with Ince's goal, in particular, a sweet one, clipped from outside the area and skidding into the net's corner. Indeed, with twenty minutes left, United led 2–1 and it looked as though the cliché about true champions not performing well but still winning might see a Sunday outing the next morning.

At that point, Cantona clearly fancied a few more headlines all to himself. He received the ball on the edge of the United area, advanced a couple of paces, looking, as always, around him. Then, as he was about to lay it off centre-circlewards, the ball bobbled away, a leg-stretch from full control. As Swindon's John Moncur came sliding in to tackle him, Cantona tried to turn past him. His legs became entangled with Moncur, still prone on the ground. As he extricated himself, he performed that neat little back-stamp he had rehearsed on John Polston's shoulder at Norwich a couple of months earlier. Only this time he hit the midriff. And this time the referee was four feet away. After a theatrical pause, during which Eric did his usual what's-all-the-fuss, scarecrow arm-stretch and Keane took the opportunity to tell the bloke in the Swindon team who is in his late thirties but wears a pigtail that he was a twat, the ref flourished his red card.

It was an X-certificate moment, replayed with salivating relish on 'Match of the Day'. We saw it from four angles, in slow motion, in real time: the only trick the producer missed was not securing the rights to fasten an under-boot camera to the bottom of Cantona's size nine to seize that rib-rattling moment of impact. For those of us who believe football is a beautiful pursuit and that Cantona is its most aesthetic practitioner, it made painful viewing. A pain perhaps not as acute as the one Moncur must have had the following morning, but pain nonetheless.

Eric later described his performance as a silly thing to do. Silly? It wasn't silly, it was inexcusable, the kind of thing you expect in a Sunday game on Hackney Marshes, only conducted with more accuracy and panache. Why did he do it? How could he do it? At that stage of the game, with United cruising to three points and Moncur doing no more than going in hard, it wasn't silly. It wasn't even unpleasant, unnecessary or dispiriting. It was barking.

The game ended up a draw, two points tossed away in a shameful final quarter-hour. Afterwards, Ferguson, unlike after the Norwich match, unlike with Hughes at Sheffield, unlike Schmeichel the previous week, said nothing to defend the indefensible. He said nothing at all, in fact, refusing to attend the after-match press conference.

Others were less circumspect. Lawrie Sanchez, newly signed by Swindon from Wimbledon and apparently scripted by Johnny

Speight, said: 'If he played for Wimbledon he would be sent off every week. He is full of niggles and nastiness. He's your typical Gallic.'

The only person to surface from the mire with any dignity was John Moncur, who said he would still vote for Cantona as PFA Player of the Year.

The United players looked less dignified as they boarded the coach home. Not that it was easy. Instead of being obscured by the star-spotters, autograph-hunters and weepy Giggsy fans who had greeted their arrival, the bus was surrounded by Swindon followers, who were baying, mocking, Istanbulling. When Cantona made his way to the vehicle there was a vomiting volley of abuse, which he appeared to ignore. But just as he was climbing aboard, someone, perhaps the only French-speaker in the West Country, said something that infuriated him so much, he turned back and started on them. He was restrained from a headlong dive into the mass by the bus driver, Sealey and Robson (this may be a slur on the bus driver, but a less likely posse of restraint would be hard to picture).

The Swindon fans loved this. As he was pulled aboard snarling, they danced and jumped and leapt around. They had niggled him into responding. They had provoked a reaction, done their part in exposing his flaws. They had touched genius.

The papers enjoyed it hugely. Never can a backlash have achieved such a head of steam so quickly. In the space of three days, United had ceased to be the greatest side to touch turf in a quarter-century and had turned into a bunch of arrogant, violent, whining curmudgeons, led by a clinically unstable Frenchman and presided over by a paranoid Scot.

'Squabbling and bitching,' wrote *The Times*, 'they marched to their draw, seeking physical contact or taking pains to avoid it, depending on individual temperament. Any thoughts of footballing greatness can be set aside for a while.'

Cod psychological and genetic analyses were dusted down to explain Eric's appalling lapse. Johnny Giles and Emlyn Hughes were trotted out to write the standard they're-not-as-good-as-we-were guff. Rather more pertinently, the old theory resurfaced that United, taking the lead from their twitchy manager, were beginning to crack under pressure. The expensive breath of Blackburn was beginning to be felt on Umbro tie-up collars. Winning every game in hand, they were just three points behind. And we were approaching Easter, that time of year again – when United had blown it in 1992.

Three days later, they were at Arsenal, the last mob you want to be playing when you're suffering from TITS (Twitchy Irritable Temperament Syndrome). All niggle and bite and Tony Adams. I'd bought the tickets originally for the Saturday fixture, and was going to take my son, but when it was put back to a midweek evening due to United's Cup tie with Charlton, it was considered he was too young, what with school the next morning. I hadn't told him where I was going that night. At breakfast he was waiting for me: 'Dad, the boys at school say it's United v. Arsenal tonight,' he said. 'But it can't be because I'm going to that.'

I didn't take him. And I felt about as big as Danny Wallace about it.

The gooners were there, though, and really up for it, chanting 'there's only one team in Europe' on the tube; there was that sense in the air that this game meant something, that it was a big night, that the course of the championship might be decided. They were confident, too, these Arsenal boys, certain that there was a chink in United that their lads could put their crowbars into.

'Treble?' a gooner said to me on the tube. 'The only treble is Blackburn in the league, Chelsea in the Cup and Villa in the Coca-Cola, mate. Your lot are going to blow it again. Lovely.'

Unlike at West Ham, this time, as Nigel, Andy the art critic and I walked to our seats and spotted the well-dressed, the well-heeled and the well-fed filing into Highbury's West stand, we said: 'Nothing to worry about here.' We saw Jeremy Beadle, there to give his lads a warm hand. We saw John Lydon at the bar. In his Rotten days he used to support nothing and no one, now he supports Arsenal. A logical progression, we thought. And when Sharpe, back in the side for the first time for seventeen games after injury, scored and, just below us, ran through a corner-post impression of Elvis – collar up, hips swivelling, the top of the flag bent over as a microphone – we were up out of our seats, in common with other reds, dotted like poppies in a meadow throughout the ground. No one, however, gave us more than a disappointed look.

'Fuckin' hell Arsenal, that was so predictable,' said the well-turned-out man behind me.

If pace alone were the pre-requisite of a great game, then this was an absolute stormer. In the pre-match build-up, much had been written about United's attitude; how they had to calm down or they were going to win nothing, red-carding their way to the unique treble of second places that had so excited the man on the tube. Roy Keane, though, he wasn't listening. He charged around, brow down, mad-eyed, looking for trouble. At one point, Bruce had to run forty yards to remonstrate with him, to pull him back from garrotting the ref with his abuse. Schmeichel, too, had the calming effect on his team-mates of a gram of speed popped into your cocoa. But no one could gainsay their commitment. There was one of the cameos of the season when Hughes and Giggs snapped at Adams' heels like hunting dogs at a wounded wildebeest, until he toppled over and they came away with the prize, the ball.

As the game got quicker, as first Arsenal equalised, then Sharpe scored again, then Arsenal equalised again and then Wright had a winner disallowed ('he was well gutted about that,' Ince told me later, laughing), only Cantona seemed to keep out of the frenzy around him. He stood on the right wing, laying the ball off quickly, a model of a man who has learnt his lesson. 'Cantona's a wanker, na na, na na,' the gooners sang on the rare occasions he touched the ball. 'I'd rather be a Frenchman than a Cockney,' came back our lads in the Clock End. And so it continued until, with five minutes left, Cantona dived in for a loose ball and sent Arsenal's Selley, who had been their man with the niggle all evening, into a pantomime of over-reaction with a late two-footer.

'Jesus,' said Nigel as Vic Callow, the ref, fumbled in his pocket. It was a yellow.

Less than a minute later, and Cantona, after forcibly robbing Jensen, the Dane with the Carmen rollers, found himself confronted by the four-square figure of Adams. He tried, it seemed to me, to jump out of the way, failed and the two of them collided. For the first time in eighty-eight minutes the action appeared to stop, everything went into slow motion as Mr Callow walked, hand fiddling with the flap of his breast pocket, in Cantona's direction. But Eric was already on his way, off the pitch, past the consoling hand of Arsenal's Dixon, past Ferguson, down the tunnel and on to the first flight to Paris by the time Callow had told him to go. This was it, we thought. He was out of love with English football now.

Around us the polite, sane-looking fans, who had tolerated opposition supporters celebrating in their midst, had all disappeared. In their place were salivating, popeyed madmen. It was like the whole stand was populated by werewolves, grown suddenly toothsome and hairy at the sight of a red card. As Callow reached into his pockets again, the man behind me began to roar.

'Yes, yes, he's sending the cunt off. He's going, he's going. Yes, yes. I don't believe it.'

I turned to look at him. He was standing on his seat, both arms outstretched, waving V-signs in the direction of Cantona's departing back, bawling with a foaming pleasure born in his stomach, making comments about Eric's nationality seldom heard outside a parliamentary debate on Maastricht.

'Yes, yes, fuck off, then, you French slag.'

After the game, as he re-knotted his tie, wiped the spittle from his chin and floated back down from planet euphoria, I asked him what he did for a living.

'I'm a chartered accountant,' he said.

I actually heard a football writer saying that United 'needed to be brought down a peg or two'. And the next day the papers did their bit in the demolition. 'He's a nutter,' was the *Sun*'s headline. Every back page, every inside page, had pictures of Cantona, in black, on his way. Alongside it were pictures of McClair, Bruce and Giggs pointing out to the referee that he had made an error of judgement, or snarling like ill-disciplined hyenas – depending on your point of view. And the columnists, justified by events, wallowed in sanctimoniousness:

'Ferguson turns his side into arrogant rabble,' said the *Express*'s man, reflecting a general view that it was all the manager's fault. 'When Ferguson discusses the misconduct of United players, he should remember that Sir Matt Busby never offered an excuse and certainly not Ferguson's absurd euphemism... "You can't stop players being competitive." Not even on other player's chests?'

The moral high-ground that newspaper columnists sought to occupy over United's ill-discipline was compromised somewhat by their colleagues' hounding of Cantona. The footballer who had been sent off in successive matches was treated to the sort of reporting a philandering government minister might expect to encounter. Teams of reporters were put on his case: the *Mirror* had two storm-troopers in France talking to his relatives ('yes, we stand by Eric,' was the revelatory discovery when they knocked on his elder brother's door); the *Express*, more careful with expenses, sent their boys to Leeds. Here they uncovered the really big news: that Eric, on £8000 a week, lived in a pebble-dashed, thirties semi in Round-hay. Just in case anyone passing may have missed the place, they printed a picture of the house, complete with the door number and both Eric's and his wife's car registration numbers clearly visible. Nice touch that. Since Eric spent most of his week in the Novotel in north Manchester, just a trouser press from Giggsy's place, his wife could deal with the Leeds fans calling to pay their respects at one in the morning on her own.

There was no doubt that the players were affected by the coverage. Steve Bruce said he was worried that Eric 'might just pack it all in'.

And Ince said to me:

'We knew when we won the title that they would come out of

the woodwork, all these old players, to have a pop at us. The gaffer told us not to let it get to us, to let our football do the talking. But when you read this, that and the other about Eric or me, or Sparky, you have to button your lip, although you really felt like retaliating. Maybe in 'ninety-two we would have done, but we'd learnt from that just to ignore it and get on with our own game.'

For two weeks in March, Eric Cantona didn't just need the concern and support of his colleagues, he needed skin as thick as Gazza. The papers tried to influence events by hounding him out, tried to get him to say sod this, I'm on my *velo*. And if he went walkies, this in itself would be news: final proof of dodgy temperament. It is called moving the story forward.

There was a sense of wish-fulfilment about the reporting; it was the dynamic of the lynch mob. '*L'Angleterre contre Cantona*' was *L'Équipe*'s reading of it. And they were not far off the mark. With a nice touch of irony, the only media outfit that came to the defence of Cantona was Lynam and Hansen, Ferguson's Liverpool supporters club, who, in slow motion on 'Sportsnight', proved he was sent off the second time unjustifiably, on reputation, perhaps.

Never mind Cantona's feelings, the papers couldn't lose in the pursuit. When United played brilliantly they could drool, and the red army would buy lots of copies. When they were naughty, they could stamp all over them and the army of red-haters would buy lots of copies. Either way, it's a great story. Several papers have two sets of employees to give voice to their schizophrenia. They have local reporters with good contacts, they ghostwrite players' biographies, they can ring Fergie at home for a quote. They write nice, uncritical, supportive things so as not to blow their privileged access – access which makes for stories that sell papers. So when there is something nasty to be done, when someone has to say United have forfeited their right to be champs, or shouldn't be mentioned in the same breath as the class of '68, or Fergie wasn't fit to lace Kenny Dalglish's brogues, it is left to two of the London-based cynics. In this way, every is angle covered, and if Fergie takes exception to something written in a tabloid then the local guy can rightly point out it wasn't him, guv, and what about that exclusive you promised me.

This is not to deny that the attacks on Cantona did not reflect a national feeling at the time. You only had to look at the relish with which communications were sent to the *Sun*'s faxline suggesting he should be deported, or how callers to David Mellor's '606 Show' rang in to say they had always known he was a cheat, to see how much Eric was loathed.

Why was this? Why did the best player to fill English grounds since Best generate such antipathy? Because he is good, he is flash, he is better than his contemporaries. And he knows it. It has been an English tradition not simply to suspect flamboyance, but to try and destroy it, to bring it down a peg or two, which goes back to Charles I – a snappy dresser who had the cut of his collar ruined by Puritan drones. Cantona, moreover, compounds his criminal excess of talent by being foreign. Thus it is that players with little ability but a capacity for limitless toil – Carlton Palmer or Geoff Thomas – are characterised as delivering positive British qualities. They are most often described as honest. The implication is that the less sweat-prone Cantona, who can achieve more with one flick of the instep than others could in ninety minutes of lung expansion, is untruthful, a purveyor of alien untrustworthiness. The double standard was even evident in the reaction to United's own catalogue of ill-discipline. When Hughes, a man whose effort could never be faulted, was sent off for kicking a Sheffield United player up the arse, the papers were not full of racist analysis about a sneaky, underhand, typical Welshman.

And, of course, Cantona compounded his foreign genius by play-ing for United. The whole potent cocktail of self-righteousness, jingoism and anti-United feeling bubbled over at Highbury. Many of us have become over-excited to the point of embarrassment when our team has scored a vital goal, or won a trophy. But that account-ant exhibited a profound joy that could not have been bettered had Arsenal won the League Cup, the FA Cup, the Cup Winners Cup and he had completed that big audit all on the one day. When Cantona was sent off, boy did that man despise United.

Once it was only Manchester City, Leeds and Liverpool followers who had a special place in their bile ducts for United. In 1994 it was everywhere. At West Ham, Bruce, the least, you would have thought, provocative of United players, was spat at square in the face as he boarded the team bus. At Swindon there was that punch thrown at Hughes ('shame he didn't hit him harder' commented the Leeds fanzine). At Chester races, on a day out, Ince had a bottle of lager poured over his head. Outside every ground the biggest selling T-shirts of the year were those which mocked United. For example: 'Galatasaray Supporters Club – Tottenham Branch'. Or the one on sale at Highbury before their game against Wimbledon: 'United Do the Treble', it said, before listing the dates of the games in which United players were sent off. 'Fergie's Red Card Army Go Marching Off, Off, Off'. Quite funny as it happens.

From what did this hatred spring? The standard United response is jealousy – the fear that this side is so good, and the club so healthy, they will stop anyone else winning things for a long time to come. And there may be some of that.

But there was something more significant at work here, too; something which prevents that grudging respect that even the most jaundiced reserve for excellence. It is a reaction against the cultural imperialism of United, the McDonaldising of the club, the march for world high-street domination driven by the engine of the commercial department. Or to put it another way, United, like dog shit, are everywhere.

I was under the impression, for instance, that there were two clubs with a reasonable pedigree in Bristol. But when I went into a sports shop there, I discovered not Rovers or City clobber for sale, but United kit in all its increasingly vulgar permutations. Walking through the Broadmead shopping centre in the town, I saw boys in black shirts, girls in grey United pro-training fleece tops (they used to be called sweat shirts in my day), United items at virtually every turn, on youths whose closest encounter with the club was the day they handed over their £32.99. Simon Marsh, marketing manager of Umbro, is delighted by this, quick to point out that United change strips are a major shifter in Milan.

For the hard-core enthusiast of another side, though, it rankles. Andy Mitten, of *United We Stand*, has a good analogy on this one. It runs like this:

Say you are a fan of Portsmouth, a home-and-away-never-miss-a-game-take-a-bottle-of-banana-milk-in-a-carrier-bag nutter. You go to a match in Birmingham, on a filthy winter Saturday, see your side go down 2–0 in a crap game against West Brom; indulge, in other words, in the kind of weekend activity which *When Saturday Comes* glorifies as heroic, but is no more than an extension of Virginia Bottomley's care in the community programme. You get back to the pub about nine in the evening and there's some bloke at the bar wearing a self-regarding expression and a United shirt.

'What you doing wasting your time with them?' he sneers, rolling a pinch of your sodden Portsmouth away shirt between finger and thumb. 'You should get yourself a decent team like me.'

And so, you ask, when was the last time he had done his bit on the terraces on a wet Saturday in January. Indeed, when was the last time he had attended a Manchester United match?

'Don't actually go to games, do I.' he replied. 'Can't get tickets, can you. They're too popular a team, see. Not like your lot. But I seen every goal they scored this season on the telly.'

Now, would you not hate United, too?

So last March, when the team that had been yomping their magnificent and unstoppable way to a clean sweep of trophies, began to lose it, began to look fragile – throwing away leads and throwing punches, stamping on chests and getting suspended, and moaning, moaning, moaning – it gave that as yet amorphous sense of grievance shape and form. Where once it had been fashionable to eulogise, so it became flavour of the month to hate United, to hope they blew it, to discover a long-suppressed admiration for Kenny Dalgish, to anticipate savouring the profound pleasure of seeing your best friend fall from a roof. It was hubris, *schadenfreude* and other foreign words.

It was summed up when Alan Mullery, of Spurs, Fulham and once a manager at Brighton – a man not to be backed in a pinpoint-

Blackburn-on-a-map contest – appeared on a television programme called 'Sport in Question' wearing a Rovers bomber jacket. When questioned about it, he said: 'I just think everyone hopes they'll win.' And he got a round of applause.

The problem was – March's dodgy middle had dropped a little seed in my stomach which was growing into a muscle-wringing knot of doubt. Cantona had now got himself banned for five matches and I was beginning to fear that United-haters everywhere were heading for a season to remember.

15

Eric The King

*Out of the field/It's almost unreal/Some of the
things that Eric does.*
      Verse from 'Eric the King' terrace chant

It was not the ideal build-up to a Cup final. Five days after the
Arsenal match, United were to play at Wembley in the Coca-Cola
Cup final. Here they would face not only Aston Villa, but most of
Fleet Street and the collective contempt of every uncommitted
supporter in the country. Alex Ferguson said to me subsequently:
'At that time, elements in the media seemed to be making a con-
certed effort to create a critical climate around the club. Possibly it
worked, maybe it affected the players for the Coca-Cola Cup final.
Who can say. It certainly didn't do us any favours.'

He wasn't being paranoid. He was underplaying wildly.

At first in the season it seemed that the Coca-Cola was not high on
Ferguson's menu. In the early stages of the competition, in games
against Stoke and Leicester, he took it as little more than an opportunity to sharpen his English reserves for the European campaign.
At that stage of the season, though, the reds couldn't lose if they
tried and the tactic of not really worrying had propelled the team
into a semi-final against Sheffield Wednesday. It was a tie noted, in
the first leg at Old Trafford, less for a Ryan Giggs wonder goal
which won the game, than for the huge brawl which took place on
the concourse afterwards: United followers started it, apparently
taking retribution on Sheffield supporters who had made fun of the
Munich air crash throughout the game. Presumably, those exacting

revenge with seventies-revivalist relish were not the same morally backboned boys who, at White Hart Lane in January, had responded to Spurs fans' wobbly aircraft impressions by immediately breaking into a gas chamber hiss.

I watched the second leg on a giant screen in a bar in Manchester. In the days before Swindon, in the days before Chelsea at home, United won 4–1. Hughes scored twice and was booked for speeding on his way home; the intervention of the traffic police came a bit late for a Sheffield team torn apart by pace. When it was won, I had wandered through St Ann's Square in the centre of town. There were three people sitting on a low wall eating Kentucky Fried Chicken, and a couple loudly discussing the merits of the art film they had just seen; behind them a tram trundled past, its fart of a horn echoing down the empty streets. It hadn't set the place alight, this Coca-Cola Cup. It wasn't Istanbul out there.

Nevertheless, once the final was reached, the competition achieved significance. Big significance. We were poised on the lip of history here. Sure, the Coca-Cola was the junior trophy, but to win it as well as the two biggies, it had never been done before, even by Liverpool in their pomp. Particularly by Liverpool in their pomp. To win the clean sweep would place the impatient Alex Ferguson, indisputably, at the summit. And you could sense he was beginning to salivate at the historic possibilities of the treble.

In public he tried to play down the expectation. 'No one has ever done it before,' he said. 'Why should we be any different?'

But in private the players knew this could the first chapter of their autobiographies.

'I think once we got to Wembley, we started to sit up and think: hey, yeah, have some of that,' said Paul Ince.

'The players were definitely up for it,' Ferguson said. 'Perhaps I should have stuck with the lads who had seen us through the earlier rounds. But once they got a sniff of Wembley and what the game might mean, the regular lads, they were desperate to be involved.'

Not that their involvement worried him too much. He said: 'I have never in my life gone into a final of any kind with a team as good as the one I'm sending out for this one.'

Ferguson may have been full of confident noises, but I wasn't. Stripped of confidence by the nervy antics of the past three weeks, a dull ache of premonition had settled in my digestive system as I made my way to the game. 'We're going to lose this one,' I said to my friend Cat when I met up with her (she's got contacts as long as an orang-utan's arms and got me a ticket).

'No we're not,' she said. 'Trust me. The treble. Good title for a book.'

Despite the historical edge to the game, the Villa fans seemed more up for it than our lot did. On the tube on the way, there were more of them in fancy dress, more with face paint and silly wigs, more in beery good voice. Along Wembley Way, the banter was high and friendly.

'You don't come from Manchester,' sang the Villa. 'Do you know where Wembley is?' countered our boys, smug in the frequency of their visits to the base camp of the overcharge (£4 for a programme, £3 to have three stripes of make-up daubed across your cheeks, £2 for a piss-warm lager).

We found ourselves sitting just in front of the United players' families: wives, children, parents, girlfriends; mistresses too, probably. I spotted Mrs Sealey, with her two Les-lookalike boys. They looked spruce and proud. Fergie had been persuaded that appealing against Schmeichel's sending-off was a whinge too far in the present climate, and so they were here to watch the old man in goal, rather than looking pained on the bench. That Les luck: we could use a dash of it.

When the teams came out to be introduced to the daughter of the European chairman of Coca-Cola ('no disrespect, but you sort of hope for a royal,' Steve Bruce said later of the League Cup's habit of bowing to the sponsor), the relish in the calls of Sealey's name made it clear Schmeichel was less than missed among the masses. The big noise though was for Cantona. After his trials, the reds did their best to let him know someone loved him: 'the Marseillaise' can never have sounded louder at Wembley. He waved back at them. It was about the last thing he did in the game.

From the kickoff the pattern was set. If their fans seemed more charged than ours, so did their players. Their man Richardson dug straight into Keane, studs into the back of his ankles, sending him plunging: rattle them, unbalance the composure, get them going, get them off, that was clearly the Villa instruction. But instead of Keane – ever the bookies' banker to take offence – continuing his goggle-eyed madman performances of the last few weeks, he got up, brushed himself down and trotted away. Whatever the tabloid know-alls had contended, Ferguson was clearly working on the discipline behind the scenes. The only problem was, Keane, not the most sophisticated of thinkers, appeared to be concentrating so hard on keeping his temper, as instructed, he let the game drift away from him. Ince's theory about his tempestuous midfield partner – 'take the fire from his belly and he's not half the player' – was being given a practical demonstration.

Gradually, Richardson began to take control of the midfield, enjoying, in front of his back four, a clean-up rate the West Midlands Police could only dream of. Giggs and Kanchelskis were smothered by two markers each, Cantona was trying to keep out of everything: trouble, controversy, this game. Ince, resolute as ever, couldn't do it all on his own. He was swamped. It seemed inevitable when, after half an hour, Sealey's first action in the game was picking the ball out of his net.

United, overwhelmed as much by the significance of the occasion as by Ron Atkinson's shrewd stifling tactics, sank. The red stands began to heave with impatience, nerves fraying like a crusty's dog lead. Whereas three months ago they were drooling over his every move, people were shouting at Giggs: 'Coomon, Giggs, get in the game,' yelled the man in front of me.

The moment you suspected this was not to be a grand day out was when, from the kickoff for the second half, Giggs's pass bounced off Cantona's heel into Townsend's path.

When Villa scored again, nobody seemed surprised. We gave up and sank into depression: no Coca-Cola fizz, no treble, no history.

Then Hughes, the man genetically programmed never to give up and sink into depression, stabbed in a goal with ten minutes to go.

For a moment, as they poured forward like it was 1979 and the FA Cup final against Arsenal all over again, it really seemed we would do it: desperation the motivating force. With three minutes to go, Hughes slammed a huge shot goalwards. I was up and ready to lose all dignity. But Bosnich, once of United's youth team and a goalkeeper who, after an outrageous foul in the semi-final, enjoyed a better relationship with referees than Schmeichel, produced a wonder save. The resulting corner was cleared, they broke upfield and what happened next summed up what had happened to our season.

Kanchelskis was the only man close enough to track back. As Saunders drew Sealey and shot, as the ball made its way towards the United net, the Ukrainian, on a goal-line, stuck out an arm. Not just a penalty, a deliberate hand-ball. The referee came towards him and, as he stared at it in smiling disbelief, showed him the red card. Kanchelskis, the least worldly, the least aggressive, the last likely to whinge, had been sent off. It had reached the level of farce now. Four off in five games. He stood in weary shame behind the goal as Saunders scored from the penalty. There was only one comfort to draw from the final whistle which came a minute later: at least Eric was still on the field at the end of the game.

In the centre circle the Villa players turned cartwheels and formed human pyramids of triumph. I watched as Cantona sought each of them to congratulate them. I watched as Fergie found Ron Atkinson and put a congratulatory palm on his neck. I watched as Giggs and Brian Kidd tried to console Kanchelskis. Not whingers all the time then.

I watched too as Les Sealey, after the medals had been presented, came over to wave up at the family section. Behind me the Sealeys' morale looked beyond the reach even of a faith healer. Les was not to play for United again; when Schmeichel was injured towards the end of the season, it was the long-serving, former youth player Gary Walsh who deputised (coming on at Ipswich to the inquiry from the home fans: 'Who the fucking hell are you?'). In his last few weeks at the club, before he disappeared in the close season, Les walked around, Paul Ince said, 'with his chin down a bit'. Not even folk heroes last for ever.

On my way out of the ground I ran into Tony the T-shirt man from Budapest. He said: 'They didn't deserve that, did they? They didn't. Did they? Not Kanchelskis. Of all people, not Andrei.' And back along Wembley Way the mood was depressed, down. Given the choice of three trophies, the Coca-Cola was the one you could do without. But the real downer was that the treble, the one thing Liverpool had never done, had gone with it. What was worse, we had fallen at the first fence; Becher's and the Chair were still to come. 'We're gonna do the double,' someone chanted on the tube south. He didn't sound convinced. How could we win anything the way morale had been punctured? More to the point, how could we win anything with Cantona out of action for five games?

Pat Crerand told me that just after Cantona had destroyed Aston Villa at Old Trafford in December, he had been at a sporting function in Manchester when the Frenchman himself had walked into the room.

'Everyone present just stood up and applauded,' Crerand said. 'I'd not seen that before with a player. Never. Not Robson, not Hughes, not even Bobby. But with Cantona, they were up. The only other person I had ever seen that happen to was Sir Matt.'

Sir Matt Busby took ten years to build a reputation of total pre-eminence at Old Trafford: it had taken Eric Cantona two. If Les Sealey had brought a bit of luck to the club, Cantona had brought conviction, certainty, an arrogant self-assurance that they were, indeed, the best team in the land.

When he arrived in November 1992, United were flagging. It looked as if the collapse in the run-in during the previous season had removed the guts from the side: they couldn't stop drawing, couldn't start scoring. Then Alex Ferguson announced an unexpected signing from Leeds. I remember exactly what I was doing at the moment the news broke (for United fans, an occasion every bit as historic as the assassination of President Kennedy): I was sitting at my desk when David Robson, my boss, a Leeds fan who had all summer taunted me with his comparisons of Cantona and Pelé, Cantona and Cruyff, Cantona and Clark Kent's alter ego, came over in shock.

'Check the Reuter wire,' he said. And walked away into his office and a three-month gloom.

There it was, called up on my computer screen, the news in fluorescent green and white. And my first thought was: shit, that means he's going to flog Hughes.

I always used to name Alan Brazil in my worst-ever United line-up (that's what masochists do in pubs, reminisce over who gave them least pleasure) because he was, well, one of the worst footballers I ever saw in a red shirt. But I stopped doing so when I discovered that during his mercifully brief sojourn at Old Trafford, Brazil would throw up before every game, his guts sent into free fall by the fearful task ahead: scoring a goal for Manchester United.

Eric Cantona, as we all soon discovered, is not like that. He did not fit into the ignominious line which stretched from Ted MacDougall through Terry Gibson to, call me unkind, Dion Dublin, of United panic-buy goal-scorers. Eric was not worried about Old Trafford. The concept of such self-doubt is inconceivable in the mighty organ that is his brain. For most of his career he had been searching for a place that he felt was an appropriate platform for his extravagant skills and he appeared to have found it.

'It can be a daunting place for some footballers and it has destroyed one or two of them down the years. But Eric just swaggered in, stuck out his chest and looked around. He surveyed everything as though he were asking: I'm Cantona, how big are you? Are you big enough for me? I knew we had something special then,' Alex Ferguson remembered.

To paraphrase JFK in reverse: Ask not what I can do for Old Trafford, but what Old Trafford can do for me.

You cannot fault Cantona for effort in his search for a satisfactory employer. In France after establishing himself as a national hero when France won the European under–21 championship, he played for six clubs in six years. Not only did he own the finest talent since Platini, he seemed to have a capacity for pushing the self-destruct button that would have impressed Kurt Cobain. Behind him in his path across the country he left a trail of flung footwear, outraged officials (he called the French national manager what most of us would have liked to call Graham Taylor) and enough video clips of Bruce Lee drop kicks and Big Daddy head butts to fill an entire series of 'Fantasy Football League'.

Plus he scored a few corking goals and won a cup or two.

In the summer of 1991 he had packed in football altogether, so unconvinced was he of domestic French football's ability to satisfy his needs. Then Michel Platini, now the national manager and a long-time believer that Cantona and talent were joined at birth, pointed out to him that there were some decent clubs in England, so why not start again. Via Chris Waddle, his old team-mate at Marseille, Sheffield Wednesday were tipped off that he was in the market. Trevor Francis invited him over for a week's trial, at the end of which he suggested that Eric might stay on for a second week. (Couldn't quite make up his mind about him, he said. You know, what with that reputation and all.) Eric was almost as baffled as he was insulted.

'Sheffield is too cold anyway,' he said, as he decided not to take up the generous Francis offer.

Something of a meteorological aberration, then, that saw him fetch up in Leeds. Initially, at least, Howard Wilkinson did not need convincing of the Cantona talent. A goal against Chelsea, where he flicked the ball off knee and toe, over heads and into the goal without it once touching the turf, was enough to convince anyone. It certainly convinced the Leeds fans, used as they were to watching Lee Chapman. They loved him, particularly when his goals took Leeds to the title in 1992. He appeared to be continuing where he had left off when, in the Charity Shield the following season, he scored a hat trick. Whole warehouses in West Yorkshire were put aside for 'Ooh-aah Cantona' T-shirts. But the swag workers, going long on Cantona staying white, had reckoned without Howard Wilkinson.

There was much ribald speculation in the United stands as to why Cantona made such a hasty withdrawal from Leeds when he was performing so spunkily. Sadly, the real reason, it appears, was more mundane. There was a disagreement – about being substitute.

Howard Wilkinson is known as Sergeant Wilko to the Elland Road fans, and aptly so. He belongs to the prevalent British football management tradition which believes in treating players like a cross between schoolboys and soldiers; give them discipline and take away decision-making. Cantona was different, he took an anarchistic view of that sort of imposition. So when Wilkinson, despite all the boy's triumphs, insisted on playing him as substitute, he complained. Wilkinson didn't like it. And so he dropped Cantona to sub again. And again Cantona complained. In a management system which, by its very make-up, centres around the manager (no one else is given the room to make decisions), any deviance is interpreted as confrontation. What with Cantona's reputation, this was confrontation.

It seems absurd in an adult world that an argument over substitution could lead to the best player for a generation leaving a club for its sworn enemies for about a fifth of his true value. But it's easy to see how it happened. Wilkinson was the boss and if he said someone was sub, they were sub. Cantona has a need to feel his peers and employers share his own high opinion of himself. He took the substitute issue as an insult, whether one was intended or not.

In his book (the title of which somehow, en route across the Channel, managed to change from the poetic – *Un Rêve Modeste et Fou:* a modest and foolish dream – to the prosaic – *Eric Cantona: My Story*), Cantona sees his battle with Wilkinson as one of ego. He claims Wilkinson drove him out of Elland Road because he was jealous of the acclaim he was attaining, of the rapport he had achieved with the fans. He wasn't the only one, he said; Wilkinson got rid of other players too – Batty, Vinny Jones, Rocastle – because they were too popular on the terraces.

When the book was published, just before the FA Cup quarter-final, it generated enough controversy to keep the publishers in lunches for a year. The *Sun*, as well as printing a picture of Eric naked in the shower, granted Howard Wilkinson a right to reply. It was not the most self-analytical piece of justification ever set to print. In it Wilkinson said he did not drive Cantona out. Cantona had not been prepared to accept decisions made for the good of the club and had got his agent to agitate for a transfer. Wilkinson had the faxes to prove it. He also, unconsciously, revealed precisely what Cantona was on about: he defended his decision to sell by claiming the Frenchman was causing unrest in the dressing room. The other players, he wrote, 'did not like the adulation he was getting'.

So one day in November 1992, Wilkinson called Alex Ferguson at The Cliff looking to buy Denis Irwin. He got short shrift. But Ferguson said he was on the lookout for a striker, was Lee Chapman available? No, said Wilkinson, but Cantona was. We'll have him, Fergie said, and left the fee bargaining to Martin Edwards. When Edwards called him later on his car phone to tell him the deal was complete, Fergie nearly crashed when he heard the price.

At Old Trafford, Eric Cantona discovered not just a magnificent stadium, not just a team of incredibly high potential, but also a manager perfectly able to accommodate him and his extravagant self-will. Since Ferguson had long since subsumed his own ego into the fabric of Old Trafford, he was never remotely threatened by Cantona's celebrity. He could be as big as he liked as long as he did the business on the field for Manchester United, because that was all Ferguson was interested in.

And do the business he did.

With his collar up, his chin thrust aggressively forwards, he strutted and clucked across the Old Trafford pitch from the off, the new cock of the walk. Arrogance is a very attractive quality if it is enlisted on your behalf. United fans immediately took to Cantona's contempt for all other forms of life, from Swiss referees to Swindon midfield players. Chants were invented, T-shirts printed, the full adoration business moved into overdrive.

The United players similarly took to their new colleague's inner certainty; after all the self-doubt they had experienced in 1992, here was someone who did not contemplate failure. What's more, his style of play perfectly complemented the personnel he found himself working alongside. Far from being bought to replace the venerable Hughes, the two struck up an understanding which had long been considered beyond the Welshman. And the Cantona ability to weight a pass for Kanchelskis, Giggs or Sharpe, to put a ball out to the wings so that they didn't have to break stride, to be able to judge almost how fast the full backs facing them were, was repaid by their willingness to run for him, and by their ability to cross the ball in time for his late run into the box. At last he could spray passes to players who could do things with them. That made a change. And they seemed mature enough to trust him. He could be the pivot and everyone let him get on with it. That really did make a change.

'He's the extra dimension,' Giggs said, in a remark that typifies the respect Cantona has earned in the United dressing room. 'Even if you try to mark him, he'll create space for himself. And while you're on him, you've got Sparky or Andrei in the extra space, loving it, so you might be better off leaving him to it.'

Cantona appeared to be good at everything: shooting, passing, heading. Alex Ferguson saw all these qualities stemming from the same salient source.

'It's his balance,' he drooled after a typical Cantona performance. 'He seems to suspend himself in the air and he still controls it. He seems to pirouette. He never goes down under a challenge.'

Cantona himself may have a florid explanation for his ability: 'I imagine the ball to be alive, sensitive, responding to the touch of my foot, to my caresses, like a woman with the man she loves.'

But others saw a more basic source for his success:

'I'm a bad trainer,' said Paul Ince. 'Me and Pallister, that's the English way, innit, moaning about work and that. Eric, he's out before us, out doing his stretching, exercising. Last back too, stays out there, working on his skills. Takes a pride and joy in being at the peak. It brushes off, that attitude.'

This was the Cantona United discovered: everything about him commands attention. According to Giggs, who clearly finds the very ground he treads on to be touched by his presence, he is 'a class dresser, can wear anything and just looks cool.'

And Ferguson, perhaps sensing this was a rapacious ego that needed constant feeding, could not stop praising him. After Cantona scored with a perfect lob at Southampton, Fergie said: 'I told Ryan Giggs when he sat next to me on the bench, when you reach that level of accuracy, you can call yourself a player. I told him he was watching a master at work.'

But this didn't mean that his colleagues understood him. Not even Peter Schmeichel with whom he shares hotel rooms on away games can put a finger on him. Particularly not Schmeichel. Whereas, when he arrives at The Cliff, the goalkeeper parks as close as he can to the changing rooms and dashes inside to avoid contact with the fans, Cantona, as at Leeds, cannot do enough for the anoraks out there. He will spend up to an hour in the car park signing autographs, chatting, posing for pictures, anxious to let the faithful know he appreciates their affection. A red I know came across him in his local pub once, where he was playing bar football. Cantona, he said, was patience itself, smiling indulgently at the lad's pathetic French, not the Gallic sneer.

In every respect Cantona is not like the others. And it isn't just the language, the fact that he hunts, or that his wife, rather than spending the day at home cleaning the house in the usual run of football wives, is a university lecturer. Nor is it the poetry, the philosophy and the painting.

'Have you seen any of Eric's paintings?' Giggsy was asked by *For Him* magazine.

'No,' was the reply. 'He lives in Leeds.'

What his team-mates find most unconventional about him is that he is not a man who takes an interest in material things. He lives in the most modest of circumstances: a house in Salford, which, the *Mirror* could scarcely believe, cost him £80,000, or six and a half weeks' wages. He drives a club Audi which carried evidence of a smash along its wings and its broken front indicator for most of the season. You can imagine how the accident took place. Cantona, driving too fast, anxious to jump a red light, accelerates into the back of the car in front, which was waiting patiently for the lights to change. As the driver gets out to swap insurance details, he is confronted by Cantona, hands outstretched, a look of contempt on his face, asking him what the bloody hell he thinks he's doing.

Eric's lack of financial fascination is not the way of his colleagues, with their new executive homes in Cheshire with private security, golf courses over the back fence and big motors in the drives. Nevertheless, he wields the tastiest contract in the club. This is because he expects to be rewarded in a manner commensurate with his value: since he is the best player, he expects the most reward. It is a coincidence that the reward happens to be monetary.

However hard Eric trained, however well he played, however fetchingly the hideous nylon smock that passes as a United shirt sat on his shoulders, however much he appeared to be playing for the sake of it and not for financial return, there were those who suspected this differentness about him.

Take George Graham, a manager who does not find skill the most persuasive of a footballer's qualities. After all, he could have boasted Merson and Limpar on his wings, but more often than not played with neither. It was no surprise that it was Graham, in a brilliant, combative interview by Joe Lovejoy, who articulated the suspicion many held. He described Cantona as 'a cry baby who will let you down at the highest level'.

What highest level Graham was talking about he did not elucidate. At most important matches, Cantona has performed: as an international, he was one of the few not to make a complete fool of himself during France's World Cup non-qualification debacle; he scored twice for United in the European Cup, saving a thirty-six-year-old record with his goal against Galatasaray at home; he scored a hat trick for Leeds at Wembley; and every week at the summit of the Premiership, he has played like a man in receipt of a special bounty from on high.

To give Graham credit, when he said it, this was not a fashionable position to take. But as Eric's stock sunk lower than shares in Millwall, it became the received wisdom. Everywhere his past performances were post-rationalised. Howard Wilkinson justified his decision to sell thus:

'He has weakness. I recall him playing at Liverpool and Ronnie Whelan had a dig at him after ten minutes. We hardly saw him after that. I used to watch Bobby Charlton, Denis Law and George Best. They would perform week in, week out.'

Which made you wonder, did Howard Wilkinson see Best in 1973?

He continued: 'They would take on unfamiliar roles that might not have been to their liking. But they had a commitment to the cause, they wanted to win for the team. How does Eric Cantona compare to them? I'm afraid he does not pass that exam.'

Unlike presumably, Brian Deane, the lumbering and labouring forward bought, for twice the money, by Wilkinson to replace him. Or the lovely Carlton Palmer, who Wilko regarded as two and a half times Cantona's worth.

In a jaunty piece of cod psychoanalysis in the *Sunday Times*, Chris Lightbown, not a United admirer, used the evidence of the Coca-Cola Cup final to reinforce the Graham view. Cantona was cast as the Graeme Hick of football, a man who could slaughter the medium pace of weekly Premiership opposition, but rarely reached double figures when exposed to the quickies of big matches. Even my boss, David Robson, joined the party.

'Of course George Graham was right,' he said. 'Cantona let us down in the European Cup.'

Leeds' failure against Rangers in 1992 has thus been mythologised as the fault of Eric, who did not manage to score and was substituted, rather than their keeper John Lukic, say, who punched the ball into his own net.

But one thing about this analysis: didn't Cantona's wild streak of ill discipline at Norwich and Swindon, the latest in a career-long catalogue of those red-mist moments, provide the clincher that it was correct? He was a man who would let you down, if only by getting himself suspended from the period of the season when you most needed his divine assistance. Alex Ferguson didn't see it like that. In public, at least, he suggested Cantona was a victim of reputation: opponents out to test his fuse; referees jumping to the wrong conclusions.

'That lad himself knows he shouldn't have done what he did,' he told his old confidant Hugh McIlvanney. 'But he has none of the calculated malice shown by others in our football. There are players in the Premier League who put photographs up on their dressing room wall before a game to focus their minds on opponents they mean to take care of. These are men who set their stall out to wind people up, sort people out. Everybody in the game knows who they are and how long they have been at it. Are Cantona's unpremeditated outbursts as bad as that?'

Whoever was right, we now faced five games without the man who made the difference.

16

One Gone, Two To Go

*Easter time is very vital/That's when we decide
the title.*
From 'Gosh It's Tosh', the collected poetry
of John Toshack

Three days after the Coca-Cola Cup went flat, Liverpool were at
Old Trafford. And behind me in the press box, the match commentator from Merseyside's Radio City station said, 'Sixteen minutes
gone and no sign of United ill discipline yet. Let's hope it stays that
way.'

That's how we were presented as the Premiership reached its
nub: a red card waiting to be presented. It was conveniently forgotten that the great Busby side was equally acquainted with the early
bath: Law, Stiles, Best – off, off, off; ten times in an eighteen-month
period at the end of the sixties. But no, our new reds were reckoned
to be uniquely morally dubious. In that climate, Alex Ferguson
decided after the treble was lost that his players would not assist
the press in their assassination attempts.

'I have no arguments with the Coca-Cola result,' he told me.
'Villa set out with very clear tactics, took the lead and defended it
brilliantly. It was up to us to take the game to them and we found
that we couldn't. In the course of a season when you play so many
games, you can't expect to be good in every one of them. And we
weren't good in that one. But the thing is, lads are coming up to
me and complaining about this or that thing which is being written
about them. About how certain journalists are putting their arm
round them and treating them as mates one week, then the next
writing . . .'

He paused to search for a sufficiently contemptuous word.

'. . . stuff. So after the final I took the decision that none of the players should talk to the press until the Premiership was finished. We decided that we should allow no one to undermine our effort and determination. I will do the talking to the press, and the players can concentrate on their football. The journalists can get whatever they need from me. As a club we can speak with one voice. My voice.'

The Liverpool fans were speaking with one voice, too. One which relished every moment of their rivals' discomfort. Liverpool–United games often involve props. Once, a busload of reds went to Anfield dressed as Harry Enfield Scousers: shell-suits, perm wigs, 'taches and cries of 'Go 'ed, eh.' For Eric's last performance before his mid-season, short break in France, the Merseyside supporters had come to Old Trafford bearing large red cards. When Schmeichel's name, Kanchelskis's name and, particularly Cantona's name were announced, before the kickoff, they brandished the cards as one and chanted, 'Off, off, off.' Whatever the poison between the two sets of supporters, you would have to have been a curmudgeon indeed not to smile at that one. Giggs was off the case, too. He was, after a listless performance at Wembley, on the subs' bench.

There had been a growing discontent in the stands with Giggs. A friend of mine, who supports Charlton, sat in the Stretford End for the FA Cup tie and he told me the thing that amazed him most about his visit to Old Trafford was that the reds around him were slagging off Giggs:

'Having a go at the best player of his generation, the best player I have ever seen in the flesh,' he said. 'Unbelievable. They should come down to the Valley sometime and see how bloody lucky they are.'

He was partly right: the impatience with Giggs and his form among the United faithful was, in a way, the product of the greedy getting indigestion.

'People forget he's only young,' Paul Ince said. 'He's so class, and people expect it every week. The last four or five weeks people have been putting him down. But you've got to remember he's only twenty and he's playing fifty games.'

But the worry in the stands was that he was not pulling his weight for reasons beyond mere tiredness. Twice I heard the rumour that he hadn't trained for six weeks and was suffering from ME – which was one more letter than the ailment which was alleged to have been the cause for another player's absence a couple of seasons ago. ME, the medical experts in the red ranks reckoned, explained it. And if it didn't, then his form was gone because he had already signed for Milan and, like Hughes in 1986 when he had enrolled with Barcelona in February and stopped scoring on the spot, was trying to keep out of the way of injury.

It later transpired that Giggs had indeed been ill – regularly succumbing to sore throats, dizzy spells, sinusitis; he was to have his swollen and diseased tonsils removed immediately at the season's end. The illness had exhausted him and his form had dipped correspondingly. But in the trench warfare of Premiership football, such information is not released; it might give comfort to enemies. And this means that rumours go forth and terrify the faithful.

The game against Liverpool was not a great United performance. Cantona was preoccupied, passes went astray more frequently than letters on a post round in Kirkby. Fortunately, though, Liverpool's Redknapp, giving a performance Ince later reckoned to be the best from an opponent all season, found none of his colleagues capable of taking advantage of his shrewd promptings and clever runs. Nothing is crueller than sporting decline. And Liverpool were in full decline. Barnes looked about fifteen stone; Whelan looked incapable of kicking the ball more than two feet; Rush looked lost; once he was at the head of the slickest animal in British football, now he was playing in front of a team of dullards.

Liverpool lacked nothing in effort, it was ambition they were short of. They took the standard tactical line against United, strung five men across the midfield to reduce the space, and then kicked. It was a battle out there. Hughes, never afraid to match robust with robust, took an elbow in the face. As he lay on the ground, Ferguson had to be restrained by a policeman from leading a one-man retribution party.

But the crucial moment came late in the second half, long after Ince had thumped home a header at the near post. Kanchelskis had just seen Giggs warming up and, assuming it was him as usual to be substituted, trotted with a resigned smile on his face, towards the touchline. He was halfway to the dugout when Ince pointed out to him that it was Sharpe to come off. Kanchelskis celebrated his reprieve by tracking Thomas back into the area and apparently hauling him to the ground: the second time in a week it was clear he might not possess the defensive wherewithal to make a sweeper in the latter stages of his career. Keith Hackett, the referee, about two yards from play, peeped for a penalty. But a linesman, forty yards away on the other side of the pitch, was waving his flag like an overexcited semaphore operator. Mr Hackett trotted over, consulted him, and changed the award to a free kick to us. The linesman had spotted Thomas getting his retaliation in first.

'We love you linesman, we do,' chanted the Scoreboard boys. Not a chant heard frequently at football grounds that one.

Ten minutes later, it was all over. Liverpool were unable to take advantage, no matter how hard they tried. At this stage of the season, a scrappy 1–0 was manna. Blackburn, the night before, had been hammered at Wimbledon. So they were back to three points behind, with eight to play. Perhaps, Alex Ferguson suggested, they were now beginning to know what pressure was themselves.

After the game, in front of the press box, a middle-aged man in a sheepskin coat danced around between the empty seats, shouting up at Fleet Street's finest: 'What are you going to write about now, yer bastards, eh? No one sent off and we bastard well won. What are you going to say now?'

In the press lounge, as we waited for Ferguson to appear, we didn't have long to find out. The television was switched directly to the BBC cameras in the ground. There on the screen, in an unedited live transmission, was – my word – John Motson. When Roy Evans, Liverpool's charisma-free new boss appeared, apparently to be interviewed by him, Mottie said: 'Well, Roy, how are you. Thanks so much for coming down, appreciate it in the circumstances.'

Evans muttered something inaudible and Mottie continued with what he assumed was unrecorded small talk.

'To be honest, Roy, I don't know how you saw it, but the linesman had no business to be flagging for a foul, none at all.'

'He'll have his trousers off next,' said one of the eavesdropping hacks standing at the bar.

Evans, fresh from Mottie's fearless, probing interrogation, was first in the press room. He seemed to have swapped roles with Ferguson. He was barely concealing his simmering fury at referees, at the media, at anyone who came in his way.

'There were players on that pitch who did so many fouls that went unpunished it was ridiculous,' he spluttered.

How did he read the penalty? an excited Liverpool-based reporter asked. ''Cos it was one, wannit?'

'On the day he refereed poorly,' said Evans. 'In fact he didn't referee at all, the linesman did it for him.'

Imagine the headlines if Ferguson had said that after being denied a penalty: 'Moan United'.

Instead, following up, Fergie oozed magnanimity, first-naming the referee like an old chum. 'Keith handled the game extremely well,' he said. 'It needed a man of his experience. It's his last game, he goes out in the knowledge that all pros will miss him. A man of his experience will be missed.'

Perhaps not down the other end of the East Lancs Road.

Someone asked him how he had seen Liverpool. They had seemed charged up.

'Liverpool's two best games this season have been against us. It's a reverse of the eighties when Liverpool were dominant and we reserved our best for against them. It's an interesting topic that. Mebbe the power has shifted. You're talking about pride. Liverpool players showed pride, they ran the extra yard, tackled the extra seven pounds harder. Exactly as United used to do against them.'

Hadn't it got a little over-hairy out there, someone said.

'Oh ay, bloody hell. You expect that, come on.'

Why had he got so upset when Hughes was downed? someone else asked. Was it an elbow?

'Youse better say something about that, because I won't,' he said, getting up to go. 'At least you won't have a go at us for a change. It's time for you media to ease off us a bit.'

We won't, someone said.

'I know you won't,' said Fergie. 'We're Christmas every day for youse lot.'

The Christmas wrapping filled the papers for the next few days, in the run-up to the Easter Saturday showdown at Ewood Park. Easter had been the crunch in the previous two seasons: in 1992, it was when we had come unstuck. In 1993 it was when Steve Bruce, at the end of injury time so lengthy it was almost Whitsun by the time they had finished, scored the winner against Sheffield Wednesday. Now it was Blackburn. And the press had convinced themselves which of the two last seasons was to get a repeat showing.

'You wouldn't back United, now, even with their three-point advantage,' said the ever-prescient John Sadler in the *Sun*. 'Well, I wouldn't. I believe the initiative has swung Blackburn's way.'

'United will crack,' reckoned Chris Lightbown in the *Sunday Times*. 'Blackburn won't.'

'It is Blackburn for me,' said jolly John Fashanu in the *Mirror*.

'At the moment we appear to be the people's favourites,' said Kenny Dalglish, interviewed everywhere. 'Maybe the behaviour of United on the pitch, and the reputation it has earned them, has gone in our favour.'

Still, one thing. At least we had accumulated enough points to avoid relegation.

If, in the future, you meet someone who says they haven't missed a United fixture for years, ask them how they got a ticket for the Blackburn game on Easter Saturday, 1994. With Ewood Park under reconstruction, less than two thousand places were given to United followers. This meant, if you wanted to go, string-pulling, contact-

stroking and visits to the cash point were required in the ferment
for a seat, tales of Blackburn fans leasing out their season tickets for
the day circulated, rumours of military campaigns to crash the
turnstiles emerged, stories surfaced of how, if you turned up in a
construction worker's helmet, you could blag your way on to the
building site which ran along one touchline.

Me, I had acquired a ticket in a particularly satisfying manner. A
fortnight before the game, my friend Simon rang to say he could
make me very happy. He had a pair: the brother of a colleague of
his was a Blackburn director and was happy to provide them, gratis.

The week of the game, Simon rang again.

'Guess what,' he said. 'My mate's brother, the Blackburn director,
he's just rung up my mate, hasn't he. He said it was unusual to hear
of two Rovers fans in London and wanted to know how long we'd
been following them. My mate said to him, they're not Rovers,
they're ManU. The bloke nearly had heart failure. He is well
unhappy.'

'Oh shit,' I said. 'So that's it. No tickets.'

'No. That's why he had heart failure,' said Simon. 'He's already
posted the bastards.'

We sat in a row in the Blackburn End stand that was populated
entirely by United supporters. I asked everyone on it how they had
got their tickets. Each had a chapter of minor corruption and palm-
lining to relate:

'I got mine from a mate who works for the match sponsors. They
got given a load, and he didn't want to come,' said one lad.

Had he paid face value? I asked.

'Oh aye,' he said, making a sarcastic face. 'Fifty pounds for a
fifteen-pound seat he charged me.'

Another man had, like us, contacts in the Rovers boardroom,
while a third said: 'I live in Blackburn, I work in Blackburn. I know
who to ask.'

I asked him how much he had paid.

'Let's just say, if you know who to ask, you know you'll be paying
for it.'

I had plenty of time to work out how much revenue an attendance

202 Are You Watching, Liverpool?

of 20,886 had generated on the black market. The kickoff was a Sky-enforced five o'clock job – which, on a Saturday, has its compensations: you could get a full afternoon's drinking in first. After asking directions to the ground from a helpful citizen of the town ('if you don't know where it is, you must be United, so I'm not sure as how I'm going to tell you'), Simon and I went to a pub, just a sing-song from Ewood Park. We stood there like hamburgers in Linda McCartney's freezer, as the local crush watched the Cup final-style build-up on the pub television, jeering every mention of United, cheering every mention of Rovers, consuming gallons of liquid atmosphere, chanting over and again their one song: 'There's only one Alan Shearer.'

Half an hour before kickoff, just as games were reaching their climax around the country, we made our way to the new stadium being built on the site of the old one by Jack Walker, Blackburn's cash-happy benefactor. It is a bizarre sight, rising in steel and concrete above the cobbles and the back-to-backs like the spaceship from *Close Encounters* had landed on the set of a 1960s film starring Albert Finney. The Blackburn End stand wasn't nearly completed. Rushed open to accommodate those with a newly discovered interest in Rovers, the banqueting suites and executive boxes lay unopened, bare and dusty: as they will do again when Rovers' success wanes. Despite the modernisation, there were one or two touches evocative of the old days about the place: the impossible queue for the programme stall, the fact that the gents can stand only seven at a time, which meant, given the afternoon's preamble, that the concourse quickly became one long, desperate line. As everyone queued everywhere, news came over the public-address system of the full-time results. As usual in these provincial parts the biggest cheer was reserved for a Burnley defeat.

Up on the moor, which looked down over the roof of the modestly named Walkersteel stand, huddles of those with fewer contacts than us stood, braced against the elements. It was a crazy April day. The weather was well in tune with United's season. The game started with crisp sunlight casting shadows of building work over the pitch: by half-time clouds blacker and more billowing than Lee Sharpe's away shorts scudded across the sky.

Though it was announced before the game that Kevin Moran had won the £500 Rovers prize draw (murmurs of fix filled the ground), it was Shearer's day. He was class. There have been many explanations as to why he went to Blackburn instead of United when both clubs were in the hunt for his signature from Southampton. The one most commonly touted at Old Trafford is that it was financial – that he was lured by the Walker booty, enough to keep him and his progeny in chicken and beans for generations to come. It is a theory summed up in the parody of the Blackburn song, which runs: 'There's only one greedy bastard.' Another, more conspiratorially, suggests that Ferguson would have met Shearer's demands, but he was held back by the United board anxious not to break the pay structure, to show a profit and pay out hefty dividends: the City-stalls-progress-on-the-field theory. Either way, on that Easter Saturday, we could have done with him. Even had Cantona been available.

Shearer scored his first – a goal which proved, judging by the affection pouring from the Blackburn sections, that money can buy you love – so soon after half-time that many were still queueing for the facilities, craning their necks to watch the action on television monitors suspended over the concourse. They were back in their seats in time for his second, however, a goal of power and precision, when he shouldered Pallister out of the way and blistered a shot apparently through Schmeichel.

At that one a bonfire was lit up on the moor. It wasn't clear if this was by Blackburn fans wanting to communicate the news over the hill to Burnley or by United fans burning their betting slips. It was soon doused by a hailstorm chucking down enough ice to chill champagne throughout Lancashire. By then, big gaps had opened up in the United supporters' section, an apt metaphor for our defence.

Actually, we had not played that badly: Ince had hit the post, Flowers had made a miracle save from Kanchelskis. This wasn't a game, like against Chelsea or Galatasaray, where we had cocked up. It was just that the opposition, and it hadn't happened before that season, were better than us: Shearer, Batty and Flowers, a spine worth its weight in steel.

Back in the pub after it was over, we stood there, Simon and I, the beer refusing to go down, watching Sky's post-mortem, as around us hundreds sang of how they were walking in a Shearer Wonderland.

'What a game that was,' the barman said to me.

'I didn't think so,' I said.

'Ha ha ha,' he replied, clocking my not-quite-as-lucky-as-it-was badge. 'Ha ha ha.'

Nineteen ninety-two it was to be, Simon and I decided. And suddenly Oldham, who we had drawn in the FA semi-final, had ceased to be a walkover and become a frightening proposition.

The only thing that cheered us up was when we left the pub. A car full of reds drove past. The lad in the passenger seat, reasonably enough assuming us to be locals, stuck his head out of the window and inquired, 'Where were you when you were shite?'

17

The Boss

The geezer never stops amazing me.
                                    Les Sealey

On the plane to Hungary, Patrick Barclay had a little football teaser to keep the members of the press occupied between passes-by of the drinks trolley:

'Which British city has had two clubs play in the European Cup?' he asked. 'Neither of which has failed to reach the semi-final.'

We all struggled there. It couldn't have been Liverpool, we thought, because surely there had been times they hadn't made it to the semis. Everton's European Cup record was modest. And it certainly wasn't Manchester. City let the side down there.

'They lost to a bunch of Turks in the first round,' I said, without the benefit of foresight.

Alex Ferguson, hearing us struggle, asked to be included: he is a librarian for a stat, a sucker for a bit of football triv.

'C'mon, Paddy,' he pleaded. 'What's the question?'

Barclay told him and he was off. As he ran through London ('nah, can't be') Manchester, Liverpool, Glasgow ('nah, Rangers got knocked out in the mini-league last year'), he kept asking Barclay to repeat the question. On one occasion, Brian McClair, sitting two rows in front of him, heard it and immediately came up with the answer.

'Dundee,' he said. 'Dundee in nineteen sixty-three, Dundee United in nineteen eighty-four.'

'Correct,' said Paddy. 'Alex, Brian's got the answer.'

'Don't bloody tell me,' said Ferguson. 'I'll get it mesself.'

And he kept at it, like a pitbull with a bone drained of marrow. Ten minutes later, when Barclay, when McClair, when everyone else had forgotten he was still on the case, he got it. And he made sure everyone knew he had.

I thought of that episode after the Blackburn game. Then, so relaxed in the company of the press boys. Now, in a state of war.

As Ferguson stood in the middle of the punctured enterprise of United's faltering season, the media portrayed him not as the man with the repair kit, but as the one with the needle. The analytical coverage was lengthy: there was the old theory rehearsed, the one about the wobbles of 1992 and him being so twitchy he could communicate nerves to a Mogadon addict. There was another, too, a new one proposed by Eamon Dunphy in *The Independent on Sunday*. He said Ferguson was to blame for United's sudden decline and the drift into ill discipline because, so in love was he with his team, he had not applied appropriate sanction at the right time. He had given the wrong signal after the Sheffield United Cup tie, when he should have publicly chastised Hughes. Instead, he had let him get away with a piece of silliness by publicly saying he was not to blame. The whole team had followed the Wrexham bull, overstepping into self-destruct. As they did so, Ferguson said they were blameless and if they weren't, then someone else's crime was greater than theirs. Even Hugh McIlvanney had grown anguished, finding it hard to arrive at an explanation for the manner in which the United boss continually defended the despicable.

'His interpretation of the troubles that beset his team is sometimes irrationally subjective to the point of being an insult to his own high intelligence,' McIlvanney wrote in the *Sunday Times*.

The media were demanding a sacrificial lamb: it was up to Ferguson to make an example of someone, to prove that he was in control of the classroom. And if he didn't do it, to their satisfaction, it was proof of his culpability.

But he wouldn't do it. Instead he hit back. He stopped his players talking and complained endlessly of unfair treatment.

'People ask you questions and you give honest answers and they call you a whinger,' he said.

At every turn, he made it worse. And it occurred to me that maybe that's the way he liked it. Maybe he was doing this on purpose. Maybe a state of siege suited him best.

I ran Mark McGhee who played under Ferguson at Aberdeen and is now manager at Reading, to ask him how Fergie had operated in Scotland, to see if he could identify the method. McGhee is widely regarded as one of the sharpest young managers around, and he is clear as to who his role model is.

'Oh aye, Alec,' he said. 'What I've taken from Alec is the fundamental values of being a manager. He won't let anything deflect him from the important issues which have to be addressed: understanding his players strengths and weaknesses, analysing the opposition and motivating his players to use their strengths to overcome them. It sounds obvious, but when you become a manager, you discover how many other things get in the way which might take your mind off that.'

How did he motivate his players at Aberdeen, I wondered?

'Alec is a terrible loser. Terrible,' McGhee said. 'Whether at cards, at a trivia quiz, at football, it hurts him physically to lose. And he makes sure you know how much it hurts him. He sees football as a cause, a cause to which he expects you to give 100 per cent. Everything else is secondary. And I mean everything else.'

How did he communicate his passion, I asked. In his team talks?

'It is not so much in his team talks, no,' said McGhee. 'To be honest, I felt towards the end at Aberdeen that his team talks were getting a little repetitive. It is more in his whole attitude. He put pressure on you to perform all the time and he expected you to have the mental strength to withstand it. If you repaid him, he was incredibly loyal to you. I think that was a quality he took from his father. But if you didn't, he wasn't slow to tell you. He's very honest. And it will be the same at United, he will only want people around him who are prepared to accept the challenge, as he calls it. To take on the cause.'

And the cause? What is the cause?
'To prove everybody wrong.'

Alex Ferguson has been convinced that the world has been conspiring against him since his youth in Glasgow when, as a teenager, he organised an illegal strike at the toolmaker's where he worked because he was certain the management were about to cut everyone's wages. He was right. When he was a player, the referees or opposition were out for him, and he often got his revenge in early. Eric Cantona wrote in his book that after he had been sent off in Turkey, Fergie told him not to be too worried about it: he told him that as a player he had not been unfamiliar with the sight of the referee's finger pointing tunnelwards. As a manager at Aberdeen, Fergie was certain it was the snide metropolitans of Glasgow who were out to get him.

'He used to keep a log of how many times we Glasgow-based journalists would come to watch his side and harangue us if it wasn't enough,' one member of the Scottish football writers' corps told me. 'When his team played he reckoned they took on far more than the opposition, they took on us, the refs, the world.'

Ferguson is a clever man, perhaps the most intuitively intelligent football manager in the game. His inner rage was channelled into a superb motivating force for his team on the fringes of Scottish football life. And he smashed the Rangers/Celtic domination, even if it meant smashing a few teacups in the dressing room in the process.

'In a way we all benefited from that,' Alex McLeish, his captain there, said of his boss's crockery demolition habit. 'It made you realise what the game could mean to someone.'

Even so, McGhee said, there was always a sense that the explosions were, in part, a management technique, a reminder of the cause. Indeed when I saw him shaking the dressing room walls with that bollocking in Hungary, his face was rearranged into a mask of composure with such speed the moment he emerged to face the press, it made you wonder which of the two emotions was the real one.

After ten years of success in the north of Scotland, as Mark McGhee had noticed, the satisfaction of proving his critics wrong was wearing thin. The cause needed a fresh challenge. It wasn't managing Scotland, who he took to the 1986 World Cup; it was in England, where he could prove himself to the doubting Jessies down south. In November 1986, Ferguson became United manager, on the recommendation of Bobby Charlton and after taking the advice of Jock Stein, who told him not taking the job when it was offered to him after Busby retired was 'the biggest mistake he had ever made'.

Alex Ferguson likes to take on every aspect of a club he manages. In his early days as boss at St Mirren, for instance, he drove round the roughest part of Paisley with a loudspeaker attached to the roof of his car, haranguing the locals into coming to watch the game. But what he found at United would take more than a bit of DIY publicity to sort out. He found not the dream job, but a mess.

His predecessor, Ron Atkinson, had lost his way. He had sold good and bought bad, the youth policy had surrendered the initiative down the road to City and, if the press thought the present United were ill-disciplined, what was going on in the background then was approaching anarchy. The core of the side had become overacquainted with licensed premises, there were fights in training and on the pitch they would collapse if anyone sneezed at them.

It would take some work to reinvigorate the place.

Alex Ferguson drives a motor which is a byword, Mercedes would have us believe, for comfort, dignity and refinement. If any passing Merc executive saw how Alex Ferguson drove their model of Teutonic sophistication, however, they would wish he ran a Jaguar. One day I was at Littleton Road and saw Fergie driving off back to Old Trafford, conducting a 'Dukes of Hazzard' getaway, scrunching up an arc of gravel into the expensive paintwork of the car behind (it was Paul Parker's Saab and he didn't look impressed). Ferguson drives without regard for shock absorbers, tyre tread or, so those who have been along for the ride suggest, the nervous condition of his passengers. There is one comfort that Merc can draw from the experience of seeing their car treated with all the respect of a

TWOCer in Newcastle, though: at least Fergie doesn't drive the thing as hard as he does himself.

When he arrived at Old Trafford, he set about the place with a gale of energy. He was determined to meet the challenge he had set himself: now the cause was to be as good as Liverpool, the acknowledged kings of English football, the team whose domination in the previous decade made Celtic and Rangers look accommodating. And this new cause would take some work.

His first task was to sort out the dressing room. Ferguson likes a drink, but only in celebration of a job done. With Atkinson's reds it had become part of the daily round. He knew a drying-out was necessary and he would do what was needed, even if it meant clearing out the fans' favourite players. Indeed the concept proposed by Eamon Dunphy, that Fergie was windy of keeping his players in order, would have Paul McGrath cracking open a beer. It would be the only thing to stop him cracking up with laughter. McGrath reckons that during binges with Norman Whiteside and the other members of the United five-a-side drinking team, he could imagine Ferguson plotting the progress on the A–Z.

'Which was just as well,' he said, 'as more often than not Norman and I were in no fit state to know where we were.'

Like many a United fan, though, I was unconvinced by Ferguson when he first came. Some of his stop-gap buys (Mal Donaghy, Viv Anderson, Ralph Milne) seemed no better than some of Atkinson's duff bits of business. He seemed to me tetchy and twitchy under fire, an unattractive proposition. I wasn't the only one – the fanzines were vociferous in their lack of conviction in his ability.

'Yes, we've got a bit of egg on our faces over that now,' said Barney Chilton of *Red News*, whose publication was at the forefront of a 'Fergie out' campaign. 'When he first arrived I thought he was the man for the job. But things started to get so bad within eighteen months that well, we thought he wasn't the man for the job. But maybe with hindsight some of the stuff we printed was OTT.'

John Daniels of *Red Issue* is equally sanguine these days.

'Well, we've had to eat our words a bit over Fergie,' he said. 'But we were never looking to wave flags. We put in the mag what people wrote to us about removing him. It wasn't necessarily the views of the editors, as they say.'

But they weren't the only ones who assumed Ferguson was primed for a close encounter with Martin Edwards's axe in January 1990, and that it was Mark Robins's goal in the third round of the Cup against Forest that saved him. Talking to insiders at the club, however, it seems that was improbable. Ferguson, unlike Atkinson, had friends and allies on the board (notably Bobby Charlton) who would have argued for more time. And in any case, few of those at the club could have failed to be impressed when they saw him at work, by his commitment and his vision. By him.

Alex Ferguson is a rarity: the closer you get to him, the more you watch him in action, the more substantial he becomes. We fans, who see him only through the window of the media, see a wholly misleading picture. He is, for instance, an unexpectedly genial presence around the club.

'Cleaning ladies talk about him as if he were a special friend,' Pat Crerand told me. 'He always has time for the people with lesser roles about the place. It's very much the Busby style.'

Is that learnt behaviour, I wondered, some management consultant technique?

'No, I don't think so,' said Crerand. 'Sure, like a lot of Scots people, he's got a bad temper. A terrible temper.'

Has he. It is an unstated given in every interview conducted with a United player – the Boss and his red mists.

'But underneath it he's warm-hearted,' reckoned Crerand. 'And he's modest, a value he learnt from his father, something people find very attractive in a man of his success.'

And he is a brilliant man-manager, so good, Sir Richard Greenbury, chairman of Marks & Spencer, lunches him regularly for tips. How he creates team spirit is by making his players know for certain that they are the most important element of the enterprise. In public he flatters his players constantly. At a dinner celebrating United's success last season, for instance, after Martin Edwards gave a generous speech about how everyone at United, the back-room staff and the commercial department, had played their part in the march to supremacy, Ferguson followed by saying he was only interested in praising the players: 'they're the ones who count.'

And he has their confidence because they respect him. They respect his abilities on the training field and on the touchline, his swift way of reading a game and remedying deficiencies.

'I sat alongside him a lot last season,' Les Sealey said, 'and I tell you the geezer never stops amazing me. He is so quick tactically. He notices things about what's going on which you haven't even seen until he points them out.'

'If I'm having no change against a full back,' Giggs said, 'or Andrei is, then he'll swap us, or get us to move forward, or drop back, whatever. And whatever he tells us to do, we usually get a better time of it after we have done it.'

What they respond to most in the dressing room is the way he protects them. The way he cushioned Ryan Giggs was not exceptional, it was typical. He believes that for players to perform, they must have their minds singularly concentrated. They need not worry about anything, from arranging a passport to a decent diet, except how they perform on the pitch. He never stops policing them, to keep them safe in their enterprise. On the flight to Hungary, for instance, a film crew recording footage for the United *Video Magazine* started to take shots of the players snoozing in their seats. Ferguson, immediately appreciating the indignity involved in footage doing the rounds of Ince asleep with his mouth open, was up and at them, telling them to stop. I saw him challenging a man on the team bus in Turkey, demanding to know who he was and why he was there with the ferocious inquisitiveness of a Glasgow bouncer. Turned out the man was a friend of a director, entitled to be there, but if he hadn't been, Fergie would have applied his boot to the seat of trousers.

And what he most protects his players from is the press, the pervasive, debilitating press. They can rely on him not to undermine them with an ill-advised public word.

'Nobody gets away with anything here,' he said, when he was challenged about the Dunphy theory. 'Make no mistake about it, there's nothing wrong with a bit of discipline if it's needed and I'm not afraid to give it. When I tell them what I think of them it is in the right place, in the privacy of the dressing room or my office. I will never start slagging players in public. Once you do that, you have lost the bolt off the dressing-room door. My job is not to criticise my players publicly. But when a manager makes a public criticism, he's affecting the emotional stability of a player and that cannot be the professional thing to do. It's more about loyalty than protection.'

When a sports editor is looking for a new football writer, one of the questions he always asks candidates is with which managers are they on special terms: who can they guarantee will give them an exclusive insight. If they say David Pleat, they don't get the job. Everyone is on special terms with David Pleat. There are some managers who love the media, are friends with reporters, enjoy their company and are happy to slip little confidences their way. Alex Ferguson is not one of them: he does not have the smooth, comfortable relationship with the lads that managers like Terry Venables or Ron Atkinson enjoy. He was at the World Cup, but not alongside Brian or John or Barry in the commentary gantry. He views us boys as the least attractive part of his job. He is polite, attentive and efficient, but distant. Always distant. There are not many things he enjoys more than getting one over on us. Once, on a friendly in Portugal, the pack missed the plane home, their coach caught in the Lisbon traffic.

Ferguson's glee that they had been left behind, those who witnessed it say, was only matched by his disappointment when the lads turned up at Manchester on the next scheduled flight almost at the same time as the official party arrived.

He doesn't believe what goes on inside the club is our business, and he will do his best to ensure we don't know any more than he wishes us to.

Thus he has learnt how to perform, something which, according to Mark McGhee, he had to do in Scotland after he found he was giving too much away to too many people. When I first started reporting on United, I dutifully watched the interviews Ferguson gave to television immediately after the game, and wrote down everything he said. Then I would attend the press conference for the print journalists, then try to eavesdrop on the pieces he did for radio. I soon learnt not to bother: he says the same thing to everyone. After a game he composes what he has to say, and sticks with it, to the point of repetitiveness. He believes it is not his job to provide exclusives, but to communicate with the fans, via the media. The only time last season he appeared to be caught off his guard was over the Jimmy Hill outburst after Cantona's first stamping. And even then I'm not sure that there was not a hint of premeditation about it.

Because he does the media no turn with juicy sound bites and pally scoops, they do him none in return. There is no old friendship to be maintained, so the knives can be applied without fear of future favours turned down. And while he might moan about his strained relations, he uses his isolation to his advantage.

'Alec will do anything to protect his players,' said Mark McGhee. 'Losing worries him far more than what people say about him. He will take any course necessary to keep the players' minds on the job in hand, even becoming the press's whipping boy.'

So when Cantona does something despicable and a pundit points it out, he calls the pundit a prat. When Schmeichel loses all sense and the referee does the right thing, he says the referee should be embarrassed. When Hughes kicks someone up the arse, he says the victim shouldn't have such a provocative arse. As a result, the press worry more about him than about the miscreant. Diversionary tactics, he calls it. It doesn't make him an attractive public figure, but the players know, whatever he might say in the privacy of his office, he will not publicly humiliate them. Among the knife-edge egos of his dressing room, such knowledge breeds absolute respect.

But it doesn't stop there: when the press has retaliated by turning up the slag-volume to deafening, he can use them as the enemy, focus the minds of his players on proving their critics wrong.

'I'm sure most of the players are very angry about the stick which has been thrown their way. I think they're a bunch of angry lads who will want to prove themselves right and everybody else wrong,' Pat Crerand suggested to me just before the 1994 FA Cup semi-final.

I only hoped he was right. Ferguson could only do so much winding up of the rubber band. Once the players were out on the pitch, it was their turn.

On Easter Monday, we beat Oldham in the league. It was 3–2, scrappy, unconvincing, but it was three points, and another game out of the way. (United played 36: 79 points; Blackburn, still there and showing no signs of going anywhere else, played 36: 76 points.) Dion Dublin scored the winner and was included by Ferguson in the team for the semi-final, against Oldham again, the following Sunday.

'Teams are beginning to work out how we play and to accommodate it,' Ferguson said. 'We need some variety, we need to work on different ways of playing.'

Over the years FA Cup semi-finals had burnt into the memory like no other games: the trips to Hillsborough, Villa Park and Maine Road, knowing that Wembley was the next stop; the proximity of glory, the buttock-clenching tension, the frantic noise and colour; pogoing down the terraces when Hill scored; watching Moran carried off after one of his head-loosening challenges and, as the stretcher passed us, seeing him thrust a clenched fist for the lads from under his blanket; leaping around and thinking Danny Wallace was king; it can do odd things to you a semi-final.

This time was different. It was announced that both semi-finals were to be played at Wembley. The first occasion this had been done was in 1991 when Arsenal had met Spurs and it seemed a logical thing: there was no other neutral ground close to where those two teams operate from which could have met the demand. In 1993, both semis had been at Wembley, and again there was a point. It was Arsenal against Spurs once more, and the other match was the Sheffield derby. But there was also a warning there, in Sheffield Wednesday's experience. They had already played in the League Cup final, then there was the FA semi, which they won, and the the final, which was drawn. By the time of the final replay, many Wednesday fans were all spent out. What with the travel, the tickets, the souvenirs and Wembley's bar prices, they simply couldn't afford it.

But what did the FA care about loyal fans' problems? There was always someone else with a pocket to be emptied.

So in 1994, it was decided both semis were to be staged again at Wembley. As one game was between Luton and Chelsea, there was some justification; it was, after all, a geographically convenient neutral location. But United against Oldham? The two clubs are only ten miles apart. And here the governing body of English football suggesting they should play their semi a mutually inconvenient two hundred miles away.

Martin Edwards complained to the FA, saying his supporters couldn't keep shelling out. But in a typical fudge compromise, the blazers of Lancaster Gate said that if either side could prove their supporters welcomed the venue, the game would go ahead at Wembley. Thus were tens of thousands put out because of a couple of hundred messages of support for the idea arriving on the Boundary Park fax machine.

How to kill a semi.

This time the crisp smell of anticipation was not in the air. This time we were surrounded by empty seats, with no one singing, mainly because they didn't know the words. There were, maybe, just a thousand more than could be squeezed into Maine Road – enough to justify the exploitation next year. And the really galling thing was the exploitation was so obvious: there was no pretence about it. Tickets at £38 for a fine view of a pillar, and no reduction for children. Me, I showed my distaste at it all by buying four of them.

The only person who seemed to be enjoying the event as we walked up a half-empty Wembley Way, a route shorn of the brouhaha that had filled it only a month before at the Coca-Cola Cup, was my son. He went up to a jolly family in blue strolling their way to the Twin Towers and told them, in his five-year-old's voice, that he hated them. I asked him why he had done it.

'Because they support Oldham,' he said.

I blame the parents.

If United had played well you could have forgotten all the crap. All season we had seen them espouse progressive football – fast, accurate, alert. Now they had gone backwards. Instead of Joe Montana throws to the feet of speedy wingers, Schmeichel was dribbling the ball out of his area like David Seaman and hoofing it in the general direction of Dion Dublin's head. Poor Dublin. So used were United to threading the ball between blades of grass, that when it came to sticking it up in the air – this new tactic, this new addition to their armoury – they lost all accuracy. They wouldn't have been able to find Dublin's head if it had had a big red cross painted on it. It was as if someone had smashed the radar. After an hour Dublin was off, and the bandy legs of Bryan Robson arrived. He couldn't stop the inevitable.

And inevitable it was. When, midway through the second section of extra time, the ball landed at Pointon's feet from Schmeichel's girlie punch, I knew he was going to score. It had been coming all game. All dreary, grim, grinding game. Not because Oldham were any good, but because it was one of those games when you know you are sunk and the Dagenham Girl Pipers could score against you.

As the Oldham fans cavorted their success, I watched Ferguson, down there in front of the Wembley bench. He was standing, shoulders sunk, about half the size he had been when I spotted him five minutes earlier – a balloon with all the air let out. In his position, I would have packed it in then, cried probably. It was gone.

But Ferguson, after a second's pause, was shouting, gesticulating, indicating to Nicky Butt to get his kit off and get on; raging, raging, raging against the death. It's hopeless, I thought as I watched him. He was exposed, open, giving everything he could when nothing he could give would make a difference. It was at times like this that that Mercedes seemed scant reward for all the grief: he was helpless. He was a football manager.

And then Mark Hughes equalised.

18

Kanchelskis Makes His Point

Andrei must stay.
> United fans, Maine Road, 13 April 1994

Things changed when that Hughes goal went in. The moment it sent the Wembley netting humming with a metallic hiss, the moment the scorer ran, face in rage, towards the United end to celebrate, the moment the Oldham fans stopped ordering the beers in – things changed. When the whistle went, the Oldham players sank, their plugs removed, heavily to the turf. The United players bounced, as if air had been forcibly pumped into the soles of their expensively sponsored boots. In the time it had taken Hughes to trigger his right leg, things had changed: the double had been saved and, that moment on a Sunday in April, the team had gone from a shower to sunshine boys.

'It wasn't just that we were losing,' Paul Ince suggested to me afterwards. 'I think a little bit of the belief had gone. If the ball had fallen to anyone else other than Sparky, it wouldn't have been a goal. So that was the luck we needed. And when it went in, we seemed to find that belief in ourselves again. Until then we'd felt unsure in the way we were playing. I tell you what it did, it reminded us who we were.'

Who they were: the best team in the land.

And, in the complex way of things, with players suspended and fixtures to be rearranged, Alex Ferguson was well pleased with a draw. It suited his purposes, he said, now that the game against

Leeds the following Wednesday had been postponed to accommodate the replay.

'Not many people understood what I was talking about beforehand,' he told me. 'But before the game I said to Brian Kidd that mebbe a draw would be the best result. He said, "You're mad, the last thing we need at this stage of the season is another game." But I didn't want to go to Leeds on Wednesday on the back of a Wembley game. It has been raining a lot in the north and Elland Road's like a paddy field. After playing at Wembley, you're drained, physically and psychologically whether you've won or lost. Leeds are fresh, they haven't played for ten days, they've been on holiday. With a draw, when we played on Wednesday, it will be on equal terms against Oldham. Of course, you don't go into a game looking for a draw, but when it came, I was not unhappy. If we'd lost, I think it would have been very hard to pick the players up for the league. And the manner in which the goal was scored and the relief shown on the players' faces showed how much the desire was there. They want to do the double.'

And another thing about a replay. United have this habit of letting the underdog see a chink, then closing it brutally in their faces. In 1983, Brighton and Smith-must-score had blown it. In 1990, Oldham in the semi and Palace in the final were within minutes of pundit-pleasing, Goliath-bashing victories, and had let their chances go. Now in 1994, had Oldham had their opportunity?

Joe Royle, the Oldham manager, made the right noises.

'We fancy our chances,' he said. 'People don't realise what good players we've got. Our position in the league is down to injury problems. The two centre backs were tremendous, and in midfield United never had an inch. Remember, no one gave us a chance. We were going to Wembley as fodder. Oh yes, we fancy it on Wednesday.'

But you could sense he didn't really believe it.

United weren't training any more. Up at The Cliff, they did a bit of jogging, perhaps some five-a-sides, but showed none of the effort of those early-season sessions. Most of the time that week, most of them were on the tables in the physiotherapy room, having their painful bits massaged: thighs, hamstrings, feet, groins. Everyone had something pulled and strained and knackered. But out on the training pitch, with the youth-team players and the reserves, one man was hard at it, brushing up his ball skills – Eric Cantona, looking like a man who had been on holiday. And with this extra game, it meant he would be back in the fray that much sooner than expected.

The replay was where the first game should have been played: Maine Road. Maine Road is not Old Trafford. It sits amid the back-to-backs of Moss Side, where the alleyways between the houses have imaginative names like 'Passage number 12'. This is the Manchester of legend, the 'Coronation Street' Manchester, the Manchester of cobbles and corner shops, not the Manchester of new trams and glossy corporate headquarters which line the triumphal route to Old Trafford. We parked, my mate Chris, me and two of his friends (one, oddly, a Spurs supporter), outside a pub near to where the coaches carrying visiting fans to City's ground used to park in the old days. Near, in fact, where there used to be the piece of graffiti which sticks most in my mind from my youth (that, and 'I am the schizoid octopus man' which was, without any explanation, sprayed on a wall near our school). Prominently painted in three-foot-high letters on a wall next to the coach park was this warning: 'All away fans prepare to die'. Anyone coming into the city centre along Princess Parkway could see it over to the left, one of the welcoming landmarks of Manchester. It disappeared overnight a couple of years ago: not the sort of image a potential Olympic city wants to project.

As we made our way through the strips of back-to-backs, touts offering thick wads of unwanted tickets at every turn, we passed a street called Horton Road, so named long before a Brian of that ilk took up residence in the City manager's office. The road sign at the entrance to the street had been vandalised: someone, a disillusioned City fan presumably, had tried to rip it away – not an easy task as it was screwed to a wall on the side of a house about twelve feet above pavement level. But, despite the concerted attack, it was still hanging on by a thread, wobbling uncertainly in the breeze. Much like City's manager at the time.

Inside Maine Road, past the heaving crush trying to buy a drink at the bar named after perhaps the least likely person to inspire a licensed premises, Tony Book, it was clear the Oldham fans seemed to share our belief that their team had missed their chance. Their stands were barely half full. But the United sections (most of the ground) were boisterous and noisy, optimism restored.

Chris and I sat in the main stand surrounded by old codgers for United – nobody in sight appeared to have followed the reds for less than forty years. Either that, or they had all been twenty before the weekend and their nerves had aged them. They were full of banter of the kind which makes the stomach ache with laughter in the middle of a crowd in a football match, but when repeated afterwards seems not so much painfully funny as just painful. When, for instance, just before kickoff, a policeman came round asking every-one to look under their seats – apparently there had been a bomb warning – an old wag shouted to him:

'What you all looking for? Trophies? Shouldn't bother, you'll find none here.'

How we guffawed.

And, five minutes into the game, spotting the line of police sitting on the pitch's edge, backs to the action, looking up at the fans, someone else yelled at them:

'It's all right, lads. You can turn round. It's not City playing.'

Laugh? I thought my trousers would never dry.

They were particularly pleased, the old stagers, that Robson was back in the side, brought in to steady things down after the frantic tear-around of the first game. A flag carrier for the value of experi-ence, from the kickoff he was in there doing his bit.

'Look at him,' purred the man behind me at a typical piece of Robson. 'I don't care how old he is, he's worth his place. Look at him, that's brilliant, absolute class.' He wasn't even kicking the ball.

He was jabbing fingers of encouragement and chivvy at the hot heads around him. Class jab, though.

But me, too, I was thrilled to see Robson there, at the highest level. It wasn't sentiment; he represented something else for me. Never mind that he was always talked about with that soft awe reserved for those performing unlikely, arthritis-defying acts of sporting longevity: eighty-year-olds retaining a decent golf handicap: fifty-year-olds running the marathon; twenty-year-olds hanging on in the women's tennis circuit. The point was, he was still playing for United and he was older than me. His presence out there gave faint hope to the pathetic fallacy that there was still time to be discovered; that once the shimmy in a park kick-around had been spotted by a passing scout I was still young enough to be considered, that it was not horologically impossible that Robson and I could be sharing crossword clues on the team bus as colleagues. He and Les Sealey were my last links with that futile dream. They were the only ones at United who were older than me: most of the current squad were born when I was already a United supporter, many were born after I went to secondary school, a couple after I had done O levels.

Robson, the old boy, was magnificent. He was directing the midfield flow, shouting a lot, steaming into the Oldham area where, on one occasion, he connected with a corner and put the ball away with – to be polite – his groin, thus maintaining his record of scoring in every FA semi he had appeared in. It was a performance good enough, he thought, to guarantee his place in the FA Cup final team. It would be his fourth for United.

But he was not man of the match: there was no doubt who that was.

Andrei Kanchelskis, returning after his suspension for his sending-off in the Coca-Cola Cup, took control of the game. It was as if he was on a mission, a mission to prove. The Oldham defence, sturdy the previous weekend, offered about as much resistance to him as a half-pound of melting butter might to an electric carving knife. Shoulders hunched, head still over the ball, he tore them apart – his control at pace giving United such an unfair weaponry advantage that you expected the UN to be called in to arbitrate. Kanchelskis set up Irwin to scorch home the first, then scored a screamer of a second himself. Taking the ball on the right, he drifted inside across three challenges and hammered in a left-foot shot, which must have had Hallworth in the Oldham goal thinking, as he removed the ball from the back of the net, that these United players were out to murder him.

'We're back, we're back, we're bloody well back,' yelled the man behind me when Kanchelskis scored. I looked round and noticed he was wearing a vicar's dog collar.

Kanchelskis continued as if divinely inspired: every time he got the ball he looked capable of something astonishing. You read about players who have the ability to lift a crowd off their seats every time they touch the ball: that night Kanchelskis had the whole of Maine Road yogic flying. In the second half he set up Giggs (who reacted so nonchalantly to scoring that for a couple of moments I thought he must have missed) and won the corner from which Robson scored with a dick-poke. At the end of a 4–1 win, with the final against Chelsea arrived at in style, with a Wembley visit achieved for the fourth time in a season, the United players did something I have never seen before on a football field. They waited for Kanchelskis and, like cricketers do when a bowler has taken more than five wickets, they formed a guard of honour and applauded him off the pitch first.

The players knew what was going on here, the crowd knew what was going on: Kanchelskis was doing a bit of negotiation out there. 'Hello, hello, Andrei must stay, Andrei must stay,' chanted the lads on the Kippax to the old Gary Glitter tune.

Kanchelskis had grown weary of the dressing-room pay disparity; it was rumoured his pay cheque was less than a quarter the size of Keane's take home. Cheap labour, these East Europeans. Moreover, he had got fed up because there was never a hint that he might be one of the foreigners selected for the European Cup; he was never quite certain even of his place in domestic competition if both Giggs and Sharpe were fit and on song. And despite the self-effacing smile and the thin, high-pitched speaking voice, Kanchelskis has heels when it comes to negotiations. He disputed himself out of the World Cup arguing against the Russian coach, and now he was making noises in the Manchester press that it was 'seventy per cent certain' he would leave Old Trafford at the end of the season. Feyenoord were alleged to be the lucky recipients of his pace. What he was saying that replay night was directed at the management bench. He was saying with every blazing run: here's what I can do, pay me and pick me. Or try explaining why you haven't to the fans when I leave.

In the event, he won. Ferguson tried him up with a contract with which he could buy up most of Kiev. But there is just a possibility that Ferguson might have won too. If all the procrastinating over a new set of conditions had been a piece of Fergie psychology to extract the best from an inconsistent talent, it was his most cunning and spectacularly successful yet.

Oldham, in the meantime, were finished. They couldn't cope. Their only moment of hope in the replay was another Pointon goal scored from a corner conceded by Robson (from a cockup with Schmeichel, after which the keeper, seeing who it was, kept his opinions as to who was to blame to himself for the first time in the season). After Hughes's life-saver, United were resurgent, born again, visited by the holy speed of Kanchelskis. And the Oldham morale never recovered. Even Joe Royle, the Houdini of the moors, couldn't effect an escape from the sinking sand at the bottom of the table. Hamstrung by pompous FA officialdom which condemned them to three games in the final week of the season, Latics were not just denied a Cup final, they were relegated. They went down with Swindon and Sheffield United. No one minded about the company, but Oldham will be missed.

'April is the cruellest month': T. S. Eliot must have been from Oldham.

But us, we were off to double land – hoping, thinking, expecting to take another step to the title the following Saturday at Selhurst

Park for the last game of Eric's absence. Arriving at the ground, we heard on the car radio that the West Indies were 16 for 2 in the test match and that Blackburn had lost at Southampton. They had drawn level on points at the top, winning against Villa the previous weekend, while we were otherwise detained. But now, with this defeat at Southampton, they had played two more than us and were beginning to show an encouraging disposition towards nerves. With only five to go, a win against the Dons would just about seal it. Some day beckoned. The coincidence with the year before, when we effectively won the title on the same ground after Villa lost at Blackburn and we beat Palace on the same night, was delightfully enticing.

When we returned to the car, the West Indies were 175 for 2 (Brian Lara went on to make the highest-ever test score in that innings) and we had lost to Wimbledon, 1–0.

'Horrible pitch, horrible game, they never let us play,' was Giggs' analysis. 'Horrible.'

19

The Cheerleader

If you follow Man United, then you're
supposed to fucking sing.
Chant, sung to the tune of the old Club biscuit
commercial

Just before Oldham came to play their league game at Old Trafford, Joe Royle was quoted saying that the stadium possessed the most intimidating atmosphere in England.

'It's worth a goal start to them,' he said, in awe.

This made you wonder if Joe Royle had been to a game at Old Trafford in recent months. If he thought it possessed an intimidating atmosphere, then he must lose all nerve when going past monasteries.

As a teenager I used to wonder what the players shouted to each other on the pitch, what pearls of filth were drowned by the wail of the terraces. Did they call each other what everyone called me on a football pitch? Or were they polite?

Last season I found out. On more than one occasion from the middle of the main stand at Old Trafford, I could hear them, clearly and precisely, saying things like 'Parks, Parks, cover, cover,' or 'Andrei, Andrei, for fuck's sake Andrei,' their voices carrying with the clarity of an actor's at the National Theatre. I could hear them because even in a season when the team was producing football sufficiently moving to write operas about, there was no other noise in the ground. At Old Trafford, we're not singing any more.

It worries the core of United fans what has happened to their noise-making. During the course of most matches at Old Trafford you can see someone on his feet somewhere in the stands, arms spread in anguish, trying to get his neighbours to sing their hearts out for the lads. One or two might join in, but eventually he will give up in resigned disgust, and sit down to shouts of 'Yeah and stay sat down' from those behind him. The fanzines have been full of letters from fans ashamed that they have found themselves at home outsung by visitors from Portsmouth, Stoke, Galatasaray, even. These correspondents find it all the more perplexing because it doesn't happen away from Old Trafford. At other grounds United followers are boisterous and hearty, getting behind their team with a non-stop welter of noise; last season their encouragement made a not insignificant contribution to the record twenty-two away victories.

But at home, the hard-core, spread around the ground, have found their efforts dissipated – no one joins in with them any more. And the players, the ones who count, have noticed the change. Although they might make pat public relations statements in the *Manchester United Magazine* about how the red fans are the best in the world, they are aware of the silence. They much prefer playing in noise.

'It makes you feel as though what you're doing's important,' is how Ryan Giggs put it. 'At Anfield, at Elland Road, the buzz, it gets you going. At Old Trafford,' he paused, choosing his words, remembering the effect a headline 'Giggs slates United fans' could have on his image, 'at Old Trafford, it's more of a family thing.'

Over the last three years, the whole sociological balance of United's home has changed. And the side effect of that has been to erode the atmosphere of the place as effectively as a glass of Champions Cola might a tooth, immersed in it overnight.

In the seventies, when I first started to go to matches, in order to guarantee admission to the Stretford End and Stretford Paddock, you would have to arrive an hour before kickoff – earlier if you wanted to secure a good view. Once inside, there was not a lot else to do to pass the time other than chant. Generally, the sing-song was directed at the opposing fans at the far end of the ground who had arrived equally punctually to ensure their position. But it might also, to pass the time, articulate internal rivalries like 'Celtic, Rangers', or the fantastically trivial, 'Left side, right side, tunnel'. So when the teams eventually emerged, they were greeted by a barrage of noise, which everybody was well warmed up to continue throughout the game.

Even in those days, the supporters in the seats, certain of their place and their view, did not arrive until two minutes from the kickoff.

Now that the whole stadium is seated, and tickets are secured well in advance, and the beneath-stand areas are packed with bars to visit and restaurants to patronise, nobody takes their place until almost time. Besides, who would want to be in position early and be forced to listen to Keith Fane, the Old Trafford DJ. Keith has a thin repertoire of dreary old hits – such as James's 'Sit Down', the most appropriate anthem for the new Old Trafford. Like every other football ground DJ he appears to be specially fond of Queen's 'We Are the Champions' and Tina Turner's 'Simply the Best'. Witty eh? True, they may be more appropriately played at Old Trafford than, say, Roots Hall, Southend, but after twenty-five airings a season they begin to cloy – especially since Keith plays his stuff at a volume which not only drowns out any chanting or any conversation, it could curdle milk at fifty paces. It occurred to me one match, as Keith's choice of material ram-raided my eardrums, that if you were a pop singer and wanted to secure your pension in PRS royalties, then you should write a rock anthem (called 'We're A Very Good Football Team') which would be guaranteed plays by cloth-eared DJs in football grounds across the globe.

Singing at football grounds is a group dynamic. Unless you are particularly drunk you tend to chant only if everyone around you does. In the days of terracing, if you were keen on participating in the communal encouragement, you could make your way across to the noisy section. And once a noisy section had been established, its influence spread. Nowadays you can't decide who you sit next to, nor can you move if you find yourself in an area allergic to chanting. Centres of noisy activity rarely build up unless, like at the Charlton game when Schmeichel was sent off or against Everton after the death of Sir Matt Busby, emotions are boiling. So voyeurs like me, who would never instigate a chant, but might be prepared to join in one, find there is seldom one to join in with. This has not just happened at Old Trafford: Newcastle fans complain the all-seater St James's Park is not what it was; the North Bank at Highbury rarely troubles the Richter scale any more; and at Spurs they couldn't create an atmosphere if they provided every spectator with a bung in a brown envelope. It seems that the *Taylor Report*, in its admirable attempt to clean up football's dirty bath water, has seen the baby slip down the plughole with it.

But at United, die-hard fans are convinced there is something more than that about it: they argue, for instance, that K stand, opposite the Stretford End was, three or four years ago, determinedly vocal, even though it was seated. Last season even K stand's 'barmy army' was on the march no more than three or four times.

The blame, as with most grassroots complaints, is directed at the commercialisation of the club, which has brought with it a different sort of clientele.

'Look at the Stretford End,' Johnny Flacks, of the militant whinge wing of United fandom, told me. 'That used to house twenty thousand. Post-Hillsborough it was reduced to fifteen thousand. When it was seated, that went down to ten thousand. You're already reducing the potential volume by half. But then three thousand of those seats are given to the family stand, and three thousand more to the club-class seats for corporate hospitality and yuppie entertainment. So twenty thousand atmosphere-builders have effectively been squeezed into four thousand seats.'

I don't share Flacks's view that the middle-class spectators drawn to Old Trafford are any less loyal: I know dozens of wealthy professionals who show psychotic levels of dedication in following United. But he's right to say they're not singers. They tend to be people who have grown out of that sort of thing; they're older, they must be to afford the prices. The type of supporter most likely to generate the atmosphere the rest of us so cheerfully absorb, is the very one most likely to be disenfranchised by the new United: the lad.

Steve Bentley, the man behind the 'L'Eric Sportif' T-shirt, put it like this to me.

'There's nothing cool about United,' he said. 'Their kit's crap, all the stuff in the souvenir shop's shite, you can't get a ticket unless you're a rich bastard with contacts as long as your arm. At United it's all families and members and librarians and queuing for days for tickets or passing over a packet to touts, which is not cool. If you're a young lad in Manchester who decides on the spur of the moment he wants to go to a match with his mates, have a few beers, then a bit of a crack, then you go to City. Simple as that. I tell you, as a red, it hurts me to say it, but more cool lads go to City.'

All this meant that when we were walking to a game one day and my son asked me who decides what songs to sing at Old Trafford, I could confidently reply: no one. Because we don't sing any more.

But then at the Coca-Cola Cup final I saw something which made me realise I was wrong. Well wrong.

That afternoon, the grass bank by the turnstile through which I was meant to enter Wembley was host to a choir. A grubby, half-drunk, dishevelled choir, but a choir nonetheless, of reds, singing. They were singing, to the tune of 'Lily the Pink', 'Eric the King', a remake of a number chanted in the golden era of terrace anthems, when Denis was King. The chorus went:

> We'll drink a drink a drink
> To Eric the King, the King, the King
> He's the leader of our football team
> He's the greatest French footballer
> That the world has ever seen.

At the end of each chorus, the chanters would all fall silent while a lad with a curtain of black hair over his face, sitting on his mate's shoulders, sang hoarsely through the verses. Verses which went:

Eric the King he's remarkably trendy
Done some modelling around tow-uh-own
Up on the cat walk, wearing the best suits
And the Leeds scum they just frown.

He once played for Marseille
But never for Arsenal
Or Liverpool or even Man City
He had a brief spell though with the Leeds scum
Until he realised that they were has-beens
There's only one way now, for Eric to go now
To the theatre of all dreams . . .

He was the lost cheerleader of Old Trafford.

As he sang on, more and more people joined the throng, tumbling down the bank in nostalgic imitation of terrace shoves. It went on for half an hour – brilliant songs, inventive songs, stupid songs, songs which traced the long-distant and recent past of United, all sung with appetite and relish, and all conducted by the lad with the hair.

Between songs he would shout that if we liked what we heard, we should all buy his tape. He was brandishing a black bin liner, from which he was pulling copies of a cassette, selling them for £4 each, stuffing fivers greedily into his pockets as the choir snapped them up.

Fighting through the scrum at his feet, I bought one. 'Songs From the Bath-tub', it was called, 'United We Sing: A classic collection of over 30 terrace favourites and more'.

Back home I played it. It was an utterly tone-deaf, foul-mouthed, amateurish production, full of juvenile invective and spleen. I thought it was brilliant. There was something old: 'If I die on Kippax Street, they'll be ten blue bastards at my feet'; something new: 'How does Ryan Giggs do it?' (sung to the tune of the 'Do-It-All' advert); something borrowed: 'Eric the King'; but nothing blue.

It didn't take Jon Pilger-levels of investigative journalism to track its perpetrator down. Peter Boyle, who, as it turned out, my son and I had seen displaying his lance in a streak across Selhurst Park during the last game of the 1993 season, is not the shyest of football supporters.

Everyone in the United hard core knew where you could track down 'The Streaker'. We arranged to meet two days before the Derby against Manchester City, in a café in the nobby bit of central Manchester. It was Boyle's favourite rendezvous, he said, because he once saw Giggsy, out on a shopping spree, having a coffee there. And you never know, he might go there again.

It was not easy to miss Boyle: the hair, the black Cure T-shirt, the shabby green cardigan held together with United badges, and the peak cap saying 'Manchester United Supporters Club: Pontypridd Branch'. Over coffee he told me about his United-watching life. Now twenty-three, he had been going to away games with the lads since he was eight. And although studying in Cardiff, he still made it to most games, jibbing his way on the train, jibbing across town on the tram, jibbing his way into the ground. Brian McClair had once answered a pleading letter from Boyle with a ticket left in an envelope to be collected from the plush reception area at Old Trafford, where the connected pick up theirs. Boyle still had the envelope: it was addressed to 'The Streaker'.

'I always used to go in the United Road section, next to the away fans, and bait them,' Boyle said. 'It's not like it was. Even K stand's been dragged down into the silence. I went there recently with about forty lads from the Pontypridd branch. I had them all singing on the bus on the way up, and we were all sat together so we got a little centre going. But in the end we got fed up with "Shurrup, sit down".'

Where had all the old singers gone? I asked him. All those who used to populate the United Road?

'I bumped into a lad recently who was always down there. He said he'd just dropped out, lost interest, stopped going when they put seats in. Just not the same.'

About six months previously, Boyle had decided to record his tape, to do something positive, not just whinge. He had sold about five hundred so far, but the object was not just to make money, he said.

'We've got this great tradition of songs at United, and if we're not careful we'll let it go. It's our responsibility. It's our heritage.'

So he had taken it upon himself to recreate the Old Trafford atmosphere, to get something going. What he most wanted to tell me was he had written a chant specifically for the Derby. 'It's well sound,' he said. 'Listen to this.'

And he began singing, arms waving as he conducted himself in the middle of the posh café in the posh bit of Manchester.

> In your bitter Blue world
> You don't go to Wembley
> You don't win no cups
> You hate Man United
> You pray for fuck ups
> In your bitter Blue world.

'What d'you reckon, sound, eh?' he said, as two heavily foundationed dollies from Kendalls' cosmetics counter at the table next to us nervously clicked teaspoon against crockery. 'I'm going to get the whole of K stand singing it, you watch me. I'm determined.'

He had got them going at the Coca-Cola with 'Eric the King'; he had conducted a United choir on the Kippax during the semi-final replay; now he was going for the big one: injecting life into the corpse. I bet him he wouldn't; I bet him he couldn't.

'All right,' he said. 'You're on. I haven't been at this long, but it's working. I tell you, you'll lose. They're desperate: desperate to start singing again.'

The Derby was on a Saturday. After another Sky-jacking, the kick-off had been put back to five o'clock. Odd, that. The season before, the kickoff at the Maine Road Derby had been midday on police insistence: there was always trouble at the Derby and drinking, it was thought, was to blame. But Sky, apparently, had more sway than the law. So five o'clock it was. This meant that Boyle had a good six hours in the pub before kickoff. He was planning to travel round various pubs in Stretford selling copies of his tape. We arranged to meet at the Dog and Partridge just by Old Trafford at one o'clock.

The Dog is central red territory. You gain admission past a couple of bouncers who look you up and down checking for any hint of blue. Inside, that afternoon, were not the well-heeled or the corporately entertained, the package tourists or the day-trippers who flood through Martin Edwards's balance sheet. Inside were the live-for-Uniteds, the working class, many of them Mancunians, the rump who clung on to the ever more expensive cause. They stood around drinking, greeting each other, playing the pinball machine, quietly succumbing to nerves.

'I don't know how they're feeling in that dressing room,' said one lad who struck up a conversation with me in the gents. 'But this is me fifth trip to the bog this afternoon.'

'We'll be all right,' I said. 'Eric's back.'

Boyle's arrival in this contemplative, tension-racked place was like that of an Alka Seltzer dropped into a glass of water. He spun into the bar, hair clamped to his face, dewy with sweat, a small entourage in tow. He was already hoarse. There was a big cheer. Everyone recognised him: 'It's that lardarse what done a streak at Selhurst,' someone said.

Everyone wanted to know him. Slapping him on the back.

'All right Boylie, lad,' people were saying. 'Got any tapes?'

He hadn't, he said. Sold out already. But what he did have was a buff envelope filled with the lyrics of his latest ditty.

'I had three hundred run off on the photocopier,' he told me. 'Told you I'd get them going. You start handing them round.'

He gave me a pile of photocopied strips of the words of 'Bitter Blue World'. As I handed them out to people coming to and from the gents, participating in the defeat of my own wager, Boyle jumped on to a chair and started the singing. Dozens immediately gathered round him, heaving at his feet, as if this was what they had been waiting for all afternoon. Young lads in Ralph Lauren, faces lit up with the buzz, went off through 'Eric the King' and 'Roy Keane's A Magician' ('he wears a magic hat/And when he saw Old Trafford he said "I fancy that" '). Boyle, as before, was conductor, deciding what to sing, indicating to the rest of us when to come in for the choruses. Sometimes he sang on his own:

'United, United, ra, ra, ra; City, City, ha, ha, ha; Leeds, Leeds, baa, baa, baa.' Everyone laughed at that one. Other songs needed a bit of prompting.

'This one you will find on the song sheets handed out by my friend here. It's sung to the tune of "In Your Liverpool Slums",' he said, before launching into 'Bitter Blue World'. He sang it five times, so everyone could learn it.

When he stopped for a drink, or to greet a mate or to tell someone he didn't have any tapes left, the young lads in his choir were uncertain what to do, looking around for leadership or starting chants of their own that were generally characterised by an absence of wit: 'Shearer is a wanker, na na na na.'

A short, stocky man in his thirties, hair curled and gelled, muscled his way towards Boyle. He was bare-chested, his back a canvas of bad tattoos. He had two-inch-deep scars linking mouth and left ear.

'I love you, mate,' he said, grabbing Boyle's hand in a fist decorated in gold sovereign rings. 'Not like a poofter, like, but I love you.' He pulled Boyle to his substantial bosom in a hug of bonding. Boyle grinned at me.

'Mark, tell my friend here how you was banned.'

He came over and stood in front of me, chin forward, head moving in quick jerks like a chicken. There was an unstable look in his eyes. I noted his forearms were bigger than my thighs.

'Don't let me get banned,' Mark said. 'Don't let me. But if I see any of them blue bastards ... Don't let me do nothing though. I don't want to get banned, I have been, you know. I have been, you know. I have, don't let me.'

He wandered off, chin first, through the crowd of singers, looking for another pint.

'That's all he ever says, repeats himself,' Boyle told me later. 'I see him in here every match and he always tells me the same story. How he was in the army and how he got banned. I'm not sure if he's shell-shocked or beer-shocked.'

Even though Boyle's choir had split up on their arrival at the ground, the Derby atmosphere inside Old Trafford was alive. It was like old times in there. It wasn't just the afternoon on the lager, or the usual Derby frenzy, there was an extra edge to things. United were poised at the top, City at the bottom. Points were vital. And, to add a tub of Tabasco to the mixture, it was Cantona's first game back. The hero was about to return from exile, and City were making noises of welcome.

'We will wind Eric up left, right and centre,' their full back Terry Phelan, a player only recently acquitted of an assault in a bar, told the tabloids. 'He won't be given an inch to play in. You have to rattle Eric, get people to take a bit out of him. That's the way you've got to operate against these temperamental foreigners.'

But Phelan's psychological warfare had backfired: his manager had dropped him.

From the City sections and the United bits adjoining them, there was a steady tide of youths leaving with their arms up the small of their backs, in the company of several policemen. Even though Keith Fane was doing his best to drown them out by playing 'We Are the Champions' loud enough so that Freddie Mercury could hear it, the songs of contempt were ringing round the ground:

'City is our name,' mocked the United fans to the tune of 'Yankie Doodle Dandy', 'City is our name, eighteen years and won fuck all, City is our name.'

In the pub before the game, a man with a Glasgow accent had come on all pedantic when Boyle had started that one.

'Listen, listen,' he said, yelling from atop a table, 'City is not our name, City is their name. It should be City is their name. Get it right.'

His song-writing sub-editing had not had any effect.

'You'll win this game,' said Patrick Barclay, sitting in the press box. 'You'll win this game and the title. That's your book on course. Now Cantona's back, you'll win. You watch him.'

He was right. It was somehow inevitable that Cantona should mark his regal return with a brace of smartly executed goals. The first was a tap-in from Kanchelskis's cross, the second a one-on-one after Hughes, on burning form now, had put him through. The pair took his total to five in three hothouse Derbies. Letting us down at the highest level again.

What in particular had you missed when Cantona was out? an innocent hack was to ask Ferguson after the game.

'Well, his goals,' came the reply.

As the game reached its end and United looked increasingly confident and vigorous – their old selves – I finally spotted Peter Boyle in the crowd. He was in K stand, just above where the City fans were gathered, his green cardigan standing out among the red-and-black nylon. He was on his feet, clapping, urging. But unlike the lost and hopeless wannabe cheerleaders I had seen for most of the season, he had the whole section around him up and chanting too, directing their song at the City fans below them. After a moment I realised, as the sound drifted across to the press box, what they were singing. It was 'In Your Bitter Blue World'. I had lost my bet.

Alex Ferguson punished the press boys by taking an age to give them their quotes after the game. He left them until they were almost drowned by the incoming deadline. He was happy enough when he arrived in the press room, full of the banter of a man who could see things working out: with both teams now having played thirty-eight games, United were three points ahead. Blackburn were at home to QPR the next day. Was Ferguson, someone asked, going to watch them on the television?

'Nah,' he said. 'I'm going to Glasgow, home of the master race. I've got to get the hell out of all this St George's Day. I seen all these guys wandering around with roses; I'm thinking what a bunch of poofs.'

'Glasgow, eh?' said the esteemed representative of a Sunday tabloid. 'Trying to get away from football altogether?'

For once, the press had got the better of him. And even Fergie had to smile about it.

It was thus about an hour and a half after the final whistle that I was walking down the Warwick Road to Old Trafford tram station and passed a man chomping at a tray of chips.

Initially I took him to be a down-and-out.

'You London?' he said as I overtook him.

I stopped and said, 'Sorry?'

'You London? Are you getting the eight-thirty? I'll come with you.'

Thirtyish, bearded in a Catweasley way, and dressed in an East German army surplus parka, he was not an enthusiast for personal hygiene. He shuffled along beside me, probing my commitment.

'You go every game?' he asked. 'I've not missed home or away for eleven year, me. You going Leeds? You going Ipswich? I got a ticket from them. Just wrote off like. 'Cos I didn't have the vouchers for our bit. There's only twelve hundred tickets, I heard. I'm in the north stand, which is next to where United are, so it'll be all right. They've given us the Portman stand, upper tier, Ipswich, haven't they. Last year I was in the Pioneer stand. Fourteen-and-an-'alf-pound ticket and I got a restricted view.'

And so he chuntered on, on the tram, off the tram, up the escalator, across Piccadilly station concourse. Out it all poured – details of tickets acquired and queues queued, a conversational technique enlivened only by a spotter's hand of violence witnessed.

'It's definitely coming back,' he said. 'Kicked off everywhere we been lately. It went off in the forecourt today. It'll go off at the Cup final. Was you in Leicester Square before the Coca-Cola? It kicked off there all right. These Villa steamed in but they got hammered, like, didn't they.'

As we approached the platform I stopped.

'You not getting the train, or what?' he said.

'Sadly,' I said. 'I'm staying in Manchester tonight.'

I was meeting Andy Mitten and when I told him of my encounter a look of fearful possibility crossed his face.

'Fuck,' he said. 'You know what, it worries me I'll end up like that. Honest, it worries me what I'll end up, where this United thing will take me. I've been to every game for two seasons and it becomes obsessive, the maintenance of the record is all that counts.'

I asked him what he meant.

'I'll give you a for instance. There was meant to be a free weekend before an international, right. So I organised for a group of us from college to go to Amsterdam for the weekend. I'd booked the coach, hotel, everything. Then United rearranged their fixture with QPR, didn't they? There was nothing I could do, I couldn't pull out of the Amsterdam visit, but I had to go to Loftus Road. So I went to a travel agent and booked a flight from Amsterdam to Heathrow and back for the afternoon. Then, on the Friday, I went in the coach overnight from Preston to Amsterdam, I left them at the hotel, legged it to the airport and got the plane over to London.

'They stopped me at customs, didn't they, because I looked suspicious, didn't have any luggage, was on me own, English, flying in from Amsterdam. They gave me a right going over, interrogating me. I explained why I was there and in the end the geezer just looked at me and said: "You are dedicated, aren't you."

'I went to the game and I had to leave twenty minutes before the final whistle to leg it back to the airport. I was completely poleaxed with tiredness and popping Pro-plus to keep me awake. But I got back in time to go out in Amsterdam with everyone that night. And I thought, what's going on?'

So what was going on?

'The thing was I thought it was worth it, in a way, for the look on everyone's face when I got to Amsterdam. They couldn't believe I'd actually done it. I suppose it gave me an identity, you know, they saw me as different.'

And what's wrong with that?

'For a while it's all right. But what worries me is that I'll end up like these lads I know older than me who've sacrificed everything for United. The thing is it takes much more dedication and investment of time to see every United game than for any other club. For a start we play more, but also because of the demand and the way tickets are allocated, you have to do a lot of planning and queuing and you can find yourself becoming obsessed by vouchers and availability. You end up like your geezer: a voucher bore. Lads I know, older lads, if they've made the decision to stick full time, they've no social life, no girlfriends, no families. They'll jack in jobs if it clashes with games. They've nothing but United. And what, at the end of things, is the point of that?'

About two weeks after the end of the season, I rang Andy to check one or two facts. I asked him what he was doing with his time now the season was over.

'To be perfectly honest,' he said. 'I'm enjoying the break from football.'

He'll be back.

20

A Night in the Stocks

Merci pour Cantona, scum.
Banner unfurled at Elland Road,
27 April 1994

On the day South Africa went to the polls, I went to Leeds. On the day F. W. de Klerk voted in Soweto, I took my chance in Elland Road. This is a place where Manchester United followers feel about as comfortable as a blue whale taking a wrong turn up a Norwegian fjord. This is a place where loathing for anything red is tangible, where you can touch it, watch it as it drips from the reinforced concrete roofs and congeals in sticky puddles underfoot.

'Do they hate us,' Giggsy said of the place. 'You go to take a corner there and you've got fifteen thousand horrible skinheads in their end yelling murder at you.'

Lee Chapman wrote in his autobiography that the matches between Leeds and United were bathed in the atmosphere of a Munich rally. He was right, except Munich was more accommodating.

And all we had to do there was win. Blackburn had dropped another two points at home to QPR the day after the Derby: Ray Wilkins said he was glad to help out his old mates. Still a good man, Wilkins. Now we were two points in front, with a game in hand. If we won, we would begin to stretch out of view. But winning at Elland Road was about as straightforward as the Scott Inquiry.

I had two tickets from my mate Chris who had decided, given the extra edge generated by the Busby memorial incident earlier in the year, that he was not prepared to don helmet and flak jacket for a football match. I took along my own sort of security: Leo, my Leeds-supporting colleague David Robson's eight-year-old son. Leo had seen Leeds play against Chelsea, Spurs and Arsenal. But what he most wanted to do was see them play United.

'It's the only one that counts,' he told his father.

Leo was wearing a Leeds shirt. When we walked into a big holding pen just past the turnstiles in the visitors' section at Elland Road, a steward came over to us.

'Excuse me,' he said. 'But you are aware this is ManU here.'

I said I was.

'But he's wearing a Leeds shirt.'

I said I had spotted that.

'That's well provocative is that.'

I doubt it, I said, he's eight years old, I am a United fan and he's with me. Or at least he was until I saw his attire.

'I'd advise you to cover it up,' he said to Leo, ignoring me. 'You know what these United fans can be like: they're bloody animals.'

We took our seats in front of three middle-aged men in suits who discussed the game with the comic intensity of speech bubbles in *Billy the Fish* ('I think you'll find it will be an emotional return for the Frenchman to the stadium where he first exploded on to the English scene').

In front of us were two elderly women who had dyed their bleached white hair in red stripes for the occasion.

'You all right, pet?' they fussed as Leo took his seat.

Ferocious, these animals.

To our right, on the lower tier of Elland Road's massive new stand, the Leeds family enclosure looked equally human – people doing provocative things like taking their places and preparing to watch the game.

Everything looked anticlimactically sane about the place. Until you looked left. On our left it was zoo time. There wasn't a single supporter in the adjoining stand that did not look as though they would willingly, cheerfully, stamp on our throats. It was a bit like being in the stocks, sitting there in the United section. People had come along specifically to throw things at us. Huge-shouldered Yorkshiremen without much hair yelled their opinion of us, fat faces a-wobble in rage. Youths in Henri Lloyd polo shirts predicted what would happen to us after the game. Small boys put their arms out in aircraft impressions and then fell over in mock crashes. And there was gob. It rained gob.

Safe behind a wall of West Yorkshire constabulary, the reds returned fire. The noise bounced back and fro. We sang 'Eric the King'; they retaliated with the intellectual footnote that he was 'just a shit French bastard.' We called them sheep-shaggers and scum; they called us scum and scum. They sang about always looking on the runway for ice. We applauded ironically. They looked confused. And this was before the teams had come on to the pitch.

As it was all going on, I read the Leeds fanzine, *The Square Ball*. It was funny, full of the sort of energy and fury United fans would recognise from their own publications. There was an attack on the Leeds manager's transfer activity: 'Big Brian [Deane]'s big attraction was that he had always wanted to play for Leeds. Well, so have I! It doesn't make me worth £300,000 less than Shearer either.' There was a pastiche of the Gloucester murder inquiry, with Howard Wilkinson as a serial killer responsible for the disappearance of talented individuals from Leeds (which was illustrated by a picture of the Elland Road pitch with the caption, 'the field after it had been dug up by police'). Also, there was a tirade against the old chestnut – third kits: 'Leeds recent visit to Ewood Park serves as a case in point; apparently blue-and-green stripes clash less than blue-and-yellow stripes with Blackburn's blue-and-white. Or in other words, any excuse will do for bringing out a new nylon creation from hell mid-season to pep up replica sales.'

It might be a touch on the precious side to suggest it, but Leeds fans and United fans have more in common than they have in antipathy: the little guys fighting an uncaring system. Maybe if they saw that, they wouldn't feel obliged to re-enact the Wars of the Roses twice a season. Yeah, but who said football was about common sense?

Meanwhile on the pitch, United gave their most complete performance of the season – which was saying something. Not as subtle or
cunning as when they played against Wimbledon in the Cup, not as
outrageous as against Sheffield Wednesday in the league, not
as dramatic as against Manchester City in the Maine Road Derby,
but, given the circumstances, given the stakes, given the opposition,
it was an effort which made jaws drop from the headquarters of
the *Sun*, via the south stand at Elland Road, to Jack Walker's office
in Blackburn.

'Maybe Blackburn were looking to Leeds to give them a bit of
help. Maybe they were expecting us to come unstuck there,' a
glowing, hard-eyed, triumphant Paul Ince said to me the next day.
'Well, maybe they were wrong.'

To come to Leeds, a good side with an unparalleled home record,
and win, was something Blackburn, for all their bonuses couldn't
do. But then United were motivated by something more than money
that night. They were propelled by a potent cocktail of pride and
power, of a hatred of losing and a greed for success. And the
constant knocking, the endless speculation about them cracking
under pressure, it had made them angry. It was as if the entire effort
on the Elland Road cabbage patch was to put two fingers up to the
world, to Sadler and Lightbown, to Dalglish and Fashanu, to everyone who had said they would falter.

'All that stuff, it got to us. Definitely,' Ince said. 'The thing is,
you'd think in a dressing room like ours, full of star players, it would
be all cliquey-cliquey and that. But it's not. We all get on real well,
so when something like this happens, we tend to close in on ourselves, to look out for each other. It's us against the rest.'

And Leeds, they got the backlash to the backlash. Ince and Keane
won everything, growing stronger as the battle lengthened.

'That's what you got to do,' Ince added. 'Against McAllister and
Speed you know you've got to be strong, but you keep at it, win
the battle, win the war: wear 'em down, wear 'em down, wear 'em
down.'

Schmeichel remembered how to catch; Irwin, Parker, Bruce and
Pallister didn't give a quarter; Kanchelskis and Giggs galloped

and sprang all night; and Cantona, booed at every turn by fans who would recently have volunteered to clean his underwear using only their own saliva, flicked and feinted, creating room for everyone else.

'They put thingy . . . Fairclough . . . on him,' explained Giggs. 'But that's the thing about Eric, even if he's being man-marked, he's still giving something to the team: extra space.'

But it was Hughes who should be mentioned in dispatches. He gave the perfect centre forward's performance. He held the ball up with bravery under fire, always long enough for the leather lungs of Keane and Ince to catch up. He passed with craft, he harried, chased and frightened defenders. He was huge.

He didn't score though. Kanchelskis, unstoppable now, got the first. And Giggsy got the second, five minutes from the end. It was a reminder that beneath the layers of packaging and marketing and heart-throb hype lurks a class footballer. On the touchline he beat Kelly, who, he remembered, had smothered him in the fixture at Old Trafford, and weaved inside to play a one-two with, who else, Hughes. When he scored from the return pass, he took his non-celebratory to new levels. He stood still, face expressionless, as if rooted to the penalty spot. Then he was buried under a human tower block of celebration – Keane, as always, forming the top floor.

'He liked that one,' Ince said of the goal. 'Giggsy's got nothing to prove, he's a great player. But at Old Trafford, people were saying Kelly had him in his pocket and I think he felt as like he had a point to prove. When he scored that goal he thought: yeah, up yours, so he done the Chris Eubank bit to show, like, "I'm back".'

'Yeah, I loved it,' Giggs confirmed. He added Elland Road was his favourite away ground. 'I always seem to do well there and we tend to win – which is pretty pleasing really, because they hate us so much.'

I thought, when the whistle went, that's it. Even though news spread rapidly that Blackburn had won at Upton Park, I reckoned we had it now. If we kept winning, they couldn't catch us. The doubts had gone, blown away as effectively as Leeds were. I just wished that John Sadler had taken his own advice and backed them.

As we left our seats at the end of the game, floating out, oblivious to the seethe of dislike just over the barrier to our left, I ran into the bearded kicking-off spotter I had recently met on Warwick Road. He had a transistor radio clamped as if by surgery to his ear, listening for news from elsewhere.

'Bloody hell,' he said, seeing Leo. 'He's a bit young for this, in'tee. It's going to kick off I tell yer. After that, they'll bloody fry us. It kicked off beforehand, last hundred United through the turnstiles got jumped by three hundred Leeds, everyone got smacked.'

The United fans were coralled in the pen behind the turnstiles, no one was allowed to leave.

Anyone in a red shirt was rapidly putting on sweat shirts or zipping up jackets. Outside in the street you could hear the baying, the police sirens, the stomach-wrenching noise of blood-lust, a sound made particularly unappealing when the blood in question is your own. Missiles started raining over the wall – bottles, glasses, bricks, an item of garden furniture. Brave stuff. It was at this point I had my first-ever jolt of sympathy for the early Afrikaners: I suspected I knew what it felt like, in the middle of the laager of wagons, the Zulus circling outside.

I took Leo to the gate where a line of policemen were holding back the tide and asked to be let out.

'I wouldn't,' one of them said. 'It's ugly out there.'

I indicated I had a child with me, and inside the enclosure was not the safest place I'd ever seen. He let me through with a-who-gives-a-stuff-you're-only-a-Manc look. Once outside among the whooping natives, I told Leo to unzip his jacket and expose his Leeds shirt, and the mass parted, ignoring us as fry of no consequence. We stood for a moment watching the maelstrom of police horses and angry home supporters whirlpooling round the entrance to the away fans' enclosure. As we walked past a Black Maria, several policemen were thrusting a man in his forties into the back.

'You should have grown out of this lark by now, anyway,' said one of West Yorkshire's finest, finally shutting the doors.

I heard the next day, that the reds had been let out forty minutes later.

'The police gave our coach an escort all the way back over the border to Lancashire,' Andy Mitten told me. 'But we wouldn't have given a stuff if they hadn't. We won it.'

During the drive home to London, Leo could not stop talking about how brilliant it all was, how great it was to hear the United fans singing 'Eric the King', the song I'd taught him on the way up. And best of all how fantastic it was to see Giggs play.

'Not only that,' he said. 'But I saw him score.'

I looked at him and saw the picture of awed excitement his face had become and said that I thought he wasn't really a Leeds fan. I said that I reckoned that he only said he supported Leeds because his dad did and he didn't want to hurt his feelings. Deep down, I said, I think you're really a United fan.

He looked at me, eight-year-old eyes watering with confession.

'How did you know?' he said.

Because they all are, son.

21

One Year Since We Last Won The Title

Robson is his name, Robson is his name,
thirteen years and won the lot.
Chant heard at Bryan Robson's last match at
Old Trafford, 8 May 1994

Like the previous year, as the end approached, United kept winning, relentlessly: 'Wear 'em down, wear 'em down, wear 'em down.' After Leeds, there was a win at Ipswich in the sun; the winner came from Giggs, who put coolness aside and celebrated his goal by leaping around like Bambi.

'The Boss was having a right go at me on the touchline just before,' he said by way of explanation for his momentary aberration. 'It's was one-all and when I scored, it meant so much and that, I just couldn't help jumping around.'

If we were winning, Blackburn had to keep winning too. But they had been exhausted by the chase and were peppering their run-in with draws and defeats. The gap at the top had now expanded to four points and we had a game in hand. The day after Giggs's giant leap at Ipswich, Blackburn went to Coventry. They had to win, otherwise the mathematics would swamp them.

'Now they might know what pressure is,' Giggs said.

It was live on the telly, their game, and I planned to watch it, the ultimate sadist's evening: no pleasure except in another's pain. Then Eugen rang up and invited me to go and watch the recording of some television game show he was involved in.

'Come on,' I said, 'I'm watching the match.'

'OK,' he said. 'But Denis Law's on it.'

It doesn't take long to get to the BBC studios from my house. I was there as they kicked off the second half at Highfield Road. The television in the hospitality suite was tuned not to the match but into the studio; the room was stuffed with the programme's researchers and producers anxious to see their effort being recorded. I had to sit there, making small talk, eating a BBC buffet, not knowing. And with relief to the not-knowing torment just a finger-push away. Occasionally I would suggest switching over. No one else in the room wanted to: they were more interested in the fate of their work than in the destination of the championship. Strange, some people's priorities. Once I went for a walk, through the warren of the BBC, trying to find an unattended telly. I couldn't.

By the time the recording had finished, so was the game. The studio guests came through to join us. Danny Baker was first in, and saying 'we've got to know the score' he flicked the television over to Sky. No one argued with him. A crowd gathered round the set. They were showing a replay of a Blackburn goal. What did this mean? Was that one of five? Or their only one and Coventry had got five? It felt like that episode of 'The Likely Lads'. There was a commercial break. It lasted for ever. Then it came back to the post-match analysis. And there it was, plain on the screen. In figures that seemed to spin out of the neon and take up a life of their own – Coventry City 2, Blackburn Rovers 1.

That was it. Manchester United were FA Carling Premiership Champions 1993–94. For the second year running, they had done it without actually playing.

At the end of a ten-month saga of grounds visited and tickets battled for, of pints sunk and burgers regretted, of travel plans made and then remade because the game was switched to a Sunday because of the telly, the moment it matters, when everything was decided, I was in a television hospitality suite in the company of a collection of game-show guests (Rick Wakeman, Mungo Jerry and one of the Nolans) who hadn't a clue why Eugen and I were embracing.

For once the players were in the same state as the fans. They, too, were helplessly detached from events, watching the thing unfold on their television screens. Sky even had a camera on hand so we could watch them watching Sky the moment the title was won. There were Bruce, Schmeichel and Parker, shaking each other by the hand while sitting on a sofa at Bruce's gaff, facing a telly the size of Jodrell Bank. I think I spotted a can or two about the place.

'I was at a mate's house, watching it on the telly,' Giggs told me. 'Year before, I'd only been able to watch the first half, but this time I watched all of it. When it was done, we went out and partied. Everyone round our way did the same.'

At BBC Television Centre, there was only one thing to do. Seek out Denis Law and congratulate him.

'Very pleased, very pleased,' the former king said. 'It's not quite as good a feeling as last year, you know with that wait and all. But good. Very good. I'm delighted for Alec after all he's had thrown at him.'

I asked him how good he thought this United team was.

'You need me to tell you?' he said. 'You've seen them. But what I will say is I'm frightened for the rest of football. I really am. I get paid to watch Premier League stuff every week, and honestly this lot are the only ones I'd pay to watch. They're streets ahead. I think they're going to dominate things like Milan have in Italy.'

But you can't object to that, I said.

He grinned.

And one more thing. Did he realise the fans now sang about Cantona in the way they used to sing about him? Did he know 'Eric the King' had succeeded 'Denis the King'.

'Bloody sacrilege,' he said, mock-spluttering into his beer. 'Actually, I couldn't think of a better successor.'

Two days later, Southampton were at United: academic for us, but they needed the points to stay up. For the nostalgia, I stood in the Scoreboard Paddock, the penultimate opportunity to stand at Old Trafford before the *Taylor Report* was fully implemented. I looked across at where my United-watching career had started. Things had changed since those early days. The Stretford Paddock, the forest of red solidarity, was now the Pontins Family Stand, where Uncle Dave entertains the patrons before the game and Mars give samples away throughout it. 'If you could mention the sponsors by name, I'd be very grateful,' Danny McGregor had said. Happy to oblige.

Out on the pitch too, it was different. There is a ludicrous pub bore's debate which suggests that Best would not have made it in today's United because the pace of the game is too frantic. It is of course a non-starter of an argument, he would have been the second name on the Fergie team sheet, after Cantona. But as for Alex Forsyth, Arnie Sidebottom and Tommy Jackson, the boys I had watched in awe back in 1975: it might be harder to make a convincing argument for their prospects in 1994.

It was an odd anticlimax inside the ground. The thing was won, but we were told by Keith Fane that the real celebrations would be on the Sunday when, for the benefit of Sky subscribers who might otherwise not see it, the trophy was to be presented. To drown out any spontaneous outbreaks of celebration, he had switched his monster PA's volume knob up to ear-bleed as he played his new favourite song – D:Ream's singularly inappropriate 'Things Can Only Get Better'.

There was an odd, otherworldly atmosphere throughout the game. After forty weeks of lurching tension, here was an outcome which didn't matter, a game without an emotional significance. It was difficult to know how to behave – which was why the series of Mexican waves took off: it was something to do. As the waves went round the ground, they would travel cheerfully through the Southampton section, then stop dead in the middle of the main stand.

'Stand up yer yuppies,' shouted the man next to me as another wave beached on the posh seats. 'I think they've lost the use of their legs, the rich,' he added.

After the game, in his role as atmosphere-generator to the masses, Peter Boyle threw a title-winning party at his girlfriend's place in Chorlton. We were to meet outside the Trafford pub, on Warwick Road. I got there to discover Boyle already surrounded by a platoon of followers, lads in their teens and early twenties, a couple of years younger than their musical director. As the huge tide of humanity washed out of the stadium past us on its way to the car parks and tram station, people shouted in our direction: 'All right, Streaker,' or, 'Boylie, nice one.' Two elderly men came out of the crowd to shake him by the hand. 'See you at Wembley,' they said. And: 'Keep up the good work, son.'

'Who are they?' I asked him.

'No idea,' he said. 'Fans, I suppose.'

At the party dozens of supporters gathered, to sing songs, drink beer, roll joints and celebrate being reds. As I walked into the house, at the bottom of the stairs sat two lads, gingerly tackling the vegetarian stew Boyle's girlfriend Sally, an anti-Fascist indie-popper, had prepared.

'What's this?' asked one, chasing a piece of courgette round his paper plate.

'I think it's cucumber,' said his mate.

'Cucumber? Whoever heard of cooking cucumber?'

In the sitting room, Boyle's tape was playing on the stereo. Mark, the old soldier in beer-shock, was sitting on the sofa, dressed in a white European Cup Winners Cup shirt, chin forward. I sat next to him.

'To be a red, eh?' he said. 'Eh? Eh?'

'Yeah,' I said. 'It's a good feeling.'

'Eh? Eh? To be red, man. Eh?'

He put out his hand to be shaken. I took it. He squeezed my knuckles as others might a grape.

'Eh?'

We sat for a few minutes in silence, listening to the tape. Then he stood up and shouted 'On, on, on,' just after Boyle's voice had been heard saying 'and the Reds go marching...' He jabbed his fists forward as he did it, sparring out his loyalty.

'Eh? Fucking hell,' he said, sitting down. 'Yes. Yes.'

There was another silence. I got up to go. Then he said:

'I was one of them once.'

'A what?' I said.

'Player. United player. Played in the youth team, back in the seventies. With Andy Ritchie. Left wing. Then I got into the pop, like,' he lifted his can of Kestrel. 'Too much pop. I blew it. They said I was the new George Best. That's what they said. I coulda done it, man. I coulda been Ryan fucking Giggs, me.'

I asked him what his surname was. He told me.

It was cruel, it was very cruel, but the next morning I rang up Old Trafford and asked if they had a record of him playing for the youth team in the mid-seventies. They'd check, they said. After ten minutes they rang me back. They said they'd asked the official club historian and no, there was no record of him.

The players had been celebrating, too. Not in the frantic way they had the year before, when it was like VE day. But they had enjoyed themselves. I went to Paul Ince's house that week, to interview him for the *Manchester United Magazine*, and he was happy, very happy – a grin which must have hurt stapled to his face. While we talked a man rang the doorbell of his house. It was a hot day, all the doors were open and he listened as his wife asked the man what he wanted.

'Have you made arrangements?' she asked. 'Have you got an appointment?'

It turned out the caller was from a local news agency; a story about a number of players being involved in a fight had reached him and he wanted 'Paul's comments on some serious allegations if at all possible.'

Ince went to the door and asked him what it was about.

'We understand there was an incident at Chester races involving you and some racial abuse.'

Ince said he had nothing to say.

'Are you denying the incident took place?' said the hack.

'I'm saying we had a nice quiet night, OK?' Ince said, all polite and noncommittal.

The man seemed happy with that and went away.

Ince came back into the room and shrugged. The next day it was the front-page story in the *Mirror* and the *Sun*: 'Soccer Stars In Race Brawl'. As the *Mirror* had it: Ince, Cantona, Bruce and Pallister had been set upon by Liverpool louts who had abused Ince, but the players behaved impeccably under provocation; the *Sun* reported that the players were acting the bigheads, causing offence and Cantona started the trouble. Had to be Eric. Goldfish Bowl United.

I asked Ince about it, the intrusions on his privacy, the fact he is such a recognised face in a town where the football team is the principal asset, where he and his team-mates are the biggest thing in the lives of people like Mark and Catweasle and Andy Mitten. And me.

'To be honest, I don't mind if a geezer wants an autograph and a quick chat,' he said, answering the phone to a mate who wanted tickets for the game on Sunday, then deciding to leave it off the hook. 'Where was I. Yeah? No problem, happy to do an autograph, lovely. But then you get blokes come up and want to talk football for hours: "What's Giggsy like? What's Fergie like? What's Robbo like?" You know, do they want to talk about their jobs after work? And the wife's standing there, maybe for half an hour, left out of it. And though she's good about it, understands it's part of the job, you're meant to be out with her, giving her some time. Instead, there's this geezer giving it some. And you feel like saying: "Look, come on, it's my night off, give me a break, mate, yeah?" But you know if you do that it'll be all "he's too big for his boots, look at him superstar, we're the people who made him and he hasn't got time for us". So you can't win.'

You can win the title though. That must be a comfort. That must make the grief easier to bear.

'Oh aye,' he said. 'I must stop saying that, "Oh aye". Back home they give me slaughter for saying it. Reckon I'm turning Manc. But yeah, we done it.'

They had won it, too, in a ruthless, efficient, nerveless manner. Of their last five games, United had won four and drawn one; of theirs, Blackburn had drawn three and lost two. United the finishers. Yet the press still harked back to that stumbling 1992 time, still suspected that they were a team with a fault line running through the middle.

'What none of them realised was how much we had learnt from

'ninety-two,' Ince said. 'In 'ninety-two we thought we'd won it, and it went out of our hands. Worse thing for me was I wasn't playing. We lost at home to Forest, drew at Luton, lost at West Ham and I wasn't out there. I'm not saying I'd have made a difference, but it was frustrating for me. The worse thing was we thought we were the best team, and we blew it.

'So this year, even when we were sixteen points ahead, and Blackburn had two games in hand, we weren't surprised that they closed it to ten, to seven, to three, to none at one point. Didn't panic us, we knew it would happen. All this shutting the bookies and stopping taking bets in January, we'd been there before, we knew it was bollocks. We never felt under pressure as they closed us. You want to know about pressure, you go talk to them lads at Oldham, fighting for their bloody lives, that's pressure. This isn't pressure.

'As soon as Blackburn got level on points and had to go to places like Coventry and Southampton, the pressure was on them to do it. We'd done it, we'd been there, so we knew what to expect and we went out and did the business when it mattered: against City and Leeds. That's what we can do. We can win when it matters.'

Wasn't there something they could learn from this year as they had from 1992? An element of self-control, perhaps?

'I know what you're getting at,' he said. 'Obviously, temperwise, we get involved too much. But if you took the fire out of the belly, we wouldn't be half the players we are. I've learnt to curb it more than, say, Keanie has, but that's maybe because I'm a bit older. You have to learn. When I was his age, I seemed to get involved in everything. He'll learn in time. But I tell you this, you don't win without competing.'

And what about Cantona?

'Eric's Eric. Enjoy it while you can, mate.'

Ince missed out on the final game of the season, rested before the Cup final, trying not to put too much pressure on a groin strain that would take an operation to sort out eventually.

The last game, it had everything. Except football. The fans were in face-paint mode. Outside the stadium they climbed the advertising hoardings and covered the posters for Reebok and Umbro with banners for 'Flixton reds'. Inside, the place was a swirl of flags – it looked wonderful. The usual ban, by which every week policemen remove enough canes from supporters' flags to keep a raspberry farm upright for a year, was lifted. Presumably, since the Manchester Royal Infirmary was not besieged by emergency admissions of detached retinas that afternoon, the ban will stay lifted. Or maybe not. Across the stands a giant flag, paid for by the fanzines, was passed overhead, Italian-style. On the pitch, a series of presentations were made: to the reserve- and youth-team player of the year.

And then Denis Law, receiving an ovation somewhat louder than the one he had got at Television Centre earlier in the week, gave Bryan Robson a long-service award, the United equivalent of a gold watch. Robbo was off to Middlesbrough as manager, and this was his last appearance at Old Trafford.

I saw his first. It was in 1979 for West Bromwich Albion when they destroyed Dave Sexton's stodgy United 5–3. Despite Regis frightening Brian Greenhoff, despite Cunningham frying Nicholl, it was Robson I noticed. He was everywhere, tearing from penalty box to penalty box, cleaning up in front of the Albion area one moment and raiding into United's the next. Even if he had stood still, it would have been hard to miss him with the Harpo Marx frizz-perm he wore at the time, perhaps the only serious mistake he has ever made.

When he came to us as part of Ron Atkinson's baggage, we found we'd signed half a team; for years he carried United. And to watch him in action was to see someone who cared. I remember an extraordinary image at Loftus Road in 1992: even from the stands you could see Robson's teeth were clenched so firmly in determination that you thought his jaw was going to snap, sending powdered molars drifting on to the turf. The irony, the deep irony, of his Old Trafford career is that a team fitting for his talents was only assembled towards the end of it, when he could only flit on its peripheries.

In this atmosphere of celebration and reflection, of memory and dedication, the United commercial department thought it the perfect opportunity to unveil what they called 'the new concept in sports marketing'. Before kickoff four girls walked on to the pitch carrying an airship load of red balloons. At the count of three, conducted over the public-address system by our frantic friend Fane, the balloons were released. There behind them, in the centre circle usually graced by Hughes, Cantona and Giggs, was a man dressed in a big, fluffy, comedy devil's outfit. He was, apparently, Fred the Red: 'the new Manchester United character mascot', the Ronald McDonald of Old Trafford. To celebrate his arrival, the crowd's attention was drawn to the Fred the Red catalogue, which had been stapled into the centre of the match programme before the news of ticket-price rises for the new season. Merchandise of a range and quantity that would need a superstore of its own were on offer: Fred pens, Fred shirts, Fred India rubbers; even a Fred television cartoon is planned. For a moment, as Fred stood there waving to the crowd, you wondered what United were more proud of here – the finest set of footballers assembled in a generation, or the invention of a new way to pay their wage bill.

The fans were underwhelmed by Fred, barely applauding his arrival (he didn't take the hint and leave, he just continued bouncing around the touchline as if he owned the place). Old-fashioned things that they are, they preferred to celebrate the players and their achievements.

The team's arrival was somewhat more spectacular: a parade of stage-managed triumphalism. Fanfares sounded, flares popped, the Coventry City team formed a guard of honour. And on they came, the players who had done it. The applause, the singing, the noise throughout the game was totally at odds with anything that went on on the pitch. With most of the first team sitting it out, it was left to the reserves to go through ninety minutes of motions before the trophy presentation.

Only one man seemed to be engaged in a football match – Bryan Robson. As the crowd sang his name, he went in a single-minded pursuit of his hundredth goal for the club. In the last few seconds

I thought he was going to get it. He bent a rising shot from the edge of the area towards the left-hand corner of the goal. It just looped round the post, the crowd groaned, and he looked as if he had just forgotten his mum's birthday.

But he got his moment. Steve Bruce invited him to go and lift the trophy with him. While the reserves who had played in the game stood in the centre circle trying not to look like spare parts, the boys who had done the business went up to receive their reward: a hold of the ugliest trophy in British football history. They also got medals this year, chunky gold medals with a modernist lion engraved on the front. Last year they had taken replicas of the trophy back home to Cheshire, miniatures in silver. Several of the players had complained, not surprisingly, that they didn't like the mini-trophies. The FA had conceded that something 'more traditional' should be presented.

Then they went down on to the pitch, to provide the next day's papers with soaraway souvenir posters. For some reason Fred the Red, by now the embarrassment of Old Trafford, was still there, bouncing around, waving as if he was the main attraction. On a signal prearranged among themselves, as soon as the pictures were finished, the players charged at him, downed him and, with a roar of encouragement from the crowd you could have heard in Liverpool, tore his monster suit off. The actor inside Fred's costume flounced off in a temper, calling our heroes all sorts of names. So that was the final score: Players 1, Commercial Department 0. For a brief moment at Old Trafford, football, as they say, was the winner.

Afterwards, in the press room, Ferguson was oddly uneuphoric. He looked like a man halfway through the task in hand.

'I don't think any of you want to talk about the game,' he said.

He was right.

'Those celebrations,' he said. 'When you see commitment and response like that from supporters, it drives you on, it really does. Sixteen defeats in three league campaigns now, that's a fabulous achievement, really fabulous. Last year we won it by ten points, this year eight. You know what, I'd be happy with a gap of six next year. I said after the Liverpool game that eighty-four points would do it and I was wrong, Blackburn got that.'

What next, Alex? someone said.

'We can achieve anything here now,' he said, 'if these players want to accept the challenge. They've only got to look to Robbo today to see what someone can achieve. He'll go on from here. It's very difficult to be a manager nowadays, with freedom of contract and the pressures from the modern media, youse lovely boys. But he can make it.'

Even here one day?

'Why not,' said Fergie. 'Aye, why not.'

It was left to Phil Neal, the Coventry manager and a member of the greatest of Liverpool sides, to have the last word. Had it been his idea, someone wondered, that his players had formed a guard of honour for United and clapped them on to the pitch.

'Yes,' he said. 'The ref said to us we should go out together. I said no way. They deserve nothing but our respect, end of story. They are far and away the best and our place is to acknowledge that.'

Praise indeed.

Now, to achieve their place in history, all they had to attend to was the minor matter of the FA Cup final.

22

The Final

Know of any spares?
                    Everyone I know, May 1994

It knocks a week out of your life, preparing for the Cup final; you have to devote seven days just to the phone calls. All week it was ringing with the same enquiry: know of any spares? I only had the one ticket, acquired from Cat-with-the-contacts, and people were ringing me. The players had twenty-four each: so no wonder Paul Ince took his phone off the hook all week. There were spares aplenty if, in that ancient Cup-final tradition, your bank balance was up to it. Andy the art critic, after three calls to my house for advice, finally gave his gold-card number to a man in the *Yellow Pages*. He paid £350 for a £40 seat and was pretty pleased with himself, he'd beaten the bloke down from £450.

Jon Shine, a long-time customer of the black market, took a moral stand.

'It's the first Wembley appearance I'll have missed since nineteen sixty-eight,' he said. 'But I refuse to pay these prices. It's just gone silly.'

The stand lasted until the morning of the game.

'Oh sod it,' he said. And went down to Wembley where, after two hours, he landed a ticket for £170. It was marked, in case anyone from the FA is remotely interested in tracking down how things arrive on the black market, 'Staffordshire FA'.

Peter Boyle, an underfunded student, unfortunately didn't have the money to take the traditional route.

'I've been to thirty-six games this season and I can't get one,' he said. 'But I'm going down there. I'll watch it on the telly in a coach outside the ground if necessary. So if you know of any spares . . .'

And we arranged to meet on the morning of the match at a function advertised in *Red Issue*, a beer-in for United fans in a big hall just two stops from Wembley on the tube.

Much of the build-up had centred on how Chelsea, despite number-ing Messrs Mellor, Major and Banks among their following, did, in fact, have a truly influential supporter – God. Not to be confused with the French one at Old Trafford, this was the bearded one up in the firmament. Glen Hoddle, born-again years ago, had experi-enced a revelation in December. In it he had been told that if he drew his brother, who played for Barnet, in the third round of the Cup, Chelsea would go all the way. Since at the time Chelsea were second bottom in the Premiership and apparently incapable of going all the way in Bangkok, this was a confident celestial prediction. Hoddle said he fell off the bed when the sibling rivalry was con-firmed in the Lancaster Gate hat while he was watching 'Match of the Day'. And Chelsea had proceeded from a scrappy victory against Hoddle junior, all the way to the final.

Then, on the Tuesday of Cup-final week, Hunter Davies revealed in *The Independent* that Gavin Peacock, the most influential con-tributor to Chelsea's Cup run and the man who had scored twice without reply against United, was of a similar spiritual inclination to his manager. Gav assiduously prayed before games, seeking gui-dance in the dressing-room lavatory. God had done well by him so far.

Once during his March wobbles, Alex Ferguson had said that he felt United were playing the world, Mars, everybody. Now another opponent had been added to the list. In the over-superstitious world of football, it was not hard to believe that Chelsea's name was on the Cup.

Paul Ince didn't believe it. He was well confident.

'Yeah, but we've got to be confident against them,' he said. 'At

Stamford Bridge it was an error that let the goal in and he was lucky, though at our place he took it well. We feel as though we owe them. Also, the last couple of times we've been at Wembley the pitch has been rather dry and there's been a drag on the ball, which has meant it's gone really slow. And that isn't our game. When I've played on the pitch for England, it had been watered just before the game and it was beautiful, you could fizz the ball about. But with it being a wet spring, they maybe didn't think they needed to water it, so it was dry. With the players we've got, the flair players, you want it to be nice and spinning. That's the way United play: attack, bang, attack, bang. I saw Graham Kelly recently, you know, the FA geezer, and I told him to water the pitch.'

Then he narrowed his eyes and added:

'Anyhow, we owe them one. Next thing I'm hearing, Chelsea have come out with "How to beat Man United". We'll see. There's not many teams who've won the double and we want to be there, we want to do it. We're confident now we've got the one trophy under our belt. I tell you, put your money on us, boy.'

That was the last word I had with the players. It was impossible to talk to them in final week unless you contributed to the pool, another quaint Cup-final ritual by which any interview had to be paid through the nose for. Poor things, they needed the extra money.

Since United had been out of bounds to the press for the latter part of the season, most of the tabloids were happy to pay away. Amid the snowstorm of expensively acquired truisms – 'great opportunity', 'dream come true', 'looking forward to it' – were a couple of illuminating exceptions.

The *Sun* ran Lee Sharpe's guide to the players' nicknames. He didn't confirm the fanzine rumour that Denis Irwin is known as Bogman in the dressing room (possibly to avoid a visitation from the Commission for Racial Equality), but he did say that Hughes, in the manner of that bloke from U2, was known as the Ledge, because he's a legend. Everyone else appeared to have names derived from facial similarities to television actors: Parker was

Benny (someone from 'Grange Hill'), Pallister was Rodney (dopey brother in 'Only Fools and Horses'), Ferguson was Taggart (ruddy-faced Glaswegian hard-man). Schmeichel, Sharpe said, had a nickname, but not one used to his face. Indeed Paul Ince told me that Schmeichel, a man not tuned into the schoolboy banter of the English professional football club, was 'just not the kind of geezer you made nicknames up for, you know what I mean?'

I also liked a picture in one of the tabloids of all the players' wives togged out in their Cup-final best. Since Giggsy wasn't married, and didn't want his girlfriend exposed, the paper had lined his mum up in the picture. Rather ungallantly they had given the ladies' ages: Lynne Giggs was a year younger than Bryan Robson's wife, Denise.

Alex Ferguson, on the other hand, gave open house at Old Trafford on the Wednesday. For the occasion in the press lounge he wore an antique red shirt – one, he said, that had been made for the European Cup final in 1968, but never worn because United had been obliged to wear blue to avoid a colour clash. He was in particularly relaxed form, as you might expect from a man who had just popped the Premiership trophy back into United's museum. The taut, preoccupied face we had seen for much of the season had softened, revealing the mellower lines which are usually only visible when he is not fulfilling his media responsibilities. His ambition, though, showed no sign of relaxing. As well as a determination not to lose thrice to 'the Cockneys', he wanted the players to seize the historical opportunity presented to them. After all, someone wins the title every year: the double had been accomplished but three times in a century.

'When people look at a match-day programme,' he said, 'the honours list is there to tell you how successful a club has been. Look at anyone's programme and it tells you what the club is all about: their tradition. Here, the double has never been done before. The big three – Tottenham, Arsenal and Liverpool – have all done it, and it would be nice to share their place in history. Let's say it is something we want to add to our list.'

However, the cool, unflustered Ferguson failed to communicate his relaxed demeanour to everyone – me, for instance. By Thursday the players were already in London, staying in a Gothic monstrosity of a hotel which had once been a location for Hammer horror movies (Peter Schmeichel looked oddly at home there), leaving their wives and mums back in Manchester to savour the preparations for a lavish weekend as guests of the club. But by now I had convinced myself that Chelsea were going to win and the double would go the way of the treble. My friend Giles, a Chelsea season-ticket holder, on the other hand, had convinced himself that United would. We had a lengthy phone conversation on the Friday in which we tried to persuade each other of the merits of our respective teams. His argument was: United were the best team he had ever seen. Mine was: Chelsea have beaten us twice this year. His was: it was a bloody fluke. Mine was: God is on your side. We did little to change each other's minds.

Then, browsing through an old programme (you do anything in Cup-final week to take your mind off future games) I noticed that the eleven Ferguson was expected to choose for the final – Schmeichel, Parker, Irwin, Bruce, Pallister, Keane, Ince, Kanchelskis, Cantona, Hughes, Giggs – had only played eleven times together before. They had won every game, scoring twenty-four and conceding four. Glenn, Gavin and God would have to be on top form to match that, I thought. Then I panicked. Overconfidence is usually punished.

My Cup-final morning preparation was exactly the same as Steve Bruce's standard match-day routine: I went to the lavatory four times. Then I went to the *Red Issue* event, which had begun at nine, in order to soften my nerves with beer. Boyle was on the stage when I walked in, leading a run-through of 'Eric the King'. It was amazing to see how many fans knew his verses as well as the chorus. After he had abandoned the stage to an amply buttocked, Deirdre Barlow-lookalike of a stripper, he told me his girlfriend had managed to use her wiles at Old Trafford to secure a ticket for him the day before, but a couple of his mates weren't so lucky, so if I knew of any spares . . .

A few pints, a few strippers and a few awful jokes from the compere later, we made our way to the tube station. There were six of us: Boyle, me, two young lads in red, a Welshman in shorts called Duane, with about a quarter-inch of limb free of tattoos, and a Shaun Ryder-lookalike with a bottle of beer, who was snapping everything with his Canon Sureshot. We were a group about as intimidating as a special needs school outing and one which I would have thought, as we sang our way through the Boyle repertoire, epitomised the party atmosphere of Cup-final day. Well, I would think that, but then I'm not a psychotic Chelsea fan.

They stood at the other end of the tube carriage, five of them, in their twenties, dressed in sports labels, without a colour between them. The moment we stepped on to the train, they started swearing at us. Boyle, not one to shrink quietly into the background, started a round of 'Eric the King', to which they replied 'Chewl-sea, Chewl-sea', sung with resentment rather than pleasure. It was perhaps not wise of Boyle to counter this with 'Chelsea is your name, Chelsea is your name, twenty-four years and won fuck all, Chelsea is your name.' But he did.

Just past Neasden station, they charged us. The first one through – a type usually found on the other end of a lead from a muscle dog – pushed Duane the tattooed Welshman and sent him flying. His lieutenant, pockmarked of face and greasy of ponytail, grabbed hold of the bottle the Shaun Ryder-lookalike was holding and snarled: 'What you doing with this?'

'I'm drinking from it, mate,' was the reply.

'Well, I'm going to smash it over your head.'

As the two of them wrestled for control of the bottle, the third in line punched one of the youths in a United shirt hard in the mouth. A middle-aged man who had been sitting down until now stood up and said:

'Hey lads, look, it's the Cup final.'

'So fucking what?' said the Chelsea worm. And he head-butted him. Then it kicked off. Everyone was on the move, sidestepping out of the way of ill-targeted blows and kicks. People were getting hit on the shoulder, the elbow, the neck. In the flail, looking past the youth who had been hit – who was holding his mouth and whimpering like a lost dog – I could just see Boyle. By now at the other end of the carriage, he had worked the Chelsea man who had led the charge on to a seat and pinned him there with his knees on his shoulders. I could see his fists rhythmically pounding downwards in a way you didn't expect from someone who likes the Cure.

Beside me, the pockmarked bloke and the middle-aged peace-maker had hold of each other's faces with their left hands, trying to work them into range of their right fists. The peacemaker was repeating as he did it: 'It's the bloody Cup final, why are you doing this?'

The pockmark didn't speak, he just made a snorting noise, rage creasing his face, spit foaming at the corners of his mouth. They both tumbled on to the carriage floor, the pockmark on top trying to wriggle his face free. A boy in a United shirt, no more than sixteen, pulled at the pockmark's beige Lacoste bomber jacket saying: 'He's me dad, for fuck's sake, he's me dad, leave him alone.'

I heard a commotion behind me and turned to see three more pushing down the aisle, swinging from the dangly handles. I think they had come through the connecting door from the next carriage. As I spun round I realised something: I would be the first person in the ruck they would come across.

'All right lads,' I said, extending my arms palm-first towards them and suddenly realising I hadn't a notion whether they were ours or theirs. 'The Old Bill will be at the station.'

They were theirs. I saw a punch coming and ducked into it. It landed on the back of my head, just behind the ear, the place where Frank Bruno's usually land. I assumed I was in for a kicking. But only two ill-aimed Timberland moccasin blows had come my way when God took time off from looking after Gavin and Glenn and intervened. As I staggered backwards, the train ground into Wembley Park. A boy in a Chelsea shirt, his face wiped of colour, hammered hard at the open-door button. The door opened and everyone was sucked out, like water down a drain. Spotting a gap, I legged it along the platform, completely uninterested in the fate of my travelling companions. As the fighters came tumbling out of the carriage, down the platform came a lone policeman, past me and into the small mob in pursuit. He grabbed the first person he could. By one of those coincidences that must happen occasionally even to the Metropolitan Police, it was the right man: the pockmark. Past the policeman I saw Boyle applying a final knee to the groin of the fight's perpetrator and running hard for the stairs. I felt a sudden surge of self-righteousness and went back, up to the policeman and said, 'It was him, he started it. Make sure he doesn't see the match.'

The policeman advised me to fuck off. So I did.

I joined the scrum heading up the exit steps and looked ahead for Boyle. I caught sight of him making exaggeratedly friendly conversation with a Chelsea fan who had blue-and-white stripes war-painted across his face.

'Good luck mate, enjoy yourself,' he said, shaking the rather surprised man by the hand. 'Have a great day, that's what's important.'

'That's how it should be,' Boyle said, as I caught up with him. 'I feel soiled by what happened back there, honestly, dirty. But as soon as that twat grabbed the bottle I knew it was going off, so I just made sure. I can't believe anyone can be that bitter.'

While Boyle bore no obvious signs of engagement, Shaun Ryder was less lucky. He had lost his Sureshot and his shades and had a crimson welt above his eye.

'Twats,' he said. 'Spoil it, don't they?'

Outside the tube station there were hundreds of police and lads running all over the place, many of them away from the stadium. A bloke in his twenties, who had no other form of identification than an enamel United lapel badge like the one I was wearing, grabbed me by the shirt. 'Come on reds,' he said, pointing in the direction everyone was running, 'it's kickin' off, it's kickin' off.'

I declined his invitation to join him.

'Got any spares, by the way?' he said as he headed off.

Boyle, Duane and I made it up a Wembley Way tense with possibility. At the top we separated, with me heading through the Chelsea throng to the section I was in. 'Take off your badge,' Boyle counselled. Not much point in that, I said, since I was also wearing a 'L'Eric Sportif' T-shirt. As I made my way to the turnstile, someone called me a 'Manc slag' and spat on my boots.

That Cup final spirit in full.

I met up with Cat, who had my ticket, by the turnstile. By now it was torrenting with rain, thumping a rhythmic pound against the stadium's roof, small brown rivers in flood from piles of police-horse muck, half-eaten burgers soggy in gutters.

The Wembley sight, though, is not one to be diminished by rain; just as it will not be diluted by the urine channelling through the concourses, or the lager at £3 a throw which tastes as if it has been siphoned straight from this tidal flow. Nor, though it was our third visit there in two months, did familiarity do anything to dull the sensation. It was wonderful in there, the thousands of individual feats of fancy dress, the extra effort football-followers make for the Cup final, merging into an impressionistic blob of colour and noise. As the crowd sang 'Abide with Me', as the busbys of the band grew bedraggled in the downpour, as the two teams emerged gladiatorially from the tunnel, you would have to had little sense of romance if your stomach did not lurch into a spinning, twisting, gastric impression of Nadia Comaneci.

The Chelsea fans had given a new edge to the traditional sight. Adopting an Italian trick, they held up coloured cards, previously left on the seats by their supporters' association, so their entire section was redecorated in blue-and-white stripes. It made the reds, at the other end, look old-fashioned and provincial with their flags and scarves.

It was raining so hard now that the players were already soaked by the time they lined up for the national anthem, unlike the minor royal they were presented to who was protected by an umbrella the size of a small tree. Ince, at least, would be pleased, the pitch was getting a good watering.

As they peeled off to start warming up, I realised Robson wasn't among them. So the great hero, the man who had carried the team for nearly a decade, the man who had scored the first genital-assisted goal seen in a Cup semi-final, was not to finish his United career at Wembley, even as a substitute. It would have been nice if he had, but Ferguson is not a man to let sentiment overwhelm efficiency. Afterwards, the manager revealed that Cantona was suffering from a sore back, and he needed McClair as a substitute in case. It was a hard decision he said, of the kind Robson would need to make when he became a boss at Middlesbrough.

'I said to him, "What would you do in my position?" '

To which Robson, not a man afflicted with self-doubt, replied: 'I'd play myself.'

Our tickets cost £60 face value, for which we were afforded a perfect view of a pillar running, with geometric precision, through the middle of one penalty spot. Fortunately, it was at the end United were attacking in the first half, during which Chelsea adopted the game plan they had used in their two Premiership victories against us. It meant deploying a brace of pacey midgets up front to disturb Pallister and Bruce, with Peacock sitting just behind to steam through on any confusion. Newton was super-glued to Cantona, as were the full backs to Giggs and Kanchelskis, leaving Wise, small and angry, to exchange with Ince and Keane – a task he approached with relish. The idea, not a new approach this season, was to smother United's attacking invention and hope to protect a snatched goal. For the first forty-five minutes the Londoners ran and ran, closing down United at every turn, allowing them no room for trickery. They were first to everything, playing as if – well – this was their Cup final. Their fans did their bit too, singing constantly and chucking sticks of celery (for some reason even Giles could not explain, a favoured vegetable at Stamford Bridge) at Giggs and Cantona when they took corners. And when Peacock's long shot hit the bar, I had a sudden surge of alarm: lightning could strike three times. We were lucky to go back up the tunnel still in it.

During the interval, Ferguson asked each of his players if they had it in them to achieve their place in history. This is apparently what he does a lot, since every match they play now is of historical significance. But from the re-start it seemed the well-trodden motivational chat might work again. The Chelsea players began to look as though they had exhausted themselves tearing around in the rain and were marginally slower about the pitch and into the tackle; they had lost what Ferguson calls the extra seven pounds; and among United's many attributes is a remarkable fitness, they are a team which grows stronger as their opponents weaken: Ince's 'Wear 'em down, wear 'em down, wear 'em down'. So Giggs, despite fifty-six games, despite the debilitations of carrying infected organs in his throat, despite the energy expended avoiding teenage girls, had the strength to find the space ahead of his full back. Twice he did it in five minutes. The first time he rasped a shot into Kharine's midriff. The second he drifted past Clarke into their area, stabbing the ball, under challenge, across to Irwin.

Mr Ellery, the referee, was three feet behind the play at this point. But he could have been sitting next to me and he would have seen what happened next clear enough. Newton, leaving Cantona's side for the first time, sent Irwin spiralling high into the north London air. Not one Chelsea player objected when the penalty was awarded. And round me, none of the United fans did either.

In Spain the same day, Deportivo La Coruna were awarded a penalty in the last minute of their last match of the season, a spot-kick which, if converted, would have won them the title for the first time. The usual Deportivo penalty-taker refused to take it, so hamstrung was he by the responsibility. The team went into a nerve-sapping huddle to decided who would do the business instead. No one would. The manager had to make a choice. When the unhappy forward who had been selected to take responsibility stepped up, he shot tamely at the keeper. In La Coruna, they went into mourning.

At Wembley, immediately the whistle sounded, Cantona – the man who George Graham said was 'a cry baby who will let you down at the highest level', the man who the *Sunday Times* described as having a temperament which faltered on the big occasion – seized the ball and walked up to place it on the spot.

Wise, clearly believing what he read in the *Sunday Times*, chittered round him, saying things, trying to put him off, moving the ball, attempting to shake him by the hand. When the Chelsea captain had finally eased off, and the ref had replaced the ball, Eric took two paces forward and replaced it again, to his own satisfaction.

While this tension-tightening performance took place, Bruce, the erstwhile United penalty man, squatted on his haunches on the half-way line with his back to the goal, looking down at his feet. As Eric walked smartly to the edge of the penalty area, turned and took seven paces forward, I said to Cat, 'He'll miss.'

He didn't.

With Kharine stranded in that humiliating flounder a goalkeeper adopts when he elects to dive the wrong way at a penalty, Cantona passed the ball precisely into the right-hand corner of the net. We jumped, we shouted, we hugged, we kissed. We wished we were down on the pitch where we could have prostrated ourselves at his feet. It was a stunning penalty, a strike of iceberg cool. It was a goal on its own worth £60, a punch to the head and gob-soaked, urine-stained boots.

'That's the thing about Eric,' Giggs told me. 'When he grabs the ball you just know.'

After the match Eric the King explained that he wasn't nervous.

'If you are nervous taking a penalty, you have no place on a football field,' he said.

And he also revealed Wise had bet him £100 he would miss, that's what all the handshaking had been about.

'He brought the money to the dressing room. I did not expect him to pay up. He is a great man.'

Three minutes later, Wise did not bother with another bet. Chelsea, their resolve as shattered as their muscles, were torn apart when Hughes invited Kanchelskis to gallop into the area in pursuit of a long pass. Sinclair paced him, nudged him and Kanchelskis made what might be described as a professional fall. Mr Ellery gave another penalty. Cantona, again showing disdain for the nerves that might afflict a mortal, produced an action replay of his first effort. Five minutes later and Chelsea were crushed like a pigeon beneath the wheels of a juggernaut, the life flattened out of them. Sinclair, the donator of the second penalty, slipped, Hughes pounced and earned himself a minor record: he had played four times at Wembley that season and scored on each occasion. By now we had exhausted our celebrations and just stood smiling the smiles of the very proud.

Like a beaten boxer lurching off the ropes, Chelsea made a brief and futile rally, Schmeichel making two smart saves. Then, Cantona broke through from the halfway line and found himself alone with Kharine. A hat trick was glimpsed, but he missed: a lapse of the God. Then Ince rounded the keeper and, showing a generosity which few others who were paid £3000 a goal by their boot-manufacturers would contemplate, squared for McClair, a late substitute, to side-foot home with almost the last touch of the game. Boyle would have been pleased for his benefactor. The double was done, Ferguson's quest for history achieved.

'Busby, Busby,' rang out the cry.

'Had he been here he would have been very proud of us today,' said Ferguson.

This was a great performance by United. Not aesthetic perhaps, and 4–0 was more than cruel on Chelsea. But the reds had shown the bite of seasoned winners, their clinical counter-attacks had destroyed opponents who had exhausted themselves in the first half. It was a paradigm of contrasting fortunes as Chelsea went up first to receive their losers' medals, drained of energy, emotion, everything. Down on the pitch, the United players were flying, larking around, popping a red wig on to Ferguson's head. He looked a proper Scotsman now.

But when Steve Bruce, a supporter's scarf dangling bedraggled round his neck, went up to lift the FA Cup, locking his elbows to thrust the oldest football trophy in the world up towards the United masses, I couldn't see him do it. Apparently, £60 is not sufficient to guarantee an unrestricted view at Wembley. The roof-top gallery cut out our view about thirty feet up (so if Sheffield United were playing you'd never see the ball). Around me, United fans celebrated the moment history was made prostrate on the terracing, squinting hopelessly in the direction of the royal box.

Down on the pitch, you could see them though: Benny, the Ledge, Rodney and Peter Schmeichel. They celebrated with abandon (though not quite as much abandon as they would show at the private party later that evening, that night and the next morning). Embracing their medals, gathering up a harvest of scarves, wearing the Cup's lid on their heads and pointing to funny banners or relatives in the crowd, they took their time circulating the ground. The Chelsea fans made themselves feel better by booing the winners with a bilious lack of grace. In contrast, United's fans cheered the losers to the rafters as they trudged their defeated way to the tunnel. Ah, the magnanimity of victory.

We stayed to file every second, every sight in our memory, making sure, as experienced Cup-finalists always say you should, that we didn't let it pass us all by. But the players were soon gone, back up the tunnel to the welcoming embrace of bottles of Gatorade and Des with his after-match interviews. Then into the Blues Brothers outfits they had decided to wear for their booze-fuelled celebration banquet. Then to the World Cup or the beach, then on to next season, when the whole thing has to be done again.

But, as we made our way home, giggling in the deluge, bumping into mates and greeting them with a fervour not normally found on the streets of London, we knew these boys had given us something. They had repaid our absurd faith, reinforced our identity, made our year, made you feel great to be a red. After Istanbul and Villa, after Swindon and Arsenal, they had recovered. And had proved that they were the greatest football team England had seen for a generation, since those soon-forgotten days when another bunch of reds, from Merseyside, won everything in sight. No one, not Jimmy Hill, not John Sadler, not Kenny Dalglish could deny our boys were the best. And when the fourth goal had gone in, the fans near me began a chant which acknowledged that this was not simply a victory over Chelsea, not just a Cup win, not just a double. The shift in power, influence and domination which had been craved so long had finally been achieved. They sang:

'Are you watching, Liverpool?'

Not A Lot Of People Know This

United records achieved in the 1993–94 season

1. United became the first-ever club to win the treble: the league, the FA Cup and the Charity Shield.

2. Bryan Robson and Les Sealey became United's third and fourth oldest post-war players. Sealey became United's oldest post-war goalkeeper. The oldest post-war player list now reads:

> John Warner, Newcastle (A) 22 April 1950: 38 years, 213 days
> Bill Foulkes, Southampton (H) 16 August 1969: 37 years, 222 days
> Bryan Robson, Coventry City (H) 8 May 1994: 37 years, 117 days
> Les Sealey, Aston Villa (Wembley) 27 March 1994: 36 years, 179 days

3. Peter Schmeichel established United's longest-ever run for a goalkeeper: 94 games. Steve Bruce now has the longest league run for a number 4: also 94 games.

4. Bryan Robson finished his career at Old Trafford eighth in the all-time United appearance table.

		Games	**Goals**
1.	Bobby Charlton	754	247
2.	Bill Foulkes	682	9
3.	Alex Stepney	535	2
4.	Tony Dunne	530	2
5.	Joe Spence	510	168
6.	Arthur Albiston	482	7
7.	George Best	466	178
8.	Bryan Robson	457	99

5. Robson was also United's longest-serving club captain – 12 years; yet his predecessor, Ray Wilkins, is still playing league football.

6. United had six sendings-off in 1993–94 (seven if you include Robson's in the pre-season tour of South Africa). They had only five sendings-off over the previous six seasons.

7. With Kanchelskis's dismissal in the League Cup final joining Kevin Moran's in the 1985 FA Cup final, United now boast the only players sent off in both Wembley showpieces.

8. United have never lost at home in 52 games in European competition. Of the 19 different teams to have won the European Cup, United are the only ones never to have lost at home in Europe.

9. United have now won the FA Cup eight times, a record shared with Spurs.

10. United have now played in a record eight FA Cup semi-final replays: 1949, 1965, 1970 (2), 1979, 1985, 1990 and 1994.

11. United have scored 28 goals in FA Cup finals, more than any other club.

12. United have appeared in 12 FA Cup finals, a record shared with Arsenal.

13. Since 1976 United have appeared in seven FA Cup semi-finals and won them all: 1976 (Derby), 1977 (Leeds), 1979 (Liverpool), 1983 (Arsenal), 1985 (Liverpool), 1990 (Oldham) and 1994 (Oldham).

14. United are only the second English side to win trophies in five successive seasons. They have some way to catch Liverpool's record of nine successive seasons: between 1976 and 1984.

15. United are now second in the all-time trophy-winning table, level with Arsenal on 20, well behind Liverpool's 33. Fourth are Aston Villa with 19.

16. United achieved a club record of 41 wins in a season (better than 38 in 1956–57) with 27 in the league, six in the League Cup, six in the FA Cup and two in the European Cup. Twenty of these were on opponents' grounds, two on neutral territory. The record for wins in a season is Everton: 43 in 1984–85.

17. United played a club record of 63 games in 1993–94. This comprises 42 league; nine League Cup; seven FA Cup; four in the European Cup and one Charity Shield. The previous record was 60 in both 1964–65 and 1982–83.

18. United are the only team to come first or second in every major domestic competition in one season.

19. Five United players each scored 10 goals or more: Cantona, Hughes, Giggs, Sharpe and Kanchelskis. The only other occasion five different United players got 10 goals or more was in 1964–65, with Best, Charlton, Law, Herd and Connelly.

20. Mark Hughes is now seventh in United's all-time goal-scorers table:

		League	Cup	Total
1.	Bobby Charlton	199	50*	249
2.	Denis Law	171	66*	237
3.	Jack Rowley	182	29*	211
4.	Dennis Viollet	152	20*	179
5.	George Best	137	42*	179
6.	Joe Spence	158	10	168
7.	Mark Hughes	112	39*	151
8.	Stan Pearson	128	21	149
9.	David Herd	114	31*	145
10.	Tommy Taylor	112	19*	131

* includes Charity Shield

21. Bryan Robson has scored at least one league goal in the last 20 league seasons for either West Brom or United.

22. Robson became the oldest man since the war to score for United. The list reads as follows:

Bryan Robson, Oldham (FA Cup semi replay), 13 April 94: 37 years, 92 days

John Warner, Charlton (H, FA Cup), 7 February 1948: 36 years, 139 days

Bill Foulkes, Real Madrid (A, European Cup), 15 May 1968: 36 years, 129 days

Jimmy Delaney, Charlton (H), 16 September 1950: 36 years, 13 days

Bobby Charlton, Southampton (A), 31 March 1973, 35 years, 171 days

We'll have to wait until November 2011 for Ryan Giggs to top the list.

23. United only lost four league games out of 42, a club record. The previous best was five in a 42-game season and four in a 38-game season.

24. United achieved their best-ever undefeated run – 34 games in all competitions – between defeats at Stoke on 22 September 1993 and at home to Chelsea on 5 March 1994. The English record is 40 (Notts Forest in 1978). United's previous record was 29 undefeated in all competitions from February–October 1956. However, they failed to overcome the record of 26 undefeated league games, also established in 1956.

25. United achieved their longest run of successive away league victories – seven – at Norwich, Coventry, Crystal Palace and Wimbledon at the end of the 1992–93 season and at Norwich (again), Aston Villa and Southampton at the start of 1993–94. The previous best was six in 1985.

26. United achieved their longest-ever undefeated home run in all competitions – 36 games – between being beaten by Wimbledon in November 1992 and by Chelsea in February 1994.

27. United also marked up a club record of 20 successive away games undefeated in all competitions, between defeat at Stoke in the League Cup in September and Aston Villa in the League Cup final in April.

28. This season saw the first time United beat one team four times in one campaign: Sheffield Wednesday 3–2 and 5–0 in the league; and 1–0 and 4–1 in the League Cup. Sheffield was definitely United's favourite away location; they also beat Sheffield United three times, and won four times in all in the steel city.

29. Just six people separated United's top four home attendances: Liverpool, 44,751; Everton, 44,750; Wimbledon, 44,748 and Chelsea, 44,745. They were out ordering pizza for the Chelsea game.

30. Peter Schmeichel has by far the best goal average of the 75 goalkeepers in United's history; an average of 0.79 goals conceded

per game. Apart from the handful who have played in five games or fewer, the only other United keepers with averages of less than one are: Gary Bailey (0.90) and Chris Turner (0.96).

31. Odd in a goal glut, but by the end of the season United had gone a record 193 games without a hat trick; the last was by Mark Hughes in the League Cup against Southampton on 23 January 1991.

32. United won 22 away games (including two on neutral grounds). This is a club record.

33. Eric Cantona is the only player to score two penalties in a FA Cup final.

34. Since 1989 United have monopolised the PFA Awards. They have won the Players' Player of the Year Award four times – Hughes (1989 and 1991), Pallister (1992) and Cantona (1994) and the Young Player Award three times – Sharpe (1991) and Giggs (1992 and 1993). What's more, in between, Platt and McGrath winners in 1990 and 1993 are former United players. Despite this, no United player has won the Football Writers' Player of the Year award since George Best in 1968.

35. Alex Ferguson is the only manager to win the double in both Scotland (with Aberdeen in 1984) and England (with United in 1994).

36. Mark Hughes has now won the most trophies of any United player – seven: two league titles (1993 and 1994); three FA Cups (1985, 1990 and 1994), one League Cup (1992) and the European Cup Winners Cup (1991).

   Next in line are Bill Foulkes with six: four titles (1956, 1957, 1965 and 1967); one FA Cup (1963); and one European Cup (1968). And Bryan Robson: two titles (1993 and 1994), three FA Cups (1983, 1985 and 1990) and one Cup Winners Cup (1991).

37. Oh, and it is now three years since United last failed to win the title.

APPEARANCES 1993–94

	FA Premiership (sub)	Coca-Cola Cup	FA Cup	European Cup	Total
Bruce, Steve	41	8(1)	7	4	60(1)
Butt, Nicky	0(1)	0	0(1)	0	(2)
Cantona, Eric	34	5	5	4	48
Dublin, Dion	1(4)	1(1)	0(1)	0(1)	2(7)
Ferguson, Darren	1(2)	1(1)	0	0	2(3)
Giggs, Ryan	32(6)	6(2)	7	4	49(8)
Hughes, Mark	36	8	7	2	53
Ince, Paul	39	5	7	4	55
Irwin, Denis	42	8(1)	7	3	59(1)
Kanchelskis, Andrei	28(3)	9	6	0	43(3)
Keane, Roy	34(2)	6(1)	6	3	49(3)
Martin, Lee	1	3	0	1(1)	5(1)
McClair, Brian	12(14)	6(1)	1(4)	0	19(19)
McKee, Colin	1	0	0	0	1
Neville, Gary	1	0	0	0(1)	1(1)
Pallister, Gary	41	9	7	3	59
Parker, Paul	39	6	7	3	55
Phelan, Mike	1(1)	2	0	1(3)	4(4)
Robson, Bryan	10(5)	5	1(1)	4	20(6)
Schmeichel, Peter	40	8	7	4	59
Sealey, Les	0	1	0(1)	0	1(1)
Sharpe, Lee	26(3)	2(2)	1(2)	4	33(8)
Thornley, Ben	0(1)	0	0	0	0(1)
Walsh, Gary	2(1)	0	0	0	2(1)

GOALSCORERS 1993–94

	FA Premiership	Coca-Cola Cup	FA Cup	European Cup	Total
Cantona, Eric	18	1	4	2	25
Hughes, Mark	12	5	4	0	21
Giggs, Ryan	13	3	1	0	17
Sharpe, Lee	9	2	0	0	11
Kanchelskis, Andrei	6	1	3	0	10
Ince, Paul	8	0	1	0	9
Keane, Roy	5	0	1	2	8
Bruce, Steve	3	2	0	2	7
McClair, Brian	1	4	1	0	6
Irwin, Denis	2	0	2	0	4
Robson, Bryan	1	0	1	1	3
Dublin, Dion	1	1	0	0	2
Pallister, Gary	1	0	0	0	1
own goal	0	0	0	1	1
Totals	80	19	14	8	123

FA Premiership Final Table

1. Manchester United Pl:42 W:27 D:11 L:4 F:80 A:38 Pts:92
2. Blackburn Rovers Pl:42 W:25 D: 9 L:8 F:63 A:36 Pts:84

Alex Ferguson

Born: 31.12.1941

Place of birth: Govan.

Previous clubs: as player: Rangers, Queen's Park, Dunfermline; as manager: East Stirling, St Mirren, Aberdeen; also caretaker manager of Scotland for the 1986 World Cup finals.

Appointed Manchester United manager: 5.11.1986

Honours: for Aberdeen: Scottish champions 1980, 1984, 1985; Scottish Cup winners: 1982, 1983, 1984, 1986; Scottish League Cup winners: 1986; European Cup Winners Cup winners: 1983; European Super-Cup winners: 1983; for

Manchester United: FA Premier League: 1993, 1994; FA Cup: 1990, 1994; League Cup: 1992; European Cup Winners Cup winners: 1991; European Super-Cup winners: 1991.

Only manager to win all domestic honours on both sides of the border, including the double.

Only manager to have won the European Cup Winners Cup with two different clubs.

With thanks to Michael Crick for this.

Index